The Most Ancient Testimony

The Most Ancient Testimony

Sixteenth-Century Christian-Hebraica
in the Age of Renaissance Nostalgia

Jerome Friedman

Ohio University Press

Athens, Ohio

Library of Congress Cataloging in Publication Data

Friedman, Jerome.
   The most ancient testimony.

   Bibliography: p.
   Includes index.
   1. Hebrew language—Study and teaching—History—
16th century. 2. Judaism—Relations—Christianity.
3. Christianity and other religions—Judaism.
4. Reformation. 5. Renaissance. I. Title.
PJ4528.F74 1983   261.2′6′09031   82-18830
ISBN 0-8214-0700-7

This book is dedicated to

Robert M. Kingdon,

my professor and teacher,

and

Roland H. Bainton,

our inspiration and guide

Table of Contents

Acknowledgments

I owe much to many people for their help and support in preparing this book. Professor Robert M. Kingdon, mentor and colleague, first suggested this topic to me while I was a student in his charge. Since that time, his advice, criticism, suggestions, and support materially aided this work through its various stages of development to completion.

Dr. Philip Bebb provided the collegial and professional advice as well as editorial criticism that one always anticipates from colleagues but rarely receives. Dr. Bebb was the first to read the manuscript for this book and the last to see it off to the press. Dr. Robert Kolb's insights and criticism provided justification for the practice of sending manuscripts to good critics. His efforts are evident throughout the final work. Thanks must be accorded to the many individuals who read separate sections and chapters and whose advice was as eagerly incorporated into the work as it was originally sought.

Special thanks to Janet L. Kronenberg whose critical reading of the final draft contributed significantly to the readability and precision of the final product. No simple statement can adequately express my thanks, respect, and gratitude for the manifold efforts of Deborah J. Klein, my wife, friend, and ally.

I am indebted to many institutions and agencies for their generous financial support during the several years this book was written. Dr. Eugene P. Wenninger, Dean of Research and Sponsored Programs at Kent State University, provided financial aid and arranged grants and academic leaves of absence. The generous grants of the American Philosophical Society, the National Endowment for the Humanities, and the Summer Institute of the Center for Reformation Research provided the financial resources necessary to acquire materials both here and abroad.

Finally, my thanks and appreciation to Helen Gawthrop of the Ohio University Press. Her efforts in producing this volume convincingly demonstrated the skill, competence, sensitivity, and attention required to turn a manuscript into a book.

Introduction

Christian-Hebraism, the use of Hebrew, rabbinic, or Cabbalistic sources for Christian religious purposes, contributed to the intellectual climate of crisis and change characterizing the fifteenth and sixteenth centuries. Use of such source material had dramatic results including the retranslation of the Old Testament (hereafter OT), the reinterpretation of the New Testament (hereafter NT), and the reexamination of historically central doctrines of Christianity. Paradoxically, these efforts entailed close intellectual cooperation with Jewish scholars who opposed Christianity in all its forms.

The Reformation was concerned with the clarification of Christian dogma and Protestant scholars abandoned centuries of established Church tradition to "return to Scripture" in its most authentic literary forms. In so doing, scholars found Hebrew knowledge necessary if the OT was to be properly translated and the NT understood in its conceptual, historical, and linguistic context. Consequently, Protestant scholars and theologians turned to Jewish teachers, grammarians, and exegetes with enthusiasm and vigor.

Yet Christian-Hebraica was not solely a child of the Reformation, for it had emerged several decades earlier under the auspices of such scholars as Pico della Mirandola and Johannes Reuchlin and others who were not primarily motivated by the reforming ideals of subsequent Protestants but who were instead devoted to the mystical theology of Provençal and Spanish Jewry known as the Cabbalah. Historians have noted yet other forms of Renaissance-Reformation-age Jewish intellectual influence in the study of critical philology at the University of Alcalá and among thinkers referred to as radicals, especially of the Italian, Spanish, and Polish-Lithuanian variety. Yet another manifestation of Christian-Hebraica was a new Christian mission to Jews consisting of works written in Hebrew and using special arguments accommodated to a Jewish reading audience.

Whether of the Catholic, Protestant, or radical sort, Hebrew study proved controversial. One is reminded of the many Europe-wide conflicts that tore at the heart of sixteenth-century academic and religious circles concerning Hebraica, including the Reuchlin-Dominican controversy at the start of the century, the Luther-Sabbatarian conflict concerning the alleged judaization of Protestantism at midcentury, and the intradenominational conflict within the Polish-Lithuanian Unitarian church at the end of the century. Certainly the concerns of the Spanish Inquisition regarding Jewish influence among Alumbrados is well known. Less well known was the raging battle between the Hebraists of Basel and those of Wittenberg concerning the proper use of Jewish sources and the best method to approach rabbinic materials.

Despite the importance of Christian-Hebraica in the sixteenth century, subsequent scholarly attention has been meager or fragmented. One cause, no doubt, has been the general lack of Hebrew and Aramaic language facility among historians of early-modern Europe. As a result, many Reformation-age personalities are studied with little regard for their interest in Hebraica. Clearly, the historian's limitations are passed on to the subject under investigation and often justified on the basis that the subject just used Hebrew for "translation," which explanation, as we shall see, is either wrong or simplistic in most cases.[1]

Another factor has been the general neglect of and disinterest in matters pertaining to Jews and Hebrew because both were associated with judaization. Martin Luther complained that "Christian-Hebraists were more rabbinical than Christian" and believed that they were perverting the course of the Reformation. Indeed, Luther wrote no fewer than five treatises attempting to nullify what he perceived as a dangerous judaization of the new religion. Yet few of his biographers raise any of the issues involved, and even Luther's translator into English made clear that discussion of Jews or Hebrew in no way constituted an endorsement of Judaism as a religion.[2]

If one can overlook the neglect of Jews by those writing of the sixteenth century from a confessional orientation or for some religious purpose, how does one understand the desire to delete Jewish-related issues even when they were important and germane? The Reuchlin-Dominican tangle has been generally converted from one scholar's defense of the Jewish right to use the Talmud for religious purposes into an academic controversy between humanists and scholastics with no mention of the Jews at all. Despite the overwhelming evidence that this latter interpretation is incorrect, only one Renaissance-Reformation historian has pointed to the essential nature of the conflict.[3]

Even more curious is the treatment accorded Charles V in his relationship with Jews, Hebrew, and the problems of judaization. Surely this great leader has been studied and analyzed from a variety of vantage points, yet hardly a single historian has noted how this champion of the Inquisition in Spain completely reversed these policies in Germany where he attempted to encourage Jewish settlement in Protestant areas as he became aware of Protestant fears of judaization and Christian-Hebraica. Even more to the point, neglect of matters Jewish has led historians to delete all mention of the Catholic belief that Protestantism was a new form of Judaism. Indeed, Protestant interest in Hebrew was proof positive that Lutheranism was a variety of Judaism.

Where literature concerning Christian-Hebraica exists, it is often out of date or severely fragmented. Geiger, Perles, Bacher, Walde, and Kluge and other nineteenth-century scholars wrote important works dealing with Christian study of Hebrew, but all of these are very general and have attempted to cover all of the Middle Ages through the end of the Reformation.[4] As a result, many provide fine listings of who knew some Hebrew and what few grammars they wrote but often fail to appreciate the intellectual significance of their subjects and the difference between early and later Hebraica. Geiger, for instance, Reuchlin's leading biographer, considered that humanist's preoccupation with, and lifelong devotion to, the Cabbalah the product of a sick mind.[5] Other nineteenth-century historians were equally strident in reflecting a general intellectual orientation precluding mysticism or any philosophy smacking of the irrational. The relationship of Hebraica to Renaissance humanism, Reformation hermenuetics, and exegesis—not to mention the ancient theology—was not considered by these authors.

Attempting to compensate for the general lack of interest in matters Jewish or pertaining to Hebrew study by Christians, Jewish historians have attempted to fill in the blanks with many articles dealing with specific issues or personalities. These scholars often bring enviable linguistic skills to their study of Christian-Hebraica but are just as often hampered by a lack of comprehension—often concern—regarding Christian systematics and Reformation theology. Consequently, much Jewish scholarship has been able to describe sixteenth-century Hebrew publication but rarely attempts to place this publication and interest within the context of Renaissance-Reformation intellectual and religious life. Amram, Galliner, Newman, Ben-Sasson, Marx, Hirsch, the three Rosenthals, and Baron have written fine descriptive accounts of Christian publication of Hebrew but have been unable to judge their subject's interest in Hebrew other than by quantifying the number of publications or the number of Jewish sources used.[6]

None has distinguished between Renaissance and Reformation interests in Hebrew, between Catholic and Protestant rabbinic study, or between Lutheran and Reformed students of Jewish sources. How radical theologians and orthodox thinkers might have used the very same Jewish sources to arrive at vastly different positions remains a mystery.

One area of Christian-Hebraica that has received more attention in recent years is the study of the Christian-Cabbalah. Blau, Secret, and Scholem have made important contributions to our understanding.[7] All, however, are limited by a variety of factors. Scholem's interest in Christian-Cabbalism is only an adjunct to his monumental contributions in single-handedly bringing the study of the Jewish Cabbalah to the forefront of scholarly attention. Blau's oft-cited work was one of the earliest to analyze this subject in English, but it did not consider the Renaissance intellectual context that made intense interest in the Cabbalah explicable. Secret, certainly the dean of Christian-Cabbalistic studies, had written about that source in general as well as about the importance of specific Cabbalistic texts such as the *Zohar* ("[Book of] Splendor"). Unfortunately, Secret has cast a wide net and has included as Cabbalists many who disavowed that study, such as Sebastian Münster and Paul Fagius, but whose importance to other areas of Christian-Hebraica was fundamental, if unexplained. Moreover, Secret's pattern of organization using separate chapters for individual countries places his subject in an artificial framework. Consequently, Secret's exemplary work does not make clear distinctions between Christian-Cabbalism and Christian-Hebraica or between advocates and opponents of Cabbalah within the framework of Christian-Hebraica and yet is not wide enough to include such Hebraists as Servetus and other radicals.

In recent years Christian-Hebraica has been fortunate in attracting the attention and abilities of some very fine young scholars. Zika and Copenhaver have correctly placed the Christian-Cabbalah within the framework of the ancient theology, that important category of intellectual perception brought to scholarly attention by D. P. Walker.[8] The fundamental connection between Cabbalah and *magia* has been noted by both authors, and it is reasonable to assume that future work in this area will be far more analytical and contextual as a result.

The area of sixteenth-century exegetica, long neglected, is finally attracting the attention it deserves and with it the Jewish component that was so important to sixteenth-century exegetes. My own work with Michael Servetus, which emphasized the systematic function Jewish sources played in his construction of a radical theology and exegesis, has been, it is to be hoped, seminal.[9] Gerald Hobbs's several contributions to the area of Bucer studies and general Christian-Hebraica are significant for the skill and sophistication, both conceptual and linguisitic, demonstrated in analyzing Bucer's Psalms publication.[10] Similarly, Bernard Roussel's work must be included in any list of new studies conducted by scholars possessing linguistic abilities, critical skills, and open minds.[11]

Standing upon the shoulders of those who came before, I hope to present in this volume the first systematic-functional analysis of Christian-Hebraica during the first half of the sixteenth-century. This is not an exhaustive work; many Hebraists are mentioned only briefly and some not at all. The overwhelming number of Christian-Hebraists learned Hebrew, wrote small grammars with which to teach students, and devoted their lives to the teaching profession. A few more wrote small glosses or published critical editions of the Psalms, with an even smaller number of scholars making truly significant contributions in terms of theory, linguistics, new scriptural method, or philosophy. It is useless to list all these many students of Hebrew since Geiger already did that over a century ago and the *Encyclopedia Judaica* has recently published an even greater list of some twelve hundred scholars familiar with Hebrew.[12] For this study, I have sought out those seminal scholars whose works influenced others, demonstrated a level of scholarship and sophistication hitherto unknown, or reflected the orientation of some larger community of scholars. In concentrating upon fewer, but significant, Hebraists, I have attempted to express the multiplicity of types and varieties of Hebraica that existed. In all instances I have attempted to demonstrate the function of Jewish sources within that individual author's religious orientation. It is important to know why certain authors used the sources they did and how these ideas of Jewish origin were amalgamated into a Christian synthesis. Knowing this will help us differentiate between Catholic Hebraica and its Protestant counterpart; between Reformed and Lutheran Hebraists and between Servetus and everyone else.

The period of the first half of the sixteenth century was chosen for several important reasons. This fifty-year timespan witnessed the greatest growth in Hebraica and the best work by the best scholars in that area. Additionally, this half century witnessed the most significant conflicts among Hebraists themselves and sits at the junction of the Renaissance and the Reformation. It was also the five-decade period in which the different varieties of Christian-Hebraica first and most clearly manifested themselves.

This study differs from all that came before not only in treating a narrow time period intensely but also in dealing with several peripheral issues of great importance to Christian-Hebraists themselves. Issues such as the judaization debate and missionary writings must receive equal attention along with scriptural exegesis, Cabbalah, and philology. And all of this must be placed within the locus of the intellectual world and framework of the early sixteenth-century.

We must similarly understand a factor comprehended all too clearly by every Christian-Hebraist of the age; both anti-Judaism and anti-Semitism were so strong that the integrity of anyone studying Hebrew would be questioned and compromised. The importance of the Reuchlin controversy was lost on no one, and virtually every Hebraist was blasted by opponents as being a secret Jew, in league with Jews, of Jewish origin, or all the above. Indeed, as we shall see, even Hebraists themselves made skillful use of anti-Semitism against one another in their attempts to clarify their own respective positions. This slur proved so amazingly successful that by midcentury, when most pioneering Hebraists were dead, Christian-Hebraica itself began to succumb to an intellectual environment they themselves had helped create. Unfortunately, treating anti-Semitism elicits varied reactions, ranging from great discomfort and regret to anger and defensiveness, thus making its discussion in an open and matter-of-fact fashion somewhat difficult. Let us accept at the very outset of this study that anti-Semitism, however unfortunate a sentiment, was an accepted fact of life in sixteenth-century Europe. Consequently, even though it is an easy matter to condemn Luther, Erasmus, or others for their hostile attitudes toward Jews, it is also quite pointless. Not only are the above-mentioned figures long removed from the concerns of this world but it would also be far more fruitful to accept their negative feelings toward Jews and proceed to discuss how this made the study of Hebrew difficult, controversial, or simply subject to peculiar restraints. However, as I have not attempted to add the polemical dimension of moral outrage to the creative uses sixteenth-century figures found for popular anti-Semitic sentiment, neither have I found it worthwhile to conceal or cloud the effective cultivation of this prejudice by many of the scholars and religious thinkers analyzed.

I have attempted to keep technical and grammatical concerns of Hebrew and Aramaic linguistics to a minimum. Consequently, the reader in early-modern European history unfamiliar with these languages should experience little difficulty in this regard. All Hebrew and Aramaic terms and expressions have been transliterated into the Latin alphabet and repeatedly translated and explained throughout the volume. Where some point of grammar is important to the reader's understanding of the issues involved, I have made every effort to explain the ideas in question, keeping in mind that most readers are unfamiliar with Hebrew.

A word is in order concerning the use of the term *Christian-Hebraica*. I have used this Latin neuter plural term in the singular throughout the manuscript. Other terms such as *Christian-Hebraism* imply not only a movement of some type but also a singular attitude or frame of mind. *Christian-Hebrewism* is no better but sounds worse. Using *Christian-Hebraica* in the plural did not look correct on the written page and was jarring to the eye and ear as in "Christian-Hebraica were, are, etc. . . . " Consequently, I hope Latin purists will tolerate this grammatically awkward but more readable use of *Christian-Hebraica* as a singular construction. After all, *Christian-Hebraica* was a rather unique expression in the history of Latin Christian thought.

NOTES

1. I refer here, for instance, to Hastings Eells's study *Martin Bucer* (New Haven, 1931), which successfully avoided any mention of Bucer's enduring interest in Hebraica and his important contributions to that field of study.

2. *Luther Works*, general ed., H. Lehman (Phila., 1955), 47:123. In introducing Luther's treatise *On the Jews and Their Lies*, the translator of this work, Martin H. Bertram, noted, "Such publication is in no way intended as an endorsement of the distorted views of the Jewish faith and practice."

3. See James H. Overfield, "A New Look at the Reuchlin Affair," in *Studies in Medieval and Renaissance History*, ed. H. L. Adelson (Lincoln, Neb., 1971), 8:165–207.

4. L. Geiger, *Das Studium der Hebräische Sprache in Deutschland vom Ende des 15 bis zur mitte des 16 Jahrhunderts* (Breslau, 1870); Otto Kluge, "Die Hebräische Sprachwissenschaft in Deutschland in Zeitalter des Humanismus," *Zeitschrift für die Geschichte der Juden in Deutschland* (1931, 1932); Joseph Perles, *Beitrage zur Geschichte der Hebräishen und Aramäischen Studien* (Munich, 1884); William Bacher, *Die Hebräishen Sprachwissenschaft vom 10 bis zur 16 Jahrhunders* (Trier, 1892); H. Walde, *Das Studium der Hebr. Sprache in Deutschland am Ausgang des Mittelalters* (Münster i. w. 1916).

5. L. Geiger, *Allegemeine Deutsche Biographie* 28:793.

6. D. W. Amram, *The Makers of Hebrew Books in Italy* (Phila., 1909); H. Galliner, "Agathius Guidacerius," *Historia Judaica*, 2 (Oct. 1940): 85–101; L. I. Newman, *Jewish Influence on Christian Reform Movements* (New York, 1925); H. H.

Ben-Sasson, "The Reformation in Contemporary Jewish Eyes," *Proceedings of the Israel Academy of Sciences and Humanities* (Jerusalem, 1971), 4:239–326; Alexander Marks, "Notes on the Use of Hebrew Type in Non-Hebrew Books, 1475–1520," *Studies in Jewish History and Booklore* (New York, 1944); Frank Rosenthal, "The Rise of Christian-Hebraism in the 16th-Century," *Historia Judaica*, 7 (April 1945): 167–91. Also see his unpublished dissertation entitled "Christian Hebraists of Latin Europe," submitted at the University of Pittsburgh in Pennsylvania in 1945; E. I. J. Rosenthal, "Sebastian Muenster's Knowledge and use of Jewish Exegesis," in *Essays Presented to J. H. Hartz,* edited by I. Epstein, E. Levine, C. Roth (London, 1945); J. M. Rosenthal, "Marcin Czechowic and Jacob of Belzyce: Arian-Jewish Encounters in 16th-Century Poland," *Proceedings of the American Academy for Jewish Research,* vol. 34 (New York, 1966); Salo W. Baron, *A Social and Religious History of the Jews,* vol. 13 (New York, 1969); *idem,* "John Calvin and the Jews" and "The Council of Trent and Rabbinic Literature," *Ancient and Medieval Jewish History* (New Brunswick, N.J., 1972).

7.   J. L. Blau, *The Christian Interpretation of the Cabala in the Renaissance* (New York, 1944); Françoise Secret, *Le Zôhar chez les Kabbalistes chrétiens de la Renaissance* (Paris, 1958); *idem, Les Kabbalistes chrétiens de la Renaissance* (Paris, 1964); G. Scholem, "Zur Geschichte de Anfänge der christlichen Kabbala," *Essays Presented to Leo Baeck* (London, 1954). See also W. J. Bouwsma, *Concordia Mundi; The Career and Thought of Guillaume Postel* (Camb., Mass., 1957).

8.   Charles Zika, "Reuchlin's De Verbo Mirifico and the Magic Debate of the Late Fifteenth Century," *Journal of the Warburg and Courtauld Institutes,* 39 (1976): 104–38; and in the same journal, Brian P. Copenhaver, "Lefèvre D'Etaples, Symphorien Champier, and the Secret Names of God," 40 (1977): 189–211. Concerning the ancient theology, see the following: D. P. Walker, *The Ancient Theology* (Ithaca, N.Y., 1972); *idem, Spiritual and Demonic Magic from Ficino to Campanella* (London, 1958); Frances A. Yates, *Giordano Bruno and the Hermetic Tradition* (Chicago and London, 1964); Brian P. Copenhaver, *Symphorien Champier and the Reception of the Occultist Tradition in Renaissance France* (The Hague, 1978).

9.   See my *Michael Servetus: A Case Study in Total Heresy* (Geneva, 1978) and the following: "Michael Servetus: The Case for a Jewish Christianity," *Sixteenth Century Journal,* vol. 4 (April, 1973); "Michael Servetus: Exegete of Divine History," *Church History,* vol. 43 (December 1974); "Servetus and the Psalms," *Histoire de l'exégèse au XVIe siecle,* ed. O. Fatio (Geneva, 1978). The best biography is still Roland Bainton's *The Hunted Heretic* (Boston, 1953).

10.   R. Gerald Hobbs, "Martin Bucer on Psalm 22: A Study in the Application of Rabbinic Exegesis by a Christian Hebraist," in *Histoire . . . ,* ed. Fatio, and his soon-to-appear "Monitio amica: Pellican to Capito on the Perils of Rabbinic Readings," in *Mélanges offerts à Jean Rott.* Of special note is Hobbs's unpublished dissertation for the Protestant faculty at the University of Strasbourg in 1971, en-

titled "An Introduction to the Psalms Commentary of Martin Bucer," undoubtedly the finest and most complete study of Bucer's Psalm exegesis.

11.   See Bernard Roussel's "Martin Bucer, exégète," *Strasbourg au coeur religieux du XVIe Siècle* (Strasbourg, 1977), pp. 153–66; and by the same author, an unpublished dissertation for the Protestant faculty at the University of Strasbourg in 1970, entitled "Martin Bucer: Lecteur de l'Epitre aux Romains."

12.   *Encyclopedia Judaica* (Jerusalem, 1971), 8: 21–67.

PART I

The Discovery of Hebraica

Chapter One

Medieval 'Hebraica Veritas' and Renaissance Hebrew Study

In the year 1550 nearly every student could find Hebrew instruction at the majority of universities in western Europe and Germany. To acquire deeper competence in Hebrew grammar and syntax, that same student had only to travel to one of many major seats of learning, such as Paris, Padua, or Heidelberg, or to any of the major Protestant seminaries and universities in Germany. By chance, should our hypothetical student have sought instruction in the intricacies of medieval rabbinic exegesis, a large number of scholars in Strasbourg, Basel, and yet other places would have been most happy to accommodate that student's needs. For the student of limited financial means or one who was unable to travel far from home, Hebrew instruction was still available. There were many elementary and advanced Hebrew grammars, a large number of dictionaries and volumes of essays describing and detailing unusual Hebrew structures, fine points of voweling, as well as the Hebrew language's historical development. There were critical editions of all the books of the OT and a large number of volumes in both Hebrew and Latin presenting major medieval Jewish exegetical writings. Sections of the Talmud had been translated, analyzed, and annotated from a Christian perspective. Moreover, the complete Talmud had been published under Christian auspices for those wishing to read that work in the original Aramaic with the aid of special dictionaries, grammars, and word-lists prepared for a Christian audience.

Rabbinic lore, law, exegesis, and major Cabbalistic texts were available in Hebrew and Latin. For those interested in the truly rarified there were discussions of Pharisaic ethics and morality (in both Hebrew and Latin, of course) and their relationship to Christian thought. Similarly, there were treatises describing the relationship between NT practices and Jewish ritual observance. Having completed the above, the voracious Christian reader might then turn to traditional Jewish literature or to one of several missionary works written for Jews in Hebrew or even to the Hebrew translation, with annotations, of the Gospel of Matthew.

In 1550 a veritable wealth of Christian-Hebraica existed whereas but fifty years earlier fewer than one hundred Christians in Europe could read Hebrew and none could even imagine writing in that strange tongue. In 1500 Hebrew books were prepared primarily at Jewish-owned and operated presses to meet specific Jewish religious needs. By 1550 all the aforementioned literature had been published by Christians, for Christians, under Christian auspices, and at Christian presses.

Since it has hardly been treated by subsequent scholars, one might suspect the intellectual revolution of Christian-Hebraica was not noticed in the sixteenth century. Yet the Reuchlin controversy at the beginning of the century and many similar squabbles later in the Reformation age give adequate testimony to the increasing number of volumes of Judaica available, a vastly increased Hebrew reading public, and the fear that such literature might have disastrous results for Christendom.

If little has been written about the phenomenal increase in Christian interest in Hebrew, even less has appeared which might explain those factors making ignorance of Hebrew in 1550 a totally unacceptable state of affairs when such was a thoroughly acceptable condition half a century earlier. This volume will present some reasons why Christians used Jewish sources and how they were used, which sources were the most popular and why, and how this new learning fit into the framework of Renaissance and Reformation intellectual and theological contexts. This is the story of an intellectual transformation so bizarre and unanticipated that once underway it could not be controlled and gave rise to terrible fears in some quarters while leading to cultural enrichment in others. Before describing those factors that made Hebrew learning possible, we must first look at those conditions and reasons that made such knowledge improbable and unpopular earlier. Though Hebraica among Christians made enormous strides from 1500 to 1550, the previous one thousand years saw very little Christian interest in Hebrew. If we are to understand why Hebrew became so popular, we must first understand why earlier it was not.

The ideal of "Hebraica veritas" was surely one of the most overstated ideals of the Christian Middle Ages. Despite Jerome's important translation of Scripture into Latin, some medieval biblical scholars expressed the need to return to the Hebraica veritas, "Hebrew truth," of the original Hebrew text to determine the meaning of God's Word. Despite the lofty idealism surrounding Hebrew competence, the fact is that probably no more than a few dozen Christians from 500 to 1500 could read Hebrew at all and perhaps a quarter of that number could use Hebrew in any constructive sense.[1] Indeed, knowledge of Hebrew may have been an ideal precisely because no one knew any. Moreover, our understanding of the work of Christians who made great contributions to medieval Hebraica, notably Paul of Burgos and Nicholas of Lyra, demands some qualification.[2] Paul of Burgos was born a Jew, ordained a rabbi, and thus brought knowledge of Hebrew *to* the Christian world. Nicholas of Lyra, often considered the greatest medieval Christian exegete, made his greatest contribution in presenting to the Christian world a more literal, less figurative interpretation of the OT, which interpretation may have been less a product of his own creative mind than that of his source, Rabbi Solomon of Troyes, whose work he copied. Other than Nicholas and Jerome before him, it is difficult to point to a single Christian who made a lasting contribution to Christian scholarship predicated upon knowledge and use of Hebrew. Considering the enormous impact of both Paul of Burgos and Nicholas of Lyra in scholarly circles and on subsequent scriptural studies, one must wonder in amazement why other Christian scholars did not learn Hebrew, the ideal of Hebraica veritas notwithstanding.

Actually, there was no lack of Hebrew learning during the Middle Ages; it was simply confined to the Jewish community where Hebrew was used for liturgical, scholarly, and literary purposes as well as in daily life. Moreover, Jewish communities existed in virtually every corner of Europe, making the acquisition of Hebrew language skills rather easy. Consequently, if Christians did not know Hebrew, only a strong lack of interest might explain why. To some extent, Christian disinterest in Hebrew reflected the reality of Christian-Jewish relations as well as very legitimate Church interests that were focused elsewhere. If one cannot discuss medieval Church development and Christian-Jewish relations in a few short pages, at least a few salient points can be made to indicate the nature of the problems involved and why these conditions abruptly changed around 1500.[3]

From the age of the barbarian conquest of Europe, the Church conceived its primary responsibility as the propagation of the faith and the establishment of Church institutions on sound political and economic bases. The many Germanic tribes had to be converted, a network of bishops and dioceses created, and some modicum of essential morality instituted in a cultural environment far removed from the age of the apostles. This monumental task of Europe's conversion to Christianity, so easily taken for granted in retrospect, was difficult, expensive, and slow to progress. This difficult missionary task was not enhanced by virtually total illiteracy among the population, the persistence of tribal belief, and the ambivalence of many local rulers whose major interest in the Church was the civil-service bureaucracy it could provide to replace crumbling tribal lines of authority. Moreover, the treatment of the Albigensian and other heresies demanded most available intellectual and organizational Church skills and talents. Whatever the value of Hebrew, other skills were required at this time, and the Church placed primary emphasis on organizational rather than intellectual accomplishment. If the Church did not emphasize Hebrew instruction at this time, one must consider that even doctrinal development was placed on a back burner with the sacraments only receiving full elucidation and definition at the Fourth Lateran Council meeting of the Church in 1215.

Even where Scripture was important, Hebrew was of little value in this frontier atmosphere. Reliance upon Jerome's Vulgate translation of Scripture made additional texts unnecessary, especially when the proper interpretation of God's word was guided by the Holy Spirit through the agency of the papacy. When Scripture seemed obscure or did not directly address Church needs and purposes, alternate methods of interpretation involving use of allegory and other figurative methods might suffice. Consequently, facility with Hebrew might have been nice but was not necessary, given Jerome's inspired work, human imagination, and the power of the Holy Spirit to make all things intelligible. Indeed, considering the difficulties encountered in maintaining some degree of Latin literacy during the Middle Ages, mastery of Hebrew might have proved more of a hindrance than a help.

Aside from problems involved with organization and reliance upon the Vulgate, a third element was the troubling relationship between Christians and Jews. Many volumes have been written about medieval anti-Semitism, and one need not dwell on the lurid details of that relationship to understand that Hebrew was the language of the Jews and little about the Jews was appreciated.[4] Essentially, Christendom suffered from an approach-avoidance complex when dealing with things Jewish. On the one hand, Jews were Christianity's oldest enemies and critics, Jesus' murderers, and the obstinate opponents of developing Church power. On the other hand, Jews were a people like any other tribal group requiring conversion and nurturing within the fold of the faithful. Whereas all other tribal and quasi-national entities eventually abandoned their old religions and joined the church militant, Jews steadfastly rejected conversion—indeed, they seemed immune to Christian overtures. Unlike others resistant to the Gospel message, Jews presented a systematic series of arguments defending their rejection of Christianity. Jewish authorities maintained that Christianity was what it always had been, a blasphemous perversion of Judaism. To aggravate matters further, Jewish leaders argued that Christianity could believe in such views as vicarious atonement, the Trinity, a Second Coming, and other cardinal points of faith only because of their unfamiliarity with the Hebrew OT. The simplistic Christian response that the OT was less important than the NT was met with the smug Jewish observation that Christians knew about as much Greek as they knew Hebrew. Consequently, whereas other heathens posed a challenge, the Jewish community proved to be an irritating obstacle.

From the Christian perspective, Hebrew was the language Jews used to oppose conversion, to oppose Church authority, to oppose all truth and light. That language may have been God's tool for communicating with man in days of old, but much as Jews were the removed-Israel while obstinately clinging to yesterday's practices, so too did they adhere to yesterday's faith expressed in yesterday's language. If the Jews were blind, surely their means of expression was not filled with wisdom. Hebrew and Jews were so closely identified that observers had to assume that Nicholas of Lyra must have been Jewish to explain the rare phenomenon of an alleged Christian's knowing Hebrew. Indeed, as late as the sixteenth century many people continued to believe that knowledge of Hebrew was proof of Jewishness and on the basis of such an association Bucer, for one, continually defended his family's honor from so horrid an accusation. Another Reformation-age Hebraist, Johannes Boschenstein (1472–1540), spent his adult years attempting to convince contemporaries that he was not Jewish; he noted, "We were born of Christian parents, but because we are somewhat acquainted with the Holy Tongue, which is so unusual in our land, we are hated by imprudent and ignorant people."[5]

The factors discussed thus far explain why Hebrew was viewed as strange and alien, but they do not explain why Christians felt precluded from learning Hebrew. To comprehend more clearly why Hebrew was avoided by Christian scholars, one must first understand how the tension characterizing Christian-Jewish relations gave way to violence and mutual hatred.

From approximately the year 1000 increasing population, shortages of land, and more widespread commerce and trade led to growing class tension and social alienation. In this charged atmosphere Christian-Jewish tension gave way to violence. The First Crusade left over 100,000 Jews dead in Alsace and the Rhineland as idealistic Crusaders made their way to port cities to embark for the Holy Land and God's war against the infidel. Surviving Jews were subject to repressive legislation forbidding Jews land ownership, entrance into most professions, and residence in most sections of cities.[6] Consequently, the Jew, always religiously different, was now economically different as he was forced into what were still highly peripheral areas of the economy, money lending and the wholesaling of goods. As these businesses grew and prospered in an increasingly trade-oriented society, they, too, were taken over by Christians, as the Franciscans did when they opened *mónte di Pietà* to replace Jewish pawnshops, thereby making the Jew unnecessary and irrelevant in the marketplace. One country after another exiled their ancient Jewish populations: England in 1290, France in 1315 and again in 1394, Austria in 1421, and finally, the largest community of all, Spain, expelled its Jews in 1492.[7] In that year over 250,000 Jews were forced to leave their homeland; an equal number of Jews were forced to convert to Christianity often only to fall to the *auto-da-fé* of the Spanish Inquisition.

The desire to isolate Jews was also visible in legislation requiring them to wear yellow stars, green hats, white strips of cloth, or other signs attached to their clothing so that they might be more easily recognized. The observance of Jewish religious rituals became increasingly dangerous as charges of desecration of the host and ritual murder spread throughout Christendom. It was maintained that Jews desecrated the host in a continuing attempt to slay Jesus yet again and again. Ritual murder, often called the "blood-libel," advanced the notion that Jews routinely kidnapped and killed young Christian boys in order to drain them of their blood. This blood was allegedly used to bake Passover bread or was consumed by Jews to avoid smelling like Jews. Charges that Jews poisoned wells explained the many outbreaks of the plague, and in general, both civil as well as ecclesiastical authorities found in the Jew a convenient means of explanation for most ills characterizing a society in transition. By the thirteenth and fourteenth centuries the Jew had been converted, not into a Christian, but into a demonic force subsisting on Christian blood in vampire fashion, bent upon the destruction of Christendom and increasingly in league with the Turks advancing in eastern Europe.[8] Fear of the Jew, his demonic powers, and his evilness is summed up in the English word *cabbal*, which signifies both magical powers and conspiratorial intent, the origin of this term being the Hebrew word *cabbalah*, meaning "Jewish mysticism." Such fears led to continual book burnings during which all volumes written in Hebrew, the language of Satan, were destroyed.

One must marvel that the Jews were so hated and so feared that even when converted they could not be accepted into the fold of the faithful. The Spanish Inquisition burned tens of thousands of New Christian converts from Judaism for observing such obvious Jewish rituals as changing personal linen on Fridays, facing the wall when hearing of a death, cooking in olive oil, refraining from eating pork, and other activities deemed seditious to Christian well being. Iberia was subject to "pure blood laws" defining a New Christian as any individual having one Jewish grandparent on either side of his family.[9] Such exclusive legislation, it was hoped, would keep the Jewish infection from spreading throughout Christendom once Jews perfidiously chose to destroy the Church by converting to Christianity.

The elimination and isolation of Jews had the desired effect; the year 1500 saw fewer Jews in western and central Europe than at any point in the previous 1000 years. Indeed, Jewish numbers were dwindling so very rapidly that Johannes Reuchlin wrote in 1506 of "the unfortunate events which we have experienced recently with the Jews—they have been expelled not only from Spain but also from our German lands. In quest of new settlements they have been forced to migrate all the way to the Beduins [Turkey]. As a result, it may come to pass that the Hebrew idiom of their sacred writings will undergo great destruction and disappear from our midst."[10] Other more tolerant areas, such as Venice, permitted Jews to reside there, but only in a specified place. In 1516 this great Italian city created the first ghetto, an institution with immediate appeal, soon found wherever there were Jews. The last two decades of the fifteenth century also witnessed Jewish expulsion from Bohemia and many German cities and states.[11]

In this atmosphere of mutual distrust there was little to make conversion to Christianity an attractive option and little to induce Christians to learn Hebrew, the language of the Jews. There was little mutual respect, less love, and even less interest in each other's religions. There was no recognition that inter-community intellectual cooperation might yield beneficial results to either religion and no impetus to carry out such endeavors.

The Renaissance was an age of transition affecting more than Christian-Jewish relations, for much of the medieval synthesis was rapidly deteriorating. Peasant rebellion, an economy marked by currency inflation and rampant strikes, and a church facing severe internal dissent were just the tip of an iceberg that would crush many old institutions. New economic and political forces found it difficult to accommodate their demands to the pattern of conservative aristocratic institutions seeking any and all solutions not involving change. Conflicts between papal centralism and the power of bishops, between monarchy and Church, between councils of the Church and the papacy created a series of occurrences such as multiple papacies, ecclesiastical rebellion, and even papal exile from Rome. The "respublica Christiana" was withering rapidly and taking with itself any concept of order and stability Europeans had known. With little awareness of the complexity of their situation and no world view that might accommodate the notion of change, Europeans, Italians in particular, took the adventurous road backward in time through systematic escapism to avoid the problems of the present.

Nostalgic Italian humanists discovered the glories of an ancient past untarnished by the corruption and rot of their own society. Medieval law gave way to Roman law, and scholastic theology came increasingly under attack on the basis of ancient religious sources. Litterateurs wrote with disdain of the artificial values of Christian society compared with the vibrant and vital values of ancient Rome, and the apologists for each city state attempted to convince others, and perhaps themselves, that they were the reincarnation of ancient virtue. If man increasingly became the measure of all things, it was because the Church increasingly came to be no measure at all.

Religious thinkers were affected by the same nostalgic intellectual dynamic that drove secularists like Machiavelli. Increasing numbers of theologians spoke of the fall of the church, and much as Petrarch spoke of returning Italy to a stylistic classical mold, Protestants dreamed of returning Christianity to an apostolic mold. For increasing numbers of scholars, "old" was good because the present was bad. Whatever the differences between Italian Renaissance humanism and Reformation theology, both shared a nostalgic view of the past based upon disgust with the present. For all that the Reformation returned to the secure bedrock of Scripture, Renaissance humanists returned to Hermes Tresmegistus, Orpheus, the Druids, and other ancients as the true and untainted wellsprings of civilization.

If Italy was the first country where systematic nostalgia was most clearly apparent, it was also the first to appreciate that among the great cultures of the past was an ancient Jewish culture. Consequently, when that collector of ancient cultures, Pico della Mirandola, included Cabbalistic theory in his amalgam of nine hundred theses that he believed expressed all truth, he issued a resounding call to reevaluate that which had been despised for so long.[12] Pico was convinced that the secret wisdom of the Jews was a lost oral tradition given man at Sinai which reflected the greatest of universal truths. And when he wrote, "There is no science that can more firmly convince us of the divinity of Christ than magia and Cabbalah,"[13] he was at the same time affirming the need to bolster traditional belief through a pattern of thought that transcended the ills of the present. When Pico wrote, "There are no letters in the entire Law which do not demonstrate the secrets of the ten *sephiroth* ["emanations of God"] in their forms, conjunctions, separations, curvature and directness and superfluity, smallness and largeness, their crowning, their closed or open form and their arrangement,"[14] he was clearly expressing what would soon become a new orthodoxy, that God's secrets, the key that could unlock the mystery of the universe, were found in a mystical interpretation of Hebrew language and literature. Reuchlin would surpass Pico, as we shall see, when he taught that when he read Hebrew, he "shook in dread and terror" because he could feel God's presence in each and every letter of that language. Antique culture was the repository of wisdom and Hebrew was the doorway to that repository.

It is not surprising that the reevaluation of Hebrew originated in Italy, for Christian-Jewish relations were basically good there even though Jews faced increasing difficulty nearly everywhere else. Jews had lived in Italy from before the time of Christ, and despite periodic manifestations of anti-Semitism, the more commercial city governments as well as the papacy were instrumental in protecting Jews from the atrocities that occurred elsewhere. Moreover, the prominent role played by Jews as intermediaries and translators of Arabic materials was appreciated in Italy, fostering a friendly intellectual community composed of both Jews and Christians. One result of this freer atmosphere was the creation of Jewish presses as early as the 1470s which provided Jews with necessary religious literature and also provided Christians with Hebrew sources. Another result of the friendly relationship between Jews and Christians was that a Christian might find Hebrew instruction in Italy although such was almost impossible to find elsewhere.

Almost every northern Christian-Hebraist complained of the difficulty involved in finding a Jewish teacher of Hebrew. Diminished Jewish numbers no doubt accounted for much of this difficulty but so did repeated medieval rabbinic prohibition against teaching Hebrew to Christians.

Under certain circumstances Jews were permitted to teach elementary Hebrew to Christians, but reading OT Scripture with a Christian student was to be avoided. Teaching Cabbalistic mysticism was usually forbidden, though such prohibitions were disregarded in Italy as much as they were upheld elsewhere. These restrictions were created for two reasons. First, the Christian student often used his newly gained information to argue against Judaism as did Nicholas of Lyra. Second, and more important, the teaching of Hebrew to Christians was often confused or interpreted as a Jewish attempt to convert Christians to Judaism. Since such conversion was a capital offense and often provided the pretext for mass expulsion, rabbinic authorities thought it wiser to avoid Hebrew instruction altogether.

If there were not a great many Italian teachers of Hebrew, those we know of were of superlative quality even though none taught Hebrew as a profession. Obadiah ben Jacob Sforno (1470–1550) practiced medicine in Rome and served as personal physician to Cardinal Domenico Grimani.[15] Born of an illustrious rabbinic family, Sforno was educated in philosophy, philology, and mathematics and wrote diversely in both Hebrew and Latin on Aristotelian philosophy, the Talmud, Hebrew grammar, and OT exegesis as well as translating extensive parts of Euclid. Quite as a favor to Cardinal Grimani, a long-time close friend, Sforno found time in an otherwise busy schedule to tutor a private student. From 1498 to 1500 Sforno was Johannes Reuchlin's private teacher of Hebrew.

Sforno was in good company. Abraham ben Meir De Balmes (1440–1523) was another prominent Jewish physician whose impact upon the Christian community, although quite accidental, was of incalculable importance. De Balmes obtained his medical education from the University of Naples from which he was graduated in 1492. In 1510 he too became a close friend to Cardinal Grimani at whose request De Balmes agreed to translate several works from Arabic to Latin. Among the many works this scholar translated were Ibn Haykonis's *Liber de Mundo*, Geminus's *Introduction to Ptolemy's Organon*, and several works by minor Arab authors. De Balmes also wrote a Hebrew grammar, the *Mikve Avram*, which appeared in Venice in 1523 in both Hebrew and Latin (in the latter under the title *Peculium Abramae*). Yet another work by this scholar was his volume *Sha'are ha-Harcava ve ha Shimush*, which was an attempt to codify Hebrew syntax. As a personal favor to Grimani, De Balmes agreed to teach a single student interested in learning Hebrew. This student, Daniel Bomberg, would later establish the first Christian press devoted entirely to publishing Christian-Hebraica materials. Bomberg was so successful that his publications soon became the absolute standard for both the Christian and Jewish communities. I shall have more to say about this remarkable man later.

Yet another important teacher was Jacob ben Samuel Mantino (d. 1549), in many ways a personal and professional rival of De Balmes. Mantino too was a physician by profession. Having earned his medical degree from the University of Padua in 1521, Mantino had the rare honor, for a Jew, of being invited to teach medicine at the University of Bologna in 1529 and at the Sapienza in Rome from 1538 to 1541. Mantino also served as personal physician to Pope Paul III from 1534. Like many other educated Jews of his day, he translated Arabic works into Latin, including Averroes and Avicena. Regard for his intellectual and religious background was so great that Mantino served as a special OT legal consultant on the issue of Henry VIII's request for an annulment. Mantino taught Hebrew to several humanistically oriented bishops.

It would be possible to expand this list of occasional Jewish tutors of Christians to include a great many others whose students played a fundamental part in the development of Christian study of Hebrew. Such names would include Elia del Medigo, Jacob ben Immanuel Provicial (also known as Bonet de Lates), Judah Abravanel, and Pico's teacher Yochanan Allemano. All had consuming professional lives either in the general areas of medicine, diplomacy, or commerce or within the Jewish community. However, as favors to important Christian friends and associates, they agreed to tutor an occasional student.

Despite the very high quality of instruction a well-connected and wealthy student might acquire, it is obvious that only a handful of individuals might benefit from working with Jewish instructors primarily engaged in other professional pursuits. Famous persons who were instrumental in the spreading of Hebraica, such as Pico, Bomberg, and Reuchlin, received their instruction in Hebrew on this informal basis, but such informal study cannot account for the widespread popularity of Hebrew outside Italy. For Christian-Hebraica to become a broad-based movement and a focus of cultural interest, the successful fulfillment of four basic requirements was necessary. Indeed, it was the satisfaction of these prerequisites which turned Hebrew study from the passion of a few individuals to a Europe-wide cultural expression.

First, Hebrew studies needed a successful campaign of popularization. It was necessary to convince large numbers of students that their university curriculum should include the study of Hebrew, and it was equally important to persuade the usually conservative university faculty and administrators that the addition of Hebrew would be appropriate to their concept of education.

Second, formal classroom instruction of Hebrew would involve a substantial capital investment for the hiring of teachers and the provision of classroom space. Such investment would have to result from the largess of important political leaders and/or church personnel. In turn, such important leaders would have to be convinced that the study of Hebrew would benefit their interests.

The third requirement was the creation of specialized presses geared to meeting Christian students' special educational needs, including Hebrew grammars and teaching texts. Reliance upon Jewish presses would prove problematic if only because these publishers were more interested in meeting the special needs of Jews: publishing prayer books and devotional literature as well as scriptural writings not necessarily suited for Christians just learning Hebrew.[16] A Christian press might encounter fewer difficulties in acquiring permits and the necessary capital investment and even in securing materials for printing. Similarly, Christian presses encountered fewer difficulties from censors and could more easily deal with such problems once encountered. Another important consideration was that a Christian press would face fewer problems in distribution and sales since Jewish presses were subject to a variety of restrictions, prohibitions, and tariffs that made their products costly and affected steady supply. Consequently, a few passionate students might rely upon Jewish presses, but a large number of students and scholars would require a larger, more stable press geared to Christian needs.

The fourth requirement was the most important in the short run. Any program of study and publication would necessitate close cooperation with Jewish scholars—not on a part-time basis but as a full-time commitment. Such cooperation could also guarantee the services of Hebrew editors, typesetters, copy readers and type makers, all of whom existed in the Jewish community but not outside it. The Jewish community would benefit from such cooperation as it might be reasonably assured a good supply of scholarly and religious materials that would be published as part of any agreement. Additionally, the Jewish community might conceivably find that certain types of literature either difficult for Jews to publish or controversial, such as the Talmud, could be undertaken by a Christian press with little difficulty.

If one considers the state of Jewish-Christian relations in the year 1500 and the impoverished state of Christian study of Hebrew around this time, there was no reason to assume that any of these four necessary elements might appear. On the contrary, by the fourth decade of the sixteenth century each of these factors had met with total and unqualified realization. How this came about will be explained in the discussion to follow.

Factor 1: Publicity and Popularization

Although Pico's impact upon the intellectual and scholarly community was great, he was neither primarily a Hebraist nor truly important to the development of Christian-Hebraica. The first great pioneer of Hebrew study among Christians and the first scholar to campaign successfully for Hebrew studies was the German lawyer, Johannes Reuchlin.[17] His interests and contributions to Hebraica extended past the Cabbalistic studies, to which he was devoted, to the creation of grammars and critical teaching texts and to defending the value of Hebrew study. Reuchlin was also the first great Christian teacher of Hebrew to other Christians; among his students one finds such important personalities as Jacob Jonas, George Simler, John Eck, Johannes Forster, Jacob Ceporinus, Johannes Hildebrand, E. O. Schrenchenfuchs, Robert Wakefield, and Reuchlin's nephew, Philip Melanchthon. Yet Rabbi Capnion, as he was called, was not a Hebraist by profession but made his living as a jurist.

Johannes Reuchlin was born in Pforzheim in 1455 and attended school in Freiberg, Paris, and Basel where he studied law and Greek. He first developed an interest in learning Hebrew during the 1480s but was unable to find a teacher. Eventually, in 1492, Reuchlin secured the services of Jacob Yehiel of Loans, personal physician to Emperor Frederick III. To advance his Hebrew studies past what Jacob Yehiel could teach him, Reuchlin journeyed to Italy where Cardinal Grimani was able to arrange for private lessons with his friend Obadiah Sforno from 1498 to 1500. Reuchlin's first Hebrew publication, his *Rudimenta Hebraica*, appeared in 1506, three years subsequent to Conrad Pellican's elementary grammar. The *Rudimenta* was a far better work than Pellican's and consisted of two parts, a grammar and a Hebrew-Latin dictionary of biblical Hebrew. To an extent, Reuchlin modeled his grammar on David Kimchi's medieval classic *Sefer ha-Shorashim* ("Book of Roots"), which was too difficult for those totally unfamiliar with Hebrew. In 1512 Reuchlin published a companion piece to his grammar consisting of the Hebrew texts of the seven penitential Psalms plus his own translation and grammatical notes and annotations.

The purpose of this volume was to provide some practice texts for the student to read and analyze so that the student might then continue to more advanced work. Six years later Reuchlin's third educational guide appeared under the title *De Accentibus et orthographia linguae hebraicae*, which dealt with the difficult subject of Hebrew *masorah*, the theory of voweling and punctuation. Unlike Latin, the Hebrew alphabet consists of twenty-two consonants and no vowels. Vowel markings, accent marks, punctuation, and musical notations were located above, below, behind, or before the consonants and affect pronunciation, emphasis, word meaning, and even sentence structure since Hebrew has no capital letters or conventional clause or sentence endings. Consequently, even after learning to read and write Hebrew letters, adjusting to reading and writing from right to left, and learning to read easy sentences, the student had to learn voweling and punctuation without which reading Scripture was almost impossible.[18] Complicating matters, many Jewish texts deleted these markings altogether and presented only the raw text with the author or publisher assuming an understanding of this apparatus on the part of the reader. Reuchlin's work was an attempt to rationalize this difficult science of punctuation taken for granted by those raised with Hebrew but mystifying to those just learning the language.

All together, these three volumes constituted a guide for the self-teaching of Hebrew, important since Reuchlin feared that Jews would soon be exiled from all of Europe. All three works reflected dependence upon such traditional Jewish sources and authorities as Kimchi, Maimonides, Nachmanides, Levi ben Gerson, and Nicholas of Lyra and his major source, Rabbi Solomon of Troyes, or Rashi.

Had Reuchlin only produced these three works he would have merited the appellation "Father of Renaissance Hebrew study," but there was another Johannes Reuchlin as well. Indeed, the other Reuchlin, the scholar advancing the cause of mystical Cabbalistic studies, had far greater impact than Reuchlin the teacher. Like Pico, Reuchlin believed Cabbalah represented a lost font of ancient wisdom entirely applicable and beneficial to Christian purposes. This Reuchlin will be discussed later when his Cabbalistic works are analyzed.

There is yet a third Reuchlin perhaps even more important than Reuchlin the teacher or Reuchlin the mystic: there is also Reuchlin the dramatic defender of Hebrew studies against the conservative Dominican order.[19] It was precisely such an encounter between the conservative religious establishment of the day and a respected scholar that Hebraica needed to attract attention and support. In attempting to hound Reuchlin, the Dominicans created a Europe-wide battle that brought Hebrew studies to the forefront of intellectual circles as no other form of publicity could have. This was not a conflict initiated by Reuchlin, nor was it one he relished, but from the vantage point of subsequent developments and history it is clear that it was a battle that Reuchlin won, and in so doing, he established Christian-Hebraica as the cause célèbre of liberal Christian scholarly circles. In the course of the struggle against censorship, Reuchlin's defenders included major humanists, important church-reform leaders, the majority of future Protestant personalities, and even major northern nationalists like Ulrich von Hutton, who simply opposed Rome and the Dominicans wherever he could do so.

The lurid details of this conflict have been told and retold often and well, and they hardly need detailed reiteration. Yet, one must at least provide the outlines of this struggle that essentially broke the back of organized resistance to Hebrew study and cleared the way for widespread creation of Hebrew-language facilities.

Events began in 1509 when Johannes Pfefferkorn, a convert to Christianity and a protégé of the Dominican friars at Cologne, obtained from Emperor Maximilian an order authorizing the destruction of all Hebrew books found in the possession of Jews in Frankfort and Cologne. Since the turn of the century several Jewish presses, most notably that of the Soncino family in Italy, had been producing significant numbers of books for Jewish religious use. Pfefferkorn argued that Jews would not convert to Christianity if they could make use of their religious writings and the emperor agreed since he saw no reason to impede Jewish conversion. To save their books, the Jews of Cologne appealed to Reuchlin to intervene on their behalf. When that lawyer was requested by the emperor to present his opinion on whether or not Jews should be able to own and use their religious writings, especially the Talmud, Reuchlin presented a forceful argument that Jews were within their rights in owning such volumes and that in any case the books caused no harm to Christendom. As a result of this presentation, the emperor rescinded his order on 23 May 1510. The issue might have been dropped here, but the Dominicans and Pfefferkorn took up the gauntlet when the latter published a venomous and slanderous attack upon Reuchlin under the title *Handspiegel*. Reuchlin responded that same year in a treatise entitled *Augenspiegel* in which he argued that Jewish religious writings posed no threat to any believing Christian and were indeed of great value. Taking that position was an act of courage on Reuchlin's part since never before had any Christian authority defended Jews on this matter. Moreover, the Dominican order envisioned itself as the solitary guardian of Christian light against Jews and other infidels and heretics. As a result of Reuchlin's direct challenge, the Dominican prior in Cologne, Jacob van Hochstraten, became involved in the controversy and Reuchlin was ordered to appear before members of the order in Mainz to answer for his *Augenspiegel*. The charges against him included heresy and slanderous untruths against the Dominicans.

By this time the entire issue had attracted a great deal of attention. The Archbishop Uriel von Gemmingen became involved and suspended the order that Reuchlin appear in Mainz. By order of the pope, the case was to be sent to the bishop of Speyer for clarification of all charges and countercharges. After reviewing the case, the bishop found in favor of Reuchlin, thus apparently bringing the controversy to a close. However, were this the case, Reuchlin would have dealt the Dominicans a humiliating slap by challenging the order's historic position as major guardian of Catholic orthodoxy. Additionally, the concomitant confluence of the defense of Hebrew studies, the cause of church reform, and the general anticlerical mood in the north forced the Dominicans to appeal to the papacy to review the decision of the lower court. It is difficult to assess the many pressures upon Pope Leo at this time. In the interval Luther, one of Reuchlin's defenders, had posted his ninty-five Theses and was aggressively criticizing papal authority on indulgences and in other areas. Perhaps Leo felt that Reuchlin had already carried the day and the time had come to restore Dominican pride, or even that too many were already willing to challenge the voice of tradition and orthodoxy. It is also possible that this leader of God's sheep who shrugged off the Reformation as a "monk's squabble" had an equal understanding of the Reuchlin affair and felt the time had come to end all this mischief making. In any event, in 1520 Leo reversed the findings of the lower court and found Reuchlin's *Augenspiegel* and his defense of Christian-Hebraica guilty of causing scandal.

In the process of defending himself against the Dominicans, Reuchlin's health had been broken, his wealth—or what there was of it—spent on his defense, and his name blackened. Reuchlin was not without his defenders, however, for he had become the man of the hour for all those seeking reform within the Church. Ulrich von Hutten's satirical volume *The Letters of Obscure Men* made a joke of the Dominicans and presented them as ignorant authoritarians whose only justification was their political power. Indeed, Reuchlin the heretic was invited to the University of Ingolstadt

where in February of 1520 he was appointed professor of Greek and Hebrew. Two years later in June of 1522 Reuchlin died at the age of sixty-five,
but not before he had broken the resistance of those who would oppose the
teaching of Hebrew in what one recent historian has correctly described as
the most important and significant intellectual crisis leading to the Protestant Reformation.[20] In the process of granting the Dominican order an
empty victory, the Church alienated some of its best talent and much of its
younger leadership and seriously weakened its ability to deal with Protestantism and the new movement toward national Catholic churches.

Christian-Hebraica owes a debt to both Reuchlin and the Dominican
order: to the former not only because he taught Hebrew, wrote grammars,
and popularized the Cabbalah but also because he defended these pursuits
against the voices of reaction and unreason; and to the latter because its
efforts to stifle Reuchlin and his supporters attracted attention to and support for Christian-Hebraica, both of which it enjoyed for the remainder of
the sixteenth century.

Factor 2: Institutional Support

Any effort to teach Hebrew on a large scale would have had to have
included the universities because that is where the students were. Late medieval universities, however, were conservative institutions, especially resistant to change in the area of language instruction. Despite the recommen-
dations of the Council of Vienne in 1311 that universities establish chairs
for instruction in Hebrew, little or no change occurred. Fortunately for
devotees of Hebrew, the battle to expand university curriculum along more
humanistic lines had already been fought in relation to Greek studies and
language. As a result, the founding of many trilingual colleges throughout
Europe during the early sixteenth century advanced the cause of Greek language instruction and Hebrew as well. Indeed, in attacking Reuchlin, the
Dominicans acquired as critics those who advanced the teaching of Greek
since Reuchlin was as much a prominent scholar of Greek as he was a
scholar in Hebrew.

Trilingual colleges were built upon the solid foundation of royal patronage, which translated into significant financial support and institutional cooperation.[21] Many Renaissance monarchs, such as Francis I and
Henry VIII, took special pleasure in founding such institutions, which
they believed reflected their own personal level of culture and learning.
Francis I founded his trilingual college in 1529. Oxford and Cambridge

reformed their curricula with the support and direction of Bishops Wolsey and Fisher. These new institutions were the first in the north to reflect the new learning that centered upon language instruction, and it is therefore not surprising to find so great a humanist as Desiderius Erasmus guiding the new trilingual college at the University of Louvain where his friend Heironymous Buclidius was appointed professor of Hebrew. In most instances it proved impossible to find competent teachers of Hebrew, and as a result most chairs of Hebrew remained vacant until the supply of Christians trained in Hebrew increased.

The scholarly possibilities represented by the new trilingual colleges were clearly demonstrated in Spain where the University of Alcalá was founded in 1516. Through strong royal patronage, Cardinal Ximenez was able to attract such exceptionally talented Jewish converts as Alphonso of Zamora and Paul Munez Coronel to teach at the university and oversee the publication of the Complutensian Polyglot Bible, printed in 1517. This project, the model for many subsequent editions of the Bible, presented the Hebrew text along with the Septuagint, the Vulgate, and the Aramaic Targum of Onkelos, also with Latin translation. The four-volume publication also presented a short grammatical guide, an index of biblical names, and other textual apparatus. The Alcalá Bible reflected some of the strengths and weaknesses of early Christian-Hebraica publication. The desire for an accurate Hebrew text was easily accommodated in Spain, yet there is something peculiar when so critical a text and apparatus annotations are accompanied by a very basic grammar for those uninstructed in Hebrew. Similarly, the Septuagint and the Aramaic translations were important for scholars, but the Latin translation of the Aramaic must have been included for the benefit of those same students for whom the basic grammar was prepared. Similarly, a better, more accurate, translation should have replaced the Vulgate. In short, the Alcalá Bible was a curious blending of skills and critical care, but the identity of the readership for which the Bible was prepared is less apparent. Still, whatever its shortcomings, it was a fine example of what might be produced with strong royal financial support, positive Church leadership, interreligious intellectual communication, and the miracle of printing.

Hebrew study was especially encouraged in France from a surprisingly early date, if one considers that France did not have Spain's vast supply of Jewish converts. Augusto Justiniani, bishop of Nebbia in Corsica, taught Hebrew in Paris from 1517 to 1522 under the sponsorship of Guillaume Petit, confessor to Francis I and a leading personality instrumental in the subsequent founding of the trilingual college.[22] In 1516 Justiniani published his *Psalterium Polyglottum*, which presented the text in Hebrew, Aramaic, Arabic, Greek, and Latin and was just one of many psalters that would appear during the next few decades. Justiniani was a typical Catholic Hebraist interested in providing adequate texts, even if no one could use them. Surely an Arabic version of the Psalms increased the cost of publication considerably and was of doubtful value since the only people who could read it were Jews who preferred the Hebrew. Moreover, with the exception of Papal Avignon, there had been no Jews in France since their expulsion in 1394.

Petit was instrumental in bringing to Paris other scholars than Justiniani. The convert Paul Paradisus, Agatha Guidecerius, and François Vatable were others receiving royal patronage through Petit's sponsorship. Both Pardisus and Guidecerius were brought to Paris from Italy, with the latter noting, "Francis I made me happier and more peaceful than all the Medici and all the popes could have done."[23] He was not exaggerating Francis's largess, for Guidacerius had fallen upon hard times in Italy when he lost his entire library and all his possessions in the sack of Rome in 1527. Guidacerius managed to keep body and soul together by residing at the Avignon residence of Cardinal Sadoleto, but he had few, if any, manuscripts from which to work. Francis's offer of employment in Paris included a very attractive salary and the promise of royal support for publication. Moreover, Petit was able to acquire for Guidacerius copies of many of the works he had lost in 1527. This investment in one scholar proved to be fruitful, and Guidacerius published a respectable number of texts.

Guidacerius's efforts were notable in two respects. First, he was the first true Hebrew scholar in France and he did much to set a standard for accurate publication. Second, his work demonstrates both the nature and the limitations of Hebrew scholarship in Catholic centers. Guidacerius's active interest in texts was not matched by an equal interest in the rabbinic commentaries on those texts. In this respect, Catholic and Protestant Hebraists differed sharply, for the latter were as devoted to rabbinic exegesis as they were to retrieving the text itself. Quite possibly, this interest in the text pure and simple reflected a continuing respect for the Vulgate as the official translation of the Church and for the papacy as the only agency qualified to interpret that translation. Once the Council of Trent affirmed the position of the Vulgate as the only recognized translation and religiously valid presentation of Scripture, interest in Hebrew in Catholic centers diminished from even this modest desire to collect and collate accurate texts.[24] Understandably, the best Catholic Hebraica was in the area of Cabbalistic studies and not in the area of Scripture.

The major accomplishment of the trilingual colleges was not in the area of publication, however, but in teaching Hebrew to large numbers of students. Indeed, Hebrew instruction was very popular, and it is reasonable to assume that after just a year or two of instruction, more Frenchmen could read Hebrew than all the Christians in Italy at the turn of the century when Reuchlin studied with Obadiah Sforno. In this sense, royal patronage was a most important factor in providing for the instruction of Hebrew in most Catholic countries.

In other parts of Europe a different, though not less successful, institutional pattern emerges. Protestant centers also exhibited interest in Hebrew studies, but the organization of these studies was often somewhat different. A good case in point was the career of Conrad Pellican.

Pellican was born in Rouffach in Alsace in 1478 and joined the Franciscan order at an early age.[25] As was often the case, his introduction to Hebrew was rather accidental. In his *Chronikon* Pellican explained that as a child he attended a public disputation at which a Christian debator was unable to better his Jewish opponent primarily because the latter was more familiar with the OT Hebrew text. The debate lingered in his mind, and he decided to learn Hebrew but "could not presently find among the Jews of Alsace, Worms, Frankfort or Ratisbone or other places, one who could resolve grammatical questions."[26] He described borrowing a copy of Johannes Behem of Ulm's small grammar, which was so poor that Pellican could learn little from it. What little Hebrew the young Pellican knew, he learned from the convert Matthew Adrian who taught at the Franciscan house in Basel in 1502. Eventually he acquired enough knowledge to produce his own short primer of mediocre quality published in Strasbourg in 1503–1504. Though it did not compare favorably with Reuchlin's work of a few years later, Pellican's little grammar was the first competent work produced by a Christian and it represents considerable skill.

Pellican's first textual accomplishment came in 1516 when he published his *Hebraicum Psalterium* in Basel, essentially a reprinting of the standard Jewish text. From 1523 to 1526 he taught Hebrew in Basel, but he assumed his most important position in 1526 when he moved to Zurich where he remained until his death in 1556. In January of 1526 Zwingli wrote to Pellican to offer employment, "You are to read daily a certain section of the Hebrew text; we are now beginning the second book of Moses. Beyond that no other burden will rest upon you."[27] In return for these services Zwingli promised a lifetime tenure and a decent wage. Already in 1526 increasing demand for Hebraists was apparent, and Zwingli noted, "We know, of course, that the printers of books will try to hold you, but do not heed these people of money." In return for leaving Froben of Basel, the group of scholars Pellican was to join included Zwingli and Bullinger as well as Leo Juda, Myconius, Jacob Amman, Rudolph Collin, and "all urge that you do not hesitate." Pellican accepted the offer and began his lectures on 1 March 1526, and his contribution to that group of scholars was assessed by Bullinger, himself a Hebraist. Bullinger noted that Pellican presented the text "in the Hebrew language indicating here and there the idioms and properties of the language. Then he discussed its meaning, often with literal interpretation and with quotations from the [Jewish] grammarians and rabbis."[28]

Pellican discharged this responsibility until his death in 1556. This group of scholars, several of whom knew Hebrew, was a model for other study groups. Oecolampadius wrote to Zwingli, "We have remodelled the theological lectures after the pattern of your church. A Hebrew professor lectures on the OT and a Greek [professor] on the NT. I myself am to add a theological exposition from Latin on both of their more purely grammatical ones."[29]

Zwingli was aware of the rare talents he had collected to study Scripture, and he noted, "There are probably in this hall men as learned in Greek, Latin, and Hebrew as at Tübingen, Basel, Freiburg and elsewhere." Regarding Hebrew study in Catholic centers, Zwingli observed, "Zurich has probably as many scholars as learned in the three languages as he [Faber] and his people in a heap, and who understand the Scripture better than those at Lyon and Paris."[30]

There are some obvious differences between Pellican's position and role in Zurich and Guidacerius's position in Paris during the same years. Pellican was well versed in rabbinic exegesis, and he willingly admitted his dependence upon such sources as Rashi, Joseph and David Kimchi, and Abraham Ibn Ezra: "In difficult passages certainly recourse must be had to the Hebrew truth."[31] The avid use of rabbinic commentary was a hallmark of Protestant Christian Hebraica, especially in the Reformed centers of Strasbourg and Basel. Oecolampadius noted, for instance, "Except I had had the ability to read Hebrew and consult the commentaries of the Hebrews, I would not have dared to undertake this" edition of Isaiah.[32] Similar sentiments were expressed in his volume of Daniel published five years later in 1530 in Basel. As we shall see in those chapters dealing with exegesis, Jewish glosses were used for interpretation and for textual criticism; we have already had opportunity to note the importance of the masorah and other apparatus. Guidacerius, on the other hand, produced texts, or more accurately, reprinted standard Jewish texts. Additionally, Protestant scholars were more interested in translating the text, as the crowning achievement of this Zurich group would indicate. The Zurich translation of the Bible was Leo Juda's project until his death in 1542, whereupon Pellican took charge of the project and pursued it to its completion. Since translation involves interpretation, Protestant scholars may have used Jewish sources to a far greater extent and in the process developed a far greater competence in Hebrew studies. Similarly, the creation of an alternate Christian theology during the Reformation demanded a reorientation of many OT ideas and images to facilitate this new thinking. This too required greater competence in Hebrew, especially in reformed Protestant centers that premised much of their covenantal approach on the old covenant of the OT.

In discussing early Hebraists, we have necessarily dealt with Paris and Zurich as two centers that successfully attracted Hebraists. In both instances existing institutional frameworks incorporated Hebraica, thereby permitting the study of Hebrew to benefit from the strengths of those institutions. How Hebrew study would benefit from existing institutions and the important role of royal patronage are indicated by the efforts of the University of Wittenberg to find a Hebraist. In May of 1518 a rather agitated monk wrote to his mentor, George Spalatin, about a series of issues but added to the end of his letter the following note: "Finally, I hope and ask of you not to forget our university; that is, that you be concerned for the establishment of a chair in Greek and a chair in Hebrew. I believe you have seen the announcement of the University of Leipzig; as usual they imitate us."[33] Luther's plea bore partial results. Philip Melanchthon filled the position in Greek and the rivalry with Leipzig remained for decades, but the position in Hebrew went unfilled.

In another letter dated 22 May 1519, Luther again ended with a request for a Hebrew teacher, "I also ask before leaving you, sound out the Most Illustrious Sovereign's [Elector Frederick's] opinion concerning a professor of Hebrew and let us know what he thinks." Never one to leave anything unsaid, Luther continued, "John Keller from Burgkundstadt has been with us; he plans to return shortly. He taught Hebrew at Heidelberg and is the author of a small grammar (which I believe you have seen) in which he shows that he does know something in this field." Aware that Hebraists commanded good salaries, Luther stated, "He [Keller] promised us he would do everything in his power to be a reliable teacher if he could be sure that he would be provided with a decent salary by our Most Illustrious Sovereign." And then Luther added what must have been truly disturbing, "At the moment he [Keller] is in Leipzig waiting for our answer."[34]

The rivalry with Leipzig involved not only institutional pride but also competition for limited resources. Keller, whose humanistic name was Cellarius Gnostopolitanus, had taught Hebrew at various institutions including Mainz, Tübingen, Heidelberg, and Louvain. The negotiations with Luther continued for over a year with the result that Keller rejected Luther's offer of fifty guilden a year for a far better offer—at Leipzig.

Fearing the same situation would repeat itself, Luther again wrote to Spalatin on 7 November 1519. This time he was more insistent and did not confine his request to the end of the letter: "Greetings. Matthew Adrian, a Jew from Louvain, has written to me, my Spalatin, as you will see from the enclosed letter. He was forced to leave there [University of Louvain] because of their tyranny and asks to teach Hebrew [at Wittenberg]."[35] Adrian had previously taught Hebrew in Tübingen, Basel, Heidelberg, Liége, and Louvain. He left the last location when he became embroiled in a Reuchlin type of controversy. It appears that on 21 March 1519 he gave a public lecture praising the three classical languages and argued that they were a prerequisite for theological study. The traditionalists, led by James Latomus, so harassed Adrian that he was forced to leave.[36] Adrian's Jewish background also seems to have been a problem, but this might have been the case at almost any other institution as well. In any event, Luther continued in his letter to praise this "Jew" Adrian: "You know the fame and learnedness of this man. Therefore, please bring to the attention of the Most Illustrious Sovereign the gifts of God of a most distinguished opportunity to promote the study of Hebrew among us. I ask you to reply as quickly as possible so that I might give him an answer."[37]

Luther wrote to Spalatin again on 19 March 1520 about another Hebraist, Werner Einhorn of Bacharach, also a convert from Judaism. In the meantime Adrian was in Berlin, but he still sought employment at Wittenberg. As a result, Luther had dealings with two Hebraists both of whom were waiting to hear from him. Once again Luther wrote to Spalatin, on 16 April 1520:

Greetings. We have agreed with Adrian, my Spalatin, that he should wait a little. He promised to remain in Berlin for 8 days and await a letter from us. Now our task is to get an answer from Werner of Bacharach as soon as possible, Adrian, of course, demands a salary of 100 guilden in all. In this whole affair we have to be extremely careful that, as the saying goes, in trying to sit on two chairs, we don't fall between them. This should be the case if we should turn this one down and the other should by chance go elsewhere, either of his own accord or because he was being called by Mainz. Many of our friends have strongly urged me to see that Matthew is hired for at least a year, they believe, if only to avoid any notoriety because of our "Eclipse" [Leipzig.]. Rumor has it they might call him just in spite of us. . . . I suspect he has made up his mind to accept a Hebrew professorship either at Frankfort or Leipzig if we do not call him. Do answer quickly.[38]

Adrian was indeed hired and called to Wittenberg at the end of April 1520. Despite his abilities and efforts to find employment at that institution, Adrian resigned a year later and moved to Leipzig.

Adrian's successor was Matthew Goldhahn, or Aurogallus as he was called. He came to Wittenberg in 1521 and remained there until his death in 1543. Reversing a trend, Aurogallus had come from Leipzig, and in addition to a good salary Luther attempted to make him as comfortable as possible. In a letter to Spalatin on 20 May 1522, Luther wrote, "Grace and Peace, my Spalatin. Aurogallus asks if possible he be honored with some venison for his wedding. . . . Do what you can."[39] Though he taught competently, Aurogallus did not distinguish himself through publication. His successor, Johannes Forster, was the most able Hebraist employed at Wittenberg and commanded a salary of two hundred guilden.

Without the financial support of his most illustrious sovereign, Luther would not have acquired the services of a Hebraist at Wittenberg. However helpful Cardinal Grimani in Italy had been just two decades earlier in arranging for Hebrew instruction for Reuchlin and Bomberg and many others, by the second decade of the sixteenth century Hebrew was available without travel to Italy and without the intercession of the rich and powerful. The Reuchlin controversy had stirred the fires and brought Hebrew to a level of popular acceptance; and in Paris, Wittenberg, Zurich, Basel, Heidelberg, Tübingen, Mainz, Liége, Louvain, and so many other places, Hebrew was being taught to large numbers of students. One problem remained: Did these students studying in so many places have grammars and texts to learn from? Obviously they did, for Christian-Hebraica was just beginning to blossom in 1520. How an active Christian-Hebraica press came about, however, is a separate story.

Factor 3: A Jewish Press for Christians

Whether in the area of critical scriptural study, Cabbalistic numerology, or the teaching of students, the services of an active and exacting press was necessary. More than any other person of the early sixteenth century, Daniel Bomberg was responsible for meeting the growing need for publications of quality.[40] Indeed, Bomberg's productions were so good and so exact that his efforts soon eclipsed the efforts of all the Jewish presses to that time and became the absolute standard for most types of Hebrew publication.

Bomberg was born in Antwerp about 1480, the son of a wealthy burgher, Cornelius Van Bomberghen. Little is known about his youth, education, or introduction to printing, but it appears he was persuaded to undertake the publication of the Psalms by Felix Praetensis, also known as Felice de Prato, in 1515. In that year Praetensis's translation of the Hebrew Psalms into Latin was published in Venice. In that same year Bomberg applied for and received a copyright for his new typeface and form of print. His letters and format became so popular that a majority of OT Bibles published by other publishers boasted of using "Bomberg print." This became the standard typeface and, only slightly modified, was used until very recently. Similarly, the Bomberg format of using different size and shape letters for different glosses in wide margins surrounding a narrow column of text was soon accepted as the basic layout for the OT and the volumes of the Talmud.

Bomberg's first major project was the *Mikra'ot G'dolot,* his famous Rabbinic Bible, found on virtually every Hebraist's desk. This was not another super-spectacular polyglot Bible offering the reader the biblical text in yet more languages. Instead, he presented the most accurate Hebrew text published up to that time, the complete *Targum* (Aramaic paraphrases) and a full array of major and minor rabbinic commentaries and glosses. The first edition of this four-volume study appeared in 1517–1518 and was so successful that an enlarged second edition appeared in 1523 with subsequent editions published in 1546, 1548, 1568, and yet again in 1618 by Buxdorf in Basel. Even this list does not take into account the many pirated editions produced by other publishers, all produced with Bomberg print but often without his accuracy.

Felix Praetensis served as editor for the first edition with later editions edited by Abraham De Balmes; Rabbi Hiyya Meir ben David, chief magistrate of the Venice Jewish Court; and Elias Levita, the greatest Jewish grammarian of the age.

The publication consisted of four volumes. The first volume contained a long introduction by Jacob ben Chayim, a co-editor, addressing the entire project and an index to the entire OT organized according to standard Jewish divisions of Scripture with the Books of Samuel, Kings, and Chronicles divided into two books each and the Book of Nehemiah published separately from the Book of Ezra. Also in the first volume was Ibn Ezra's introduction to the Five Books of Moses. The Hebrew text was accompanied by the Aramaic interpretations, rabbinic glosses, and the complete masoretic apparatus for the Pentateuch.

Volume two presented the text of earlier, historical prophets from Joshua through the Second Book of Kings along with glosses, Targum, and masorah. Volume three presented the same format and commentaries for the remaining prophets with the last volume presenting the hagiographic writings also with glosses, Targum, and masorah. The fourth volume also presented a treatise on masoretic markings as well as the debate between Ben Asher and Ben Naphtali concerning the different markings of the Jerusalem and Babylonian manuscripts according to these two tenth-century Jewish exegetes.

The significance of this publication lay in its exactness of text, in its freedom from typographical error, in its quality of ink and materials, and most important, in its presentation of something of a distillation of major Jewish exegesis on the OT. Rather than produce a translation, Bomberg published the consummate text along with all the critical apparatus necessary for true scholarly work and study of the OT.

The success of this project led Bomberg to undertake an even more difficult and demanding task, if one somewhat more peripheral to the vantage point of this volume. In 1523 Bomberg published, for the first time and with papal permission, the complete Babylonian and Jerusalem Talmud. Though such Jewish publishers as Gershom Soncino had previously published individual tracts of the Talmud, no attempt had been made to publish the entire corpus of writings with commentaries and glosses. Bomberg was extremely proud of this undertaking, and the edition was so successful that most subsequent editions of the Talmud retained Bomberg's format and pagination.

Other than these masterpieces, both of which attracted attention in Jewish and Christian scholarly circles, Bomberg's greatest contribution lay in his production of high-quality grammatical guides for Christian use. In 1529 and 1545 Bomberg published David Kimchi's *Book of Roots* as well as Kimchi's more advanced grammar, the *Michlol*, along with critical notes and discussion by Elias Levita. As early as 1523 this Venetian press published Abraham De Balmes's *Mikve Avram* along with its Latin translation, the *Peculium Abramae*. Similarly, much of Levita's best work was produced by Bomberg, including his revolutionary *Masoret ha-Masoret* and *Tub-Taam*, both of which were published in 1538 and will be discussed below. Equally noteworthy, however, was the publication of Isaac Nathan ben Kalonymous's *Meir Netib* in 1523. This work was a complete concordance to the OT and was the first such work published for a mass audience. It was edited by Jacob ben Chayim and enjoyed both wide regard and wide popularity within Christian and Jewish scholarly circles.

One reason Bomberg's publications were so much better than anything else being published at the time was that he elicited the cooperation of the finest Jewish scholars available to him. A very gentle man of tolerant disposition, Bomberg was not infected with anti-Semitic feeling and thereby became both a close friend of and good colleague to his editorial staff. Consequently, whereas Parisian Hebraists gave the world a never-ending series of editions of the Psalms and a few elementary grammars, Bomberg produced a variety of critical editions of rabbinic commentary, the best-quality grammatical thought, and other resource material necessary for scholars wishing to read more than the Psalms.

Factor 4: Jewish Cooperation

The role of Jewish converts in the early years of Christian-Hebraica was fundamental in several senses. Many of the earliest itinerant teachers, such as Matthew Adrian and Werner of Bacharach, were converts, as were almost all the staff at Alcalá. Indeed, to some extent, one might consider early Christian-Hebraica a function of large-scale Jewish conversion to Christianity during the Renaissance, for these converts brought to their new religion many of the skills previously retained only within the Jewish community. Jewish converts played the same important role in the area of publication with Bomberg, for instance, making extensive use of the skills of such scholars as Felix Praetensis and Cornelius Adelkind, both eminent Hebraists.

Less apparent was the important role Jews played in Christian-Hebraica, though that role was far more fundamental perhaps because there were far more skilled Jews than there were converts. Jews were a hidden element in the development of Hebraica if only because society was not ready to admit the Jew to anything resembling full legal status and because Jewish cooperation was not something most Christians wished to publicize. Among publishers, only Bomberg was willing to turn operations over to Jews who made up a majority of his staff at all levels.

Before dealing with some of the more significant Jewish scholars involved with early Christian-Hebraica, it would be well to discuss those qualities many Christian Hebraists lacked which only Jewish Hebraists or Jewish converts might supply. This discussion will help explain some of the obstacles Christian students of Hebrew would have to overcome and give some hint of those Jewish intellectual tendencies that Christian scholars would accept and develop.

For a great many Christian scholars, Hebrew was a one-dimensional language in which Scripture was written. Because Hebrew was God's language and God never changes, it was easy and perhaps logical to assume that Hebrew had a uniform character and personality and was not subject to either internal or historical development and change. Indeed, the notion of linguistic development was less than a century old. Lorenzo Valla did much to demonstrate how Latin usage changed from one age to another when he exposed *The Donation of Constantine* as a forgery. Two factors made the study of "historical Latin" possible: first, there was at hand an abundance of Latin materials from classical times as well as from the Middle Ages; and second, widespread familiarity with the Latin language and its continuing widespread use in the areas of Scripture, law, medicine, philosophy, and literature provided ample opportunity for scholars to view the differences in usage employed by different disciplines in different ages. Compared to the sophistication demonstrated by scholars in Latin studies, scholars in Hebrew studies were either naive or ignorant in terms of their understanding of Hebrew development. We shall see in later chapters that as many Christian scholars became aware of the differences that exist in the Hebrew used in different ages, they argued that Jews "perverted" Hebrew.

There was little awareness of the development of the Hebrew language through its many separate phases of growth and stagnation and renewed growth. The earliest books of Scripture had been written well over a thousand years before Christ, with the last writings composed only shortly before his birth. Some hagiographic writings were the product of Jewish exile whereas others were written in Judea but reflect intense Hellenistic influence in both style and format as well as word usage. In turn, rabbinic

glosses were written during the Middle Ages and reflect a Hebrew development far removed from apostolic Judea. Some rabbis were influenced by the
Latin culture of western Europe while others reflected the Arabic culture in
which most Jewish scholars were immersed.

Aramaic posed another dimension to this problem of the historicity of
Hebrew. Gaining competence in that language was an essential task for the
Christian-Hebraist and not an overly difficult one once Hebrew had been
fully mastered. More difficult was appreciating the continuing mutual influence Hebrew and Aramaic exerted on each other after the Pharisaic age.
It was entirely common for medieval sources to use Aramaic and Hebrew
somewhat interchangeably in the same sentence, reflecting yet other permutations and combinations of meaning and intent.

Jewish scholars were traditionally understood by Christians to be "too
historical" in their interpretation of Scripture. Certainly there were many
theological and systematic reasons for this belief, as when a historical interpretation of the Psalms was used by Jews to deflate any Christian prophetic interpretations that centered upon Jesus. Yet, even without the systematic considerations, the historical quality of Jewish exegesis and
religious thought was part of an awareness of the historical development of
Hebrew. Consequently, one of the hallmarks of much Christian-Hebraica
was an increasing awareness that Scripture had to be interpreted within the
context of the age in which it was written and not limited to the vantage
point of systematic theology developed at a later time. This growing historical awareness was not altogether popular. Many scholars hoped to leave
the rocky shoals of medieval Church tradition for the secure bedrock of
Scripture as the Word of God only to discover that the bedrock was not so
secure and that the Word of God was not without its own variety of expression and diversity of meaning.

The quality that Jewish scholarship brought to Christian-Hebraica
was precisely the same concept of linguistic development that Valla had
brought to Latin studies earlier. This was especially true in the early sixteenth century since the most exciting and revolutionary work being done
within the Jewish community concerned itself with Hebrew's historical
development. Bomberg made one of his greatest contributions when he
acquired the services of Elias Levita, the greatest Jewish grammarian since
David Kimchi, whose most significant contribution lay in the area of the
masorah and in developing an even more historically critical sense of Hebrew development.[41]

Elias Levita was born in Southern Germany in the year 1468 but spent most of his life in Italy where the intellectual and social atmosphere was significantly more liberal in both Jewish and Christian scholarly circles. He lived in Padua for a number of years but lost his possessions and manuscripts when that city was conquered by the League of Cambray. Escaping to Rome, Levita found refuge in the home of Cardinal Egidio de Viterbo, a prominent ecclesiastic and scholar. Temporary refuge soon turned to personal friendship and Levita stayed with the cardinal for thirteen years where, in exchange for Greek lessons, Levita taught the cardinal Hebrew. During this thirteen-year period Levita wrote some of his most important early works. His *Sefer ha-Bahur* of 1518 was a basic but very comprehensive grammar and his *Sefer ha-Harcava* was a complete compilation of all biblical irregular verbs. Indeed, Levita's linguistic interests focused largely on the unusual and irregular features of Hebrew grammar. In attempting to provide the student of Hebrew with a good grasp of Hebrew's peculiarities, Levita wrote his *Pirkei Eliyahu* consisting of essays on various points of Hebrew structure and development.

Levita again lost all his possessions in the sack of Rome in 1527 and found refuge in Venice with Daniel Bomberg. For the next decade and a half Levita was employed by Bomberg in a variety of capacities which utilized that scholar's rare talents. Under Bomberg's sponsorship Levita again produced some very fine work. He began work on his volume *Sefer ha-Zichronot*, which dealt with the masorah and which was to take him some twenty years to complete. Subsequent works in this period also dealt with masoretic theory. His *Masoret ha-Masoret* of 1538 argued that vowel and punctuation markings were the product of the post-talmudic age and were not composed during the scriptural age itself. This was a revolutionary theory, for essentially Levita was claiming that this important key to understanding the Bible text was neither divinely originated nor known to the authors of Scripture.

The implications of Levita's theories were far reaching. Not only did Levita breach the wall of divine authorship of Scripture but in one swipe he also made irrelevant many exegetical systems, such as the Cabbalistic, which often used masoretic markings in their mystical arguments. Another implication was that the basic OT text was less reliable than previously thought because certain values and approaches to the text had been determined by a postscriptural age. Levita continued this line of reasoning in his small volume, *Tub-Taam*, where a similar argument was made regarding all voweling and accent markings. This argument was even more radical insofar as Levita left only the consonants as attributable to possible divine authorship. For Christians, Levita's arguments meant that any return to OT Scripture would necessarily rely upon earlier Jewish scholarship.

In 1540 Levita was invited by a former student, Paul Fagius, to oversee the latter's press at Isny in Württemberg, and later in Constance. Once again his scholarship broke new ground and was useful in serving both Jewish and Christian needs. Accommodating Fagius's own interests in talmudic literature and Aramaic, Levita brought out his *Meturgeman* in 1541. This volume was a complete Aramaic dictionary which, though it was completed in 1531, was not published until this later time. Sebastian Münster had already published his Aramaic dictionary in 1527. In the preface to that work Münster claimed that Levita had been the source for most of the information presented in his dictionary. Levita's dictionary, finally published fourteen years later, was far more complete. Levita noted in his own preface, "I have not added nor subtracted anything, nor have I omitted one word, be it easy or difficult, from all the Targums of the Bible." In fact, not a single word from the Targum had been deleted and, compared with Münster's fine work, Levita's work was both broader and deeper. For the first letter of the alphabet Münster listed 128 entries to Levita's 278. Where Münster referred to the verse in Scripture, Levita quoted the entire phrase in Hebrew and Aramaic.

Two other works published in this period reflect Levita's interests in Christian needs. His *Tishbi* of 1541 was a dictionary of 712 difficult terms, their explanations, and their comparative usages. In that same year he also produced another important work, the *Aruch*. This alphabetical listing of 1,000 difficult terms and expressions, with corresponding German and Latin forms and usages, was extremely valuable to any scholar hoping to translate Scripture from Hebrew.

Levita also produced several works intended only for the Jewish community, such as his Yiddish translation of many parts of Scripture and his *Bovo-Buch*, a volume of romances stylistically reminiscent of Boccaccio's work. Levita was so respected and well known in scholarly circles that Francis I offered him the chair of Hebrew at Paris. Levita declined the offer, explaining that he would feel uncomfortable in any country forbidding Jewish residence.

Other than Levita, Bomberg employed several other Jewish scholars of note. We have already had occasion to mention Jacob ben Chayim Ibn Adonijah, author of the general introduction to the Rabbinic Bible, editor of that edition, and general editor of the second edition of that work. He also served as a co-editor of the Babylonian Talmud of 1523 and general editor of the Palestinian Talmud of 1522–1523. Additionally, Jacob ben Chayim had full responsibility for preparing the concordance of 1523 for publication. In short, Jacob ben Chayim took responsibility for most of Bomberg's most exciting projects. Indeed, he was responsible for conceiving these publications, work that would have been considered nothing short of spectacular for any other press.

Part of his value to Bomberg lay in ben Chayim's uncanny ability to locate and purchase exact texts in the different Jewish communities around the world, including Salonika, Poland, and Palestine. Half a century earlier the finest manuscripts would have come from Spain, but with the exile of 1492 virtually the entire literary wealth of this community had been lost. Consequently, the ability to locate alternate texts of quality was not merely fundamental to Christian-Hebraica but extremely important to the Jewish community as well. Much as Bomberg made it possible for Jews to reproduce much of their lost intellectual heritage, ben Chayim made it possible for Bomberg to produce the best copy of the best texts. Searching for these texts was expensive, and ben Chayim wrote, "His [Bomberg's] hand was never closed nor did he draw back his right hand from producing the gold from his purse to defray the expenses of the books and of the messengers who were engaged to search for them in the most remote corners and in every place where they might possibly be found."[42] It is likely that without ben Chayim, Bomberg would have produced only grammars by Levita and many more editions of the Psalms.

Another Jewish scholar of great importance to Bomberg was Hiya Meir ben Meir, a *dayan*, or "chief magistrate," of the Venice Jewish Court. After leaving that position in 1520, ben Meir was employed by Bomberg as a general editor, but his talents were especially significant in the publication of the Talmud. As a magistrate, ben Meir's knowledge and understanding of the Talmud, Jewish civil and canon law, was unparalleled. The ordering of texts, the volume organization of this multivolume corpus of writings, and the selection of glosses were entirely ben Meir's responsibility. The choices this scholar made were very fortunate; this edition became the standard format and pattern reproduced for several centuries.

A third noteworthy Jewish scholar was Cornelius ben Baruch Adelkind. This man was employed by Bomberg for twenty years, from 1524 to 1544, during which time he worked in every possible capacity from co-

editor to proof reader, from financial manager to personal confidant. Adelkind converted to Christianity before his death and willed to his son his
new religion and all his skills in printing and Hebrew publication.

These three examples should suffice to make one central point. Aside
from being indispensable to a richer appreciation of Hebrew linguistics,
Jewish scholars were necessary to locate accurate texts for publication, to
select glosses and organize their arrangement, and to proofread the results
after the type had been set. In the early years of the sixteenth century Christian talents in these areas had not yet matured, though by midcentury many
non-Jewish scholars would possess these abilities. Much as Reuchlin's
campaign to popularize Hebrew was extremely important and much as the
institutional support given Hebrew studies through royal patronage was
fundamental, so, too, were Bomberg's efforts in securing Jewish cooperation with Christian-Hebraica, for without this mutual effort and cooperation no adequate press would have been created.

There was one other Christian press active in Christian-Hebraica publication, Froben of Basel. The moving spirit behind almost all the work
carried on by this important press was Sebastian Münster, the greatest
Christian-Hebraist of the first half of the sixteenth century. Although his
early work, as we shall see, was entirely dependent upon Jewish scholarship, Münster's later publications reflected increasing Christian independence and a growing *Christian*-Hebraica. Consequently, Münster and
Froben represent first fruits of the Bomberg-Levita tree of Hebrew learning.

Sebastian Münster was born in Ingleheim in 1488 and died in Basel in
1553.[43] He studied under the noted Hebraist Conrad Pellican at the Franciscan monastery at Roufach, which he joined in 1505. After converting to
Protestantism in 1524, Münster accepted a teaching position at the University of Heidelberg but moved to the University of Basel in 1528 where he
held the position of professor of Hebrew and theology until his death
twenty-five years later. The scope of Münster's interest in Hebraica was
immense, and by the end of the sixteenth century over 100,000 volumes of
his work were in circulation. With the exception of Jewish Cabbalistic and
mystical studies, for which he had no patience, Münster contributed to
virtually every aspect of Hebraica, and we shall have occasion to deal with
his many types of writings in many chapters of this book.

Münster's almost three-score publications in Hebraica cover a period
of over three and a half decades. During the 1520s and 1530s Münster composed grammars as did every other Hebraist of the age. These works served
two purposes: the instruction of students and the demonstration of the au-

thor's competence in Hebrew. Münster's grammars, however, were by far the best produced by any early Christian-Hebraist. His first work was entitled *Epitmoe Hebraicae Grammaticae* and was published by Froben in Basel. Four years later a much revised and improved grammar appeared under the title *M'lechet ha-Dikduk: Institutiones Grammaticae in Hebraeam Linguam*. In 1525 an even better and yet more complete grammar appeared with the title *Sefer ha-Dikduk: Grammatica Hebraicae Absolutissima*. This last work marked a turning point in Münster's Hebrew development, for this "absolutissima" volume was in fact a translation of Levita's *Sefer ha-Bahur*. To this point Münster's publications were better than those produced by other Christian-Hebraists, but they were essentially variations on the same theme. There is little reason to doubt that Münster would have progressed past this level of competence had he continued to work on his own since his basic linguistic skills were so much superior to any other Christian-Hebraist's abilities. Yet, in the preface of this pirated 1525 grammar Münster wrote, "Simon Grynaeus kindly promised and sent me the book [*Sefer ha-Bahur*] printed in Rome and known only to a few in Germany. I postponed all other studies and not without the greatest effort, I most dilligently translated it into Latin." Up to that time Münster had depended upon Abraham De Balmes: "I found that its author Elias, deserves—in my opinion—so much more praise than Abraham De Balmes whose recent grammar is less satisfactory. I feel that all those who wrote grammars previously had very little learning compared with him." Though Münster was already considered a prominent teacher of Hebrew, he noted, "I openly admit and I am not ashamed to say so, that I knew very little Hebrew grammar before I read this Elias, and indeed, that I owe much if not most of my knowledge to the elucidations of his books." In great modesty, Münster wrote, "We have become teachers before being students."[44]

After this time Münster did not bother to compose his own grammars but simply translated Levita's work into Latin or reprinted it as it was. At times sections of different works were brought together, it seemed, according to his students' needs. In 1525 Münster published Levita's *Sefer ha-Harkava* dealing with irregular verbs and nouns. Two years later he published his first "compendium" of Levita's works, the *Compendium Hebraicae Grammaticae ex Eliae Judaei Variis et optimis libris*, which was in turn followed by the *Isagoge Elementalis per quam succincta in linguam Hebraicam a Sebastian Münster nunc primum conscripta* in 1535. Over the next several years others of Levita's works appeared from the Basel publisher, and finally, in 1547, Münster published the finest and most complete single grammar to come from any press. The *Opus Grammaticum Consummatum ex variis Elianis libris concinnatum* went through repeated editions and reprintings and became the most widely used grammar book for the teaching of Hebrew to Christians. More complicated and esoteric points of grammar were deleted and the student was referred to other works by Levita. The preface to this work explains why Münster undertook the creation of one more grammar: "It appeared advisable to combine in one volume all the grammatical rules previously found here and there in several books. One integral unit was created out of separate pieces. . . . " Here as elsewhere Münster acknowledged his dependence upon Levita, noting, "As you know, I have nourished and promoted this study in the Christian world, making full use of the various books of Elias, which, with my little talent, I have put into Latin and which I have made available to all students." Considering the many grammars composed by Christian scholars, Münster felt the need to justify his continuing use of Levita's works: "In all the grammatical works written by Christians before Elias began his work, the true fundamental [grounding] was missing."[45]

Not wishing to diminish the work done by others before him or the work of contemporary Christians, his colleagues, Münster added, "I do not say any of these things to denigrate the men who attempted to promote Hebrew studies before Elias. Every real scholar does as much as he possibly can do and no one should be deprived of his due praise." Among those noteworthies singled out for mention were Capito, John Campen, Reuchlin, Pellican, and Pagninus, but none could compare with Levita, and in almost religious tones Münster wrote, "The Lord awakened a certain Jew in Italy, who was really born in Germany, . . . this man, Elias by name—who was requested by his Jewish brothers to do so—composed a most excellent grammar about 1518, for which he made use of the best Hebrew texts and sources. He called this book *Bahur*, Liber Electus, in which he describes and explains the entire basis of Hebrew grammar." After describing this work, Münster wrote a few words about Levita's other works: "After the *Bahur*, the most valuable work to me and all other students is the *Capitula Elias*. In this treatise he discusses the vowel points, silent letters, and gutturals. . . . Finally, the book *Ta'amim* [*Tub-Taam*] which is appended to the *Masoret ha-Masoret*. . . . "

Münster was one of very few scholars who could appreciate Levita's theories regarding vowel points and accents and the religious implications of Hebrew cultural and linguistic development. Later in this volume we shall observe how these issues caused deep splits between different schools of Hebraists, some of whom refused to accept the historical development of Hebrew-language use while others, like Münster and Fagius, accepted these progressive views to develop a rich understanding of historical Hebrew.

In attempting to discover the intellectual and cultural background of the OT Hebrew idiom, Münster was as devoted to Aramaic studies as he was to the pure Hebrew idiom itself. Indeed, at an early date Münster demonstrated an interest in Aramaic study for both OT and NT scriptural purposes. In 1523 Münster published his first attempt in the difficult area of Aramaic language study in his *Dictionarium Hebraicum . . . adiectis Chaldaicis vocabulis*. This minor work, more an appendage than a complete study, was superseded just a few years later in 1527 with a complete grammar, the *Chaldaica Grammatica*. Münster was also aware of the need for rabbinic opinion and commentary for a clearer view of scriptural Hebrew and for determining the quality of the cultural background of the NT. In 1525 Münster published his important *Dictionarium Hebraicum ex Rabbinorum commentariis Collectum . . .* , and ten years later he presented an adaptation of David Kimchi's classic medieval rabbinic dictionary in his *Dictionarium Hebraicum Sefer hashorashim im Nigzarim*. This work proved immensely popular and was reprinted in 1539, 1548, 1564, and in the following century. Münster's most important dictionary for Christians, however, was his 1530 production of *Shilush L'shonot, Dictionarium Trilingue*, which presented scriptural Hebrew to those familiar with Greek and Latin. This work too proved popular and was reprinted in 1543 and again in 1562.

Münster's contributions to scriptural study were no less significant than his grammars and dictionaries. He published accurate texts of many OT books of Scripture along with David Kimchi's commentary for Joel and Malachi (1530), Amos (1531), and Isaiah (1535). Münster's most important contribution in this area was his translation of the entire OT into Latin together with his own annotations, which were filled with various rabbinic commentaries. He also translated from Greek to Hebrew the Gospel of Matthew to which he added his own notes and annotations. Both of these works will be analyzed in greater detail later.

Far more controversial was Münster's publication of Jewish religious thought. As early as 1527 he brought to print Ibn Ezra's commentary on the Ten Commandments, with Maimonides' thirteen principles of faith following two years later. Both works presented a classic Jewish understanding of the requirements of the Law and represented what Münster felt were the highlights of Pharisaic religion. For similar ends, Münster published Moses ben Jacob of Coucy's catalogue of the six hundred and thirteen commandments of the Law in 1533 and two different versions of Josephus's writings in 1541 and 1551. All these works provided much information about the Pharisaic notion of the Law, an intellectual pattern and framework from which the apostles and earliest Christians emerged. For reasons less clear Münster also published a volume on Jewish astrology, the complete Hebrew calendar, some mathematical writings, and Abraham bar Chija's geographical writings.

Another area of publication was the composition of missionary treatises directed toward the Jewish community. These works too will be treated later.

With Münster's death in 1553, Christian-Hebraica had come to full maturity. Before his collaboration with Levita the study of Hebrew was still largely confined to Jews with a few Christians nibbling at the edges of Hebrew grammar. By the middle of the century enough Christians had learned Hebrew that Jewish participation was no longer absolutely necessary. Indeed, from this point on, one can truly speak of *Christian*-Hebraica, and for the first time in over 1500 years, the ideal of Hebraica veritas had been realized.

The study of Hebrew among Christians developed in a very short period from very modest beginnings. We have noted several factors that facilitated this rapid growth in Hebrew competence. Royal patronage, institutional support, the new printing press, and a unique expression of Jewish-Christian cooperation all helped bridge the traditional chasm separating Jew from Christian and Christian from Hebrew.

From its inception Christian-Hebraica was varied and motivated by different desires and aims. Many Catholic scholars sought good texts whereas Protestant scholars sought to understand these texts through the use of rabbinic commentaries to a degree unknown in the Catholic community. Reuchlin and others were less concerned with Scripture but were devoted to Jewish mysticism as a font and source of ancient wisdom necessary for Christianity. And yet this summary is far too simplistic because Lutheran and Reformed Hebraists differed as greatly as did Catholic and Protestant scholars of Hebrew. Radicals such as Servetus transcended any of these definitions and orthodox theologians like Paul Fagius were the most extreme judaizers in the sense that Münster was not. In short, thus far we have really only discussed one issue: How Hebraism and Hebraica were transferred from the Jewish to the Christian community. These many dictionaries, grammars, works of rabbinic exegesis, mystical writings, and so much more yet undiscussed were just sources from which to draw conclusions, not an end in themselves. We have, however, accomplished one important goal. We have established the fact of Hebraica veritas and the fact of Christian study of Hebrew. We must now determine what *sort* of truths these Christian scholars drew out of Hebraica veritas. We must discover their method of argument in developing these truths, and last we must determine the conceptual relationship among the many different forms, types, and expressions of sixteenth-century Christian-Hebraica and how they meshed and related to the intellectual and religious context of the age. In essence, we are ready to embark upon the sixteenth-century nostalgic search for the Jewish past.

NOTES

1.   Concerning medieval Hebraica, the reader might consult the following in addition to works already cited in the introduction: B. Smalley, *The Study of the Bible in the Middle Ages* (Oxford, 1941); H. Hailperin, "Jewish Influence on Christian Biblical Scholars in the Middle Ages," *Historia Judaica*, vol. 4 (1942); *idem*, "The Hebrew Heritage of Medieval Biblical Scholarship," *Historia Judaica*, vol. 5 (1943); Bernhard Blumenkranz, *Les Auteurs chrétiens latins du Moyen Ages sur les juifs et le judaisme* (Paris, 1963); *idem*, *Juifs et chrétiens dans le monde occidental* (Paris, 1960); H. Hirschfeld, *Literary History of Hebrew Grammarians and Lexicographers* (Oxford, 1926).
2.   Concerning Paul of Burgos, see his listings under his Christian name Pablo de Santa Maria in R. Singerman, *The Jews in Spain and Portugal: A Bibliography* (New York and London, 1975), pp. 113–14; concerning Nicholas of Lyra, see Hailperin above, but especially his *Rashi and the Christian Scholars* (Pittsburgh, 1963).
3.   Concerning medieval Jewish history, far and away the best source is Salo W. Baron's sixteen-volume study, *A Social and Religious History of the Jews*. Still useful, though old, is H. Graetz, *History of the Jews*, 11 vols. (Philadelphia, 1894).
4.   The number of works dealing with anti-Semitism is enormous, but the reader might consult any of James Parkes's books, especially *The Conflict of the Church and Synogogue* (New York, 1934) and *The Jew in the Medieval Community* (New York, 1938); Guido Kisch, "The Jew in the Medieval Law," in *Essays on Anti-Semitism*, ed. K. S. Pinson (New York, 1946); *idem*, *The Jews of Medieval Germany* (Chicago, 1949); Leon Poliakov, *The History of Anti-Semitism from the Time of Christ to the Court Jews*, trans. R. Howard (New York, 1974).
5.   Citation of Joh. Boschenstein taken from Geiger, *Studium* . . . , p. 49. Bo-

schenstein produced a small grammar entitled *Elementale introductorium in he-breas literas* . . . (Augsburg, 1514; Wittenberg, 1518).

6.   Concerning Jewish legal status, see Kisch above plus his "Medieval Italian Ju-ris Prudence and the Jews," *Historia Judaica*, vol. 6 (1944). His works cite a great many books the reader might consult.

7.   Concerning the Spanish Inquisition and Jewish expulsion from Spain, see Singerman above, and Y. Baer, *A History of the Jews in Christian Spain*, 2 vols. (Philadelphia, 1961); A. A. Neuman, *The Jews in Spain*. 2 vols. (Philadelphia, 1941), reprinted by Octagon Books in New York in 1969; Cecil Roth, *The Spanish Inquisition* (London, 1937); *idem, A History of the Marranos*, 4th ed. (New York, 1974). H. C. Lea's four-volume study *A History of the Inquisition in Spain*. (New York, 1906–07) remains a standard.

8.   The classic work on Jews and superstition is Joshua Trachtenberg, *The Devil and the Jews* (Philadelphia, 1943; reprint 1961.) See pp. 256–67 for an excellent bibliography.

9.   See the following for a discussion of this early form of racism: Albert A. Sciroff, *Les Controverses des Statuts de 'purité de sang' en Espagna du XVe au XVIIe siècles* (Paris, 1960); C. Roth, *Marranos and Racial Anti-Semitism* (London, 1940); A. D. Ortiz, *Los Judeoconversos en Espagne y America* (Madrid, 1971), especially chapter 5, "Los estatutos de limpieza de sangre."

10.   Joh. Reuchlin, *Briefwechsel*, ed. L. Geiger (Tübingen, 1875), p. 140.

11.   Concerning the ghetto, see Cecil Roth, *History of the Jews in Venice* (New York, 1930), in addition to works above. See S. Baron, 11: 275–77, for a list of cities expelling Jews from 1432 to 1520. See S. Baron, *SRH* 13: 255, for those cities expelling Jews during the 1560s. Also see Phillip N. Bebb, "Jewish Policy in Sixteenth Century Nürnberg," *Occasional Papers of the American Society for Reformation Research*, 1 (1977): 125–36.

12.   Concerning Pico, see the following: Chas. E. Trinkaus, *In Our Image and Likeness*, 2 vols. (London, 1970); E. Cassirer, "Giovanni Pico della Mirandola," *Journal of the History of Ideas*, vol. 3 (1942); E. Garin, *Giovanni Pico della Miran-dola: Vita e Dottrina* (Florence, 1937); P. Kibre, *The Library of Pico della Miran-dola* (New York, 1936); G. Massetani, *La filosofia Cabbalistica di Giovanni Pico della Mirandola.* (Empoli 1897) and Secret, Blau.

13.   Pico della Mirandola, *Opera Omnia* (Basel, 1572), 1: 105, 9, and 1: 166. Also 1: 167 and 1: 239.

14.   *Ibid.*, 1: 82.

15.   Concerning Grimani and the Hebraists mentioned in these pages, see Amram, Geiger, Walde, and other works cited in the introduction.

16.   There had long been an active Jewish press in Italy, and the reader might consult the following regarding the most active of these: the Soncino family press— see Amram, p. 51–146; G. Manzoni, *Annali Tipografici dei Soncino* (Bologna, 1883–86); F. Sacchi, *I Tipografi Ebrei de Soncino* (Cremona, 1877); M. Soave, *Dei*

Soncino Celebri Tipografi Italiani nei seculi XV, XVI (Venice, 1878). A more recent work is Joshua Block's *Venetian Printers of Hebrew Books* (New York, 1932).

17.   Concerning Reuchlin, see the following: L. Geiger, *Joh. Reuchlin: Sein leben und Seine Werke* (Leipzig, 1871); Max Brod, *Johann Reuchlin: Sein Leben und sein Kampf* (Stuttgart, 1965); Guido Kisch, *Zasius und Reuchlin* (Constance, 1961); Antonie Leinz von Dersauer, ed., *Gutachen über Jüdische Schriften* (Stuttgart, 1965); Manfred Krebs, ed. *Johannes Reuchlin, 1455–1522* (Pforzheim, 1955); Karl Christ, *Die Bibliothek Reuchlins in Pforzheim* (Leipzig, 1924); other works will be cited in other parts of this volume concerning specific aspects of Reuchlin's life and accomplishments.

18.   Concerning these markings, see Robert Gordis, *The Biblical Text in the Making; A Study of the Kethib-Qere* (Philadelphia, 1937); for a discussion of sixteenth-century views, see Gg. Schneruemann, *Die Controverse des Lud. Cappelus mit den Buxdorfen über das alter der hebräischen Punctation* (Leipzig, 1879).

19.   Aside from the literature in note 17, the best recent account is Overfield, "A New Look at the Reuchlin Affair," pp. 165–207. Also, H. Graetz, *Geschichte der Juden*, 4th ed., 9 (Leipzig, 1907): 63–195; for a complete bibliography of the older literature, see Ulrich von Hutten, *Operum Supplementum*, ed. E. Bocking, 2 vols. (Leipzig, 1864, 1869).

20.   Concerning the relationship of this crisis to the Reformation, see Charles G. Nauert, "The Clash of Humanists and Scholastics: An Approach to Pre-Reformation Controversies," *Sixteenth Century Journal*, vol. 4 (April 1973).

21.   See Hastings Rashdall, *The Universities of Europe in the Middle Ages*, 2 vols. (Oxford, 1895); S. Ozment, *The Age of Reform, 1250–1550* (New Haven, 1980).

22.   Concerning Justiniani, see Amram, pp. 226 ff.

23.   See H. Galliner, "Agathius Guidacerius," p. 91.

24.   Concerning the effect of the Council of Trent on Christian study of Hebrew, see the following article, even though it deals primarily with the publication of Jewish sources for Jewish use: S. W. Baron, "The Council of Trent and Rabbinic Literature," *Ancient and Medieval Jewish History* (New Brunswick, N.J., 1972), pp. 353–71.

25.   Concerning Pellican, see Chr. Zürcher, *Konrad Pellicans Wirken in Zürich* (Zürich, 1975); E. Silberstein, *Conrad Pellican* (Berlin, 1900); E. Nestle, *Nigri, Bohm und Pellican* (Tübingen, 1893).

26.   Conrad Pellican, *Das Chronikon des Konrad Pellican*, ed. Bernhard Riggenbach (Basel, 1872), see pp. 10–46 for the early years.

27.   J. C. Moerikofer, *Ulrich Zwingli* (Leipzig, 1867–68), p. 321.

28.   Cited in B. J. Kidd, *Documents Illustrative of the Continental Reformation* (Oxford, 1911), pp. 449–50, from Bullinger's *Reformations-geschichte*, 1: 160.

29.   *Oecolampadii et Zwinglii Epistolarum libri IV*, 1536, vii, 629, and ii, 209.

30.   S. M. Jackson, *Selected Works of Hulderich Zwingli* (Philadelphia, 1901), p. 105.

31. Pellican, *Chronikon*, p. 160.

32. See J. Oecolampadius's "Isaiah," in *In Iesaiam Prophetam Hypomnematon* (Basel, 1525), dedicatory letter f.*a*3.

33. *Luther Works*, 48, ed. and trans. G. G. Krodel, (Philadelphia, 1955): 63; concerning the peculiar development of Wittemberg Hebraica, see chapter nine of this volume. (Hereafter cited as *LW*.)

34. *Ibid.*, p. 123.

35. *Ibid.*, p. 135.

36. Concerning Adrian's conflict, see *ibid.*, p. 132, no. 1.

37. *Ibid.*, p. 132–33.

38. *Ibid.*, p. 160.

39. *LW*, 49: 5. Aurogallus, who studied in Leipzig, produced a small grammar entitled *Compendium Heb. et Chald. Gram.* (Wittenberg, 1525).

40. Concerning Bomberg, see Amram, Bacher, and H. F. Brown, *The Venetian Printing Press* (New York and London, 1891).

41. Concerning Levita, consult Gérard Weil, *Élie Levita: Humaniste et Massorète* (Leiden, 1963); also useful, M. Peritz, *Ein hebräischer Brief El. Levitas an Sebastian Münster* (Breslau, 1894); J. Levi, *Elia Levita und seine Leistungen als Grammatiker* (Breslau, 1888); C. D. Ginsberg, *The Masoreth Ha-Masoreth of Elias Levita* (London, 1865).

42. C. D. Ginsberg, ed., *Jacob ben Chayim's Introduction to the Rabbinic Bible* (London, 1865).

43. The best biography of Sebastian Münster is Karl H. Burmeister's *Sebastian Münster: Versuch eines biographischen Gesamtbildes* (Basel and Stuttgart, 1963), though V. Hantsch's *Sebastian Münster: Leben, Werk, Wissenschaftliche Beduntung* (Leipzig, 1898) is still useful. Also see D. Pulvermacher, *Sebastian Münster als Grammatiker* (Berlin, 1892). For a complete listing of all of Münster's publications, see Burmeister, *Eine Bibliographie mit 22 Abbildungen* (Weisbaden, 1964), and concerning Münster's relationship with the publisher Froben, see C. W. Hechthorn, *The Printers of Basel in the XV and XVI Centuries* (London, 1897).

44. Sebastian Münster, *Grammatica Hebraica Absolutissima* (Basel, 1525), preface. Reprinted 1532, 1537, 1542, 1543, 1544, 1552, 1563.

45. S. Münster, *Opus Grammaticum* . . . (Basel, 1547), preface.

PART II

Christian-Hebraica: The Most Ancient Testimony

Chapter Two

Overview: The Past as Pattern

A brief glance at the work of Johannes Reuchlin, Michael Servetus, and Paul Fagius should give adequate evidence that the usual explanation for the popularity of Christian-Hebraica, the need for more adequate translations of Scripture, is too limiting. Certainly such explanations do not clarify the interests of such radicals as Michael Servetus who made profound use of rabbinic sources but did not translate anything at all. Similarly, the Protestant-based need for better translations does little to explain the fascination exerted by the Cabbalah and other Jewish mystical writings over such scholars as Reuchlin, Agrippa, Postel, and many others. This interest in rabbinic conceptual sources appeared before the Reformation, continued through that tumultuous age, and remained after Reformation needs for better OT translations had long been satisfied.

Clearly, Christian-Hebraica entailed a conceptual dimension that complemented but transcended scriptural studies. The rabbis were consulted not only on points of grammar but also for more adequate definitions of faith and even guidance concerning the meaning of the NT. Despite the universal claim that Jews were blind in not seeing how Jesus fulfilled their messianic hopes and in misinterpreting Scripture, Christian scholars consulted these blind sources to a degree unrecognized by historians of the sixteenth century. Moreover, those appealing to Jewish conceptual sources ran the gamut from radical to orthodox, indicating that the appeal of these sources was widespread and not confined to obvious judaizers like Reuchlin or Servetus-like disturbers of the peace.

It may seem ironic that Jewish sources would be so valued by an age concerned with more concise dogmatic definition of Christian truth, but this was a reflection of the nostalgic desire to rediscover a pristine Jewish past. As indicated in the last chapter, both Renaissance and Reformation thinkers shared the conviction that a return to ancient sources of wisdom was absolutely necessary for the reconstruction of an alternately aesthetic, political, or Christian truth. The Renaissance return to the past that concentrated upon ancient political and legal writings saw such sources as meaningful to Europe's new urban awareness in legal, economic, political, and social senses that removed them from their feudal, rural, and agricultural past. Similarly, ancient literary and artistic forms were praised for their so-called natural grace and expression. Abuse within the religious establishment of the times stimulated a desire and a yearning for simpler times and a return to a pristine apostolic past when Jesus' simple morality was better understood. In the process of retrieving this past, much medieval tradition would need cutting away since there were many practices and beliefs that had no scriptural foundation. The Protestant "return to Scripture" was predicated upon the notion that the medieval Church had gone awry and that this erroneous pattern of development would find its cure in reinstituting the past. This nostalgic mechanism was not far removed from Petrarch's belief that the aesthetic appreciation of life characterizing the ancient world had been destroyed during the Dark and Middle Ages and in turn required restoration. In both its literary and religious dimensions, restoring a sense of truth and quality involved a return to some set of basics presumably lost but retrievable if only medieval developments could be cut away. Not coincidentally, early Italian Renaissance humanists and literary figures wrote of the fall of civilization, as Hans Baron has indicated, and religious thinkers believed in the fall of the Church in which NT truth and simplicity were lost. Different thinkers posited the actual date of this fall at different times running from the fourth to the ninth centuries, but all shared the sense of nostalgia. Jewish sources and wisdom, Jewish literature, the very intellectual milieu from which the Christian message emerged, were important parts of the pattern of sources appealed to by Hebrew scholars. Consequently, Christian-Hebraica was a Hebrew version of humanism not different from the more common Latin and Greek versions, though emphasizing religion rather than aesthetics. This specific sort of nostalgia took three different forms.

Historical Nostalgia

Michael Servetus saw in medieval church history and development nothing less than the victory of the antichrist over NT truth. Since 325, the date of the Council of Nicaea, Christian belief and practice were so corrupted by Satan that no amount of reform could alter that situation. The reconstruction of Christianity would be on the basis of the NT, of course, but what the NT meant had been clouded by a church tradition no less corrupt than the official dogma of the Church. In essence, the only road one could travel in effectively cutting away medieval corruption and rebuilding Christianity on the basis of the NT was to go back to the rabbinic opinion that predated the NT and from which the NT emerged. For example, Servetus conceived of the doctrine of the Trinity as not only unwarranted by the NT but as a polytheistic teaching of the devil carefully implanted at the Council of Nicaea by the antichrist. To understand what the first Christians believed, one had to see what Jewish thought of the period was. Hence, in reconstructing his own antitrinitarian formula, Servetus relied heavily upon rabbinic thought and concept merged with apostolic thought from the Gospels along with the earliest of Christian testimonies. One basis of determining the validity of a Christian view was whether or not Jewish sources would have accepted that point of dogma. Jewish opinion was not to be trusted on most matters, of course, but certainly Jewish monotheism was an adequate foundation upon which to build an acceptable view of God—unless one was actually willing to concede that Christianity was not essentially monotheistic. Since trinitarianism was a return to polytheism, Servetus's antidote for this religious infection was to return to a truer tradition. In using select Jewish sources, Servetus hoped to restore the true apostolic tradition, a tradition with solid Jewish feet.

Mystical Nostalgia

Not all scholars unhappy with the religious state of affairs in Europe understood the problem in a chronological sense in which a certain date marked the downfall of truth. Some, like Johannes Reuchlin, accepted as truthful all the historically important dogmas of Christianity as well as the major structures and institutions of the Roman Catholic church. The appeal of Jewish sources for Reuchlin lay in the methods of Cabbalism, and he believed that both God and Christianity would be better understood if viewed and analyzed through the numerology of Cabbalistic mysticism. Reuchlin did not seek an alternate theology as did Servetus, but an alternate method of proving accepted theology. Hence, Reuchlin and others believed that such central dogmas as the Trinity, virgin birth, the Incarnation, and the Resurrection could be proved by using Cabbalistic devices. Rather than gut the sum total of Christian belief, Reuchlin hoped to build a scaffolding around the Church to strengthen an institution experiencing problems of credibility. In fact, Reuchlin was actually weakening church institutions and beliefs by appealing to Jewish methods and teachings, though this was not apparent to him any more than it was apparent to Descartes that he too was weakening the supernatural truth of the Church in building his religious proof on the shoulders of human rationalism.

Unlike later rationalists, however, Reuchlin believed he had solid divine reason to use Jewish mystical sources. Christian devotees of Cabbalah believed it was an ancient system of truth and an oral tradition given to Moses on Mt. Sinai at the same time the written Law was given to Israel. This position would make Cabbalah very ancient and of divine origin as well, but Reuchlin went even further and taught that Cabbalah was taught to Adam in the Garden of Eden, thereby making this system the oldest in existence. Consequently, Reuchlin believed he had rediscovered a secret wisdom not only compatible with Christianity but necessary for its definition and proof as well. Moreover, Cabbalah could provide a basis of synthesis between Christianity and other ancient philosophies such as Pythagoreanism, Platonism, Hermetism, Orphism, and yet other philosophies of wisdom. While other adherents to what D. P. Walker has described as the "ancient theology" believed in Egyptian or Greek sources of wisdom, Reuchlin pioneered the Jewish basis. Unlike Servetus, Reuchlin did not believe the Church had fallen, and he remained a Roman Catholic until his death. Cabbalah was simply a better tool to define Christian truth. Additionally, if the NT was proving difficult to understand by competing Protestant and Catholic theologians, devotees of the Cabbalah took comfort in the fact that their system of truth was based upon the OT.

Apostolic Nostalgia

Some scholars saw value in Jewish sources for purely orthodox Christian ends. Unlike Reuchlin, Paul Fagius believed the NT was the sum total of religious truth and did not consider the Cabbalah of value. Unlike Servetus, Fagius did not entertain dramatic views of the Church falling to the antichrist though he did recognize that medieval Christianity was a far cry from the apostolic message. Essentially, Paul Fagius was typically orthodox in accepting historically important Christian dogmas as understood in Protestant circles. Yet, unlike Bucer, Pellican, and other Protestant Hebraists who appealed to rabbinic sources for a clearer understanding of the OT text, Fagius believed that rabbinic sources were of great value in elucidating and clarifying many thorny NT issues. Such divisive issues as proper celebration of the Lord's Supper, faith versus works, and the nature of grace had been discussed by the rabbis and Pharisees; and their rejection of Jesus as messiah did not make their views on these other issues any less valuable in determining how the apostles and earliest disciples approached these concepts. Moreover, Fagius accepted the Reformed orientation to Protestantism which saw strong lines of continuity between the old covenant and the new one. Much of Judaism may have become irrelevant and meaningless, yet it could still provide a pattern that was understood by the apostles and even accepted by some like James and possibly Peter. If Paul and the other apostles—indeed, if even Jesus himself—were part of the Pharisaic interpretative approach to the Law rather than the more stultifying Saducee literalist approach, an understanding and investigation into first-century Jewish ritual and practice could do much to elucidate what the first Christians took for granted as a norm of religious behavior. To this end, Fagius and others studied Aramaic, the language of the Pharisees, the rabbis, and the apostles, as well. Whereas Servetus sought Christian truth buried in Jewish truth and Reuchlin believed an arcane and mystical Jewish numerology might yield a rich Christian bounty, Fagius sought out the intellectual milieu of the old covenant to better understand the new covenant.

Of these three forms of conceptual use of Jewish sources, only the last was orthodox because it alone was predicated upon the NT understood in traditional senses as the sole source of religious truth. The Jews might provide background, milieu, and cultural depth to apostolic truth much as the rabbis might provide grammatical and linguistic insight into the language of the OT. Jewish sources always remained a tool and a resource, however, and never a source of truth in itself. In Fagius's mind the apostles never conceived of the trouble experienced by Reformation-age Protestants concerning such practices as the Lord's Supper. In the absence of any possibility of solving such disputes once and for all, Fagius felt the best alternative was a religious form of cultural anthropology, especially since most NT practices found their origin in OT Jewish ritual and observance.

At this point let us turn to the views and writings of each thinker to observe in greater detail the full significance of Christian nostalgia in its different manifestations.

Chapter Three

Michael Servetus: The Reconstruction of the Christian Past

Michael Servetus was born in Villanueva de Sijena, Spain, in either 1509 or 1511 and died in Geneva in 1553. During his short lifetime he was burned in absentia by Catholic authorities and in the flesh by Protestants.[1] The Spaniard's tumultuous life led George Williams to observe that Servetus "was indeed the veritable effigy for Catholic and Protestant alike of all that seemed execrable in the Radical Reformation."[2] Even in an age of widespread dissent, Servetus's writings were considered an outrage. His name was so well known all over Europe that he assumed an alias in his search for refuge.

Not a theologian by profession, Servetus made his living as an editor and a physician. He has been credited with discovery of the pulmonary circulation of the blood a century before William Harvey, and several authors have maintained that Servetus was a pioneer in the area of comparative geography as well.

Two charges were continually leveled against Servetus. The first, and clearly most serious, accusation concerned his antitrinitarian views. The second charge was that he was a "judaizer," that is to say that he exhibited an inappropriate tendency toward Judaism which he attempted to pass on to his readers. Such charges were often made against anyone holding unpopular views, but in Servetus's case there was good reason to believe that he did in fact express Jewish opinions regarding the Godhead. In his early writings as well as in his mature works, Servetus coupled extensive condemnation of the Trinity with praise for Jewish resistance to this theory of divine expression. Yet it is not known where and how Servetus learned Hebrew and rabbinica. In order to understand why Servetus made extensive use of Jewish sources, we must first appreciate how he viewed the contemporary state of the Christian religion.

Protestantism attributed contemporary Christianity's poor intellectual, moral, and religious condition to the Roman See's many departures from the written Word of God. The result was a babel of contradictory beliefs and practices for which no divine sanction might be found. The proposed solution was at once obvious and simple: An ailing Christianity might be rectified by returning to Scripture in order to verify those practices and beliefs demanded of man and to eliminate those resulting from papal imagination. For Servetus, however, the problem was at once similar yet far more severe. Constantly referring to orthodox theologians as "sophists" and condemning all medieval developments as dangerous innovations, Servetus held peculiar views regarding the cause of Christianity's ills and their manifestations. Luther regarded the Church as having fallen into error during the papacy of Gregory I in the sixth century, but Servetus saw evil permeating Christ's body in the fourth century at the Council of Nicaea.[3] Moreover, whereas Luther and other Protestants understood church error as human responsibility as well as satanic influence, Servetus saw the image of Satan alone lurking behind the errors accepted by that council. Simply put, Pope Sylvester and Emperor Constantine called that meeting into session for the single purpose of perverting true teaching at the behest of the antichrist who controlled the Church from that time. All the subsequent councils were the tools of the devil, and the views propounded were nothing less than the evil teachings of Satan. The result of satanic domination over the Church was Roman Catholicism; if Protestantism was somewhat helpful in destroying satanic papal innovation, it too misunderstood both the true cause of error and its manifestations. There was little Servetus could do on his own. However, the Church might still be purged by cooperating with the Archangel Michael, due to return in 1585 to destroy the antichrist and all evil. For the present, all Servetus could do was await the angel's return and attempt to think through what the Christian ought to believe. Had a simple return to Scripture been beneficial or even possible, Servetus might have been a Protestant, but discovering the true church demanded radical surgery upon the body of historical Christianity. It was necessary to clean away the shards and remains of the early councils and the traditions of belief which had developed upon this faulty foundation. The most faulty view of all, though by no means the only one manifesting the evil of Satan, was the doctrine of the Trinity, for what could be more fundamentally wrong with a perverted religion than its notion of God. In order to cut the faulty from the true, the surgical blade had to be sharp and it had to be carefully used. Servetus was unique among reinstitutionists in that the blade of his knife was a Jewish blade.

The Trinity was so obviously erroneous and without merit that Servetus could ask, "Pray, what Turk, Scythian, Barbarian could bear these disputes of words . . . without laughter?"[4] After attacking trinitarian wording, which emphasized that three could be one and one could be three, Servetus again noted that "not only Mohammedans and Hebrews but the very beasts of the field would make fun of us if they could grasp our fantastic notion."[5] Servetus, a Spaniard, was well read in both Jewish and Islamic literature, and in his earliest writings he noted, "How much this tradition of the trinity has, alas, been a laughing stock to the Mohammedans, God only knows."[6] Others might be dubious of using Mohammed as a religious source, but for Servetus this theologian was an adequately reliable witness, "for he says in his Koran that Christ was the greatest of prophets . . . moreover, that the apostles and evangelists and the first Christians were the best of men and wrote what is true and did not hold the trinity or three persons in the divine being but [that] men in later times added this."[7] In his mature writings, published over two decades later, he again noted that Mohammed taught that "the first disciples of Christ were great and honest men who wrote what is true, not holding the trinity but adding this later by corruptors of sacred doctrine."[8] To preempt anticipated criticism for use of so strange a source, Servetus wrote, "More reliance is to be given to one truth which an enemy confesses than to a hundred lies on our side."[9] Indeed, because outside observers' criticism of the obviously ridiculous Trinity has gone unheeded, "countless monstrosities have arisen, countless questions have come about, not only doubtful, insoluble and knotty, but also most absurd."[10]

Servetus's non-Christian sources also indicated exactly when this abusive theology was introduced, and Servetus wrote, "Mohammedans and Hebrews affirm that there was a change in the Christian religion at the time of Constantine . . . [and Rabbi] Ibn Ezra affirmed this in Genesis 27 where he makes mention of Constantine and Sylvester."[11] For Servetus there was but one option regarding proper method: To regain ancient truth one needed "to investigate the causes from the beginning, what view tradition formerly held regarding *persons* [of the Godhead] and how all things have been corrupted through the damage of time."[12]

One had to return to basics—to the NT and the confessions of the apostles and yet other early writings. But since ancient Christian writings never mentioned the concept of the Trinity and the earliest church fathers were also ignorant of this view, one could only return to the Jewish monotheistic base from which the NT, the apostles, and the early church fathers emerged. Before analyzing this Jewish base, however, we would do well to devote a paragraph or two to describing Servetus's theological views.

Servetus rejected the orthodox notion of three distinguishable persons in the Godhead in favor of the modalistic concept of three separate modes of divine expression, or three manifestations of God. In one location he might use the term *person* despite its orthodox connotations, and somewhere else Servetus might speak of a "first thing, second thing, third thing" and reject the orthodox idea of persons.[13] In yet another location Servetus would write about "three wonderful dispensations or dispositions of God in each of which His divinity shines forth," only to speak of a "threefold invocation of the divine name" somewhere else, only to correct himself yet again by describing the Godhead as "manifold aspects, diverse forms and kinds of deity."[14] Use of so many different terms and expressions has made Servetus somewhat difficult to follow, but all, at base, express the very same idea that God is solitary and unitary in Himself but various in His manifestations. The very same God appeared throughout history, but He appeared differently at different times to different peoples in different contexts. Orthodoxy was mistaken in believing that God's different modes of manifestation reflected separate entities or beings within Himself.

Servetus observed that the OT, unlike the NT, made use of many different names to refer to God. These appellations constituted the key to understanding the nature of the Godhead and also provided the reader of Scripture with an analysis of God's ever-changing role within the human and cosmic context. Servetus assumed that God used His different names in a historical-contextual sense with each name implying some religious or theological message. Servetus wrote this about the name "El Shaddai":

> For God appeared to the partriarchs and was known under the name *El Shaddai*. And from the meaning of these names in this passage it is ascertained that far more is conveyed through the name *Jehova*, for *Shaddai* comes from the verb *shod*, which means desolation as though He were a desolator and able to lay all waste. . . . Likewise, *El* means strong and powerful, whence, *El Shaddai*, as though He were a mighty desolator and under this name He was first manifested to Abraham and for this reason, that Abraham might be stronger in not fearing others.[15]

Servetus was certain that these aliases were not simply literary devices but presented what God wanted man to know of Himself at any given time. He wrote, "Therefore, although I have appeared to them under this name

"El Shaddai" and although they have realized that I have laid waste Sodom and Gomorah, yet they have not fully known hitherto that I am omnipotent, [they] have not known me under the name *Jehova.*"[16] At any given time, man's knowledge of God coincided with, and depended upon, God's role in the world. By knowing how God referred to Himself, an age could understand one additional aspect of His nature.

Servetus found names other than "El Shaddai" which expressed yet other meanings: "The other name, most holy of all, YHVH, some say means essence, others begetting. Yet it includes both and can be interpreted thus: YHVH, that is, source of all being, parent of being, one who causes to be, gives being, cause of being."[17] Still another name was "Elohim": "The more notable names of divinity are *Elohim* and *Jehova.* . . . I have interpreted Elohim as meaning God and His Word."[18]

The most apparent function of these names was to indicate to man some knowledge otherwise impossible to impart to him. We can appreciate Moses' query when standing before the burning bush as well as his specific wording: "Who are you?" Similarly, we can understand that God-ness was inexplicable to man and His answer was "I am that I am," or "YHVH." God also used different names to indicate to man that He was subject to His own dynamic of change governed by laws and conditions applying only to Him. Servetus wrote, for instance, "During the six days of creation God was never called by that name ["Jehova" or "YHVH"] because creation was not yet completed. But on the seventh day creation was completed and He first began to be called by that name, the names of creation and generation repeated."[19]

Using different names did not mean that God's nature changed or that he had more than one nature but that he wished to be understood in different contexts. Consequently, when God referred to himself as "Sabaoth," this was yet more information available to man, for "*Jehova* is called *Sabaoth,* that is, hosts, because His essence fights in the number of multitudes."[20] Servetus was quick to see an inherent relativism in God's relationship with mankind, for "God spoke differently to Noah, differently to Abimelech, differently to Job, differently to Ninevah, and differently to others."[21] This relativism was not limited to His favorite OT personages, however, but to all people of the ancient world. Antiochus of Assyria knew God under the Hebrew name "Oz" or the Latin "Ferox" though He could have been known under the corresponding Hebrew name "El Shaddai." Similarly, many Greek philosophers wrote of a "Demiurge" or "Wisdom," though "Elohim" might have expressed the same meaning.[22]

When God used the name "Jesus" to refer to Himself, He was using one more name in a long list of self-descriptive terms through which man could know God. Servetus noted, "Let us say for the present that God can share with a man the fullness of His deity and give him the name which is above every other name."[23] Servetus must have realized that in referring to Jesus as simply one more name in a long list, he was essentially placing the man in the same position as the burning bush, the pillar of fire, or any other divine manifestation: one more vehicle for God. Drawn to its logical conclusion, this view might have stripped Jesus of much of the autonomy and independence granted Him in orthodox trinitarian thought, for Servetus understood Jesus as only a reflection of God used in a specific context. But "Jesus" was a special name, for it was reserved for His greatest manifestation to that time, and Servetus wrote, "He is expressly called Emanuel, that is, God with us; even more, He Himself is called *El*."[24]

Man could only understand who God was when all these different names were put in their proper progressive order, for each name granted greater and greater knowledge of God. Servetus divided past human history into four phases that covered the period of OT names of God. In all these phases God used His names in ways that man could understand; Servetus noted, "He adapts Himself to us under some form which we are capable of perceiving."[25] The last phase was the Incarnation, in which God progressed from total incomprehensibility before Creation to total manifestation in a man. Writing about this last phase of God's self-revelation to man, Servetus stated, "Fourth, from what has been said above, learn what has been clearly and distinctly manifested to us; for the oracle has come to be flesh and we have seen Him."[26]

We can now understand why Servetus considered the Trinity a "threefold invocation of the divine name" or a "disposition" of God. Similarly, we can appreciate why Servetus hesitated in using the term *person*, which implied an eternal being within God, for clearly "Jesus" was a name for a manifestation, limited in time and place much as any other name was.

Servetus's main problem was explaining his views to a Christian audience unfamiliar with Hebrew and therefore unaware of God's use of different names. When criticizing medieval theologians, Servetus noted, "Ignorance of the divine names deceives the philosophers."[27] Even if true, such condemnation of medieval ignorance of Hebrew did not help explain his own position.

Attempting to start with basics, Servetus noted, "For you must bear in mind that all things written about Christ took place in Judea and in the Hebrew tongue and in all other languages but that there is a poverty of divine names."[28] Further complicating matters, Christianity spread to Greek-speaking peoples who were ignorant of Hebrew and of the manner of OT Jewish expression. "Because of the poverty [in Greek] of divine names, the apostles could not express this matter to the Greeks other than by the word 'theos' although they rarely use it. All these things should be carefully weighed; nor should they have caused us so much trouble had the Greeks learned Hebrew."[29] The worst problem of all was that Jews were quite correct in dismissing the Trinity as a figment of the Christian mind rather than accept this view as scriptural: "The Jews also shrink from adhering to this fancy of ours and laugh at our foolishness about the trinity and on account of its blasphemies they do not believe this is the messiah who was promised in their Law."[30] And just a few pages away Servetus again noted, "The Jews are supported by so many authorities that they naturally wonder at the great division of God."[31] From Servetus's vantage point, Christian belief regarding Jesus and his place within the Godhead had become so estranged from scriptural truth that even the blind Jews made good points against Christian theology. Servetus wrote that "the reason they [the Jews] give for denying that Christ is God is the distinction made in the incorporeal deity,"[32] which position was Servetus's as well.

Only by returning to the Jewish roots of Christianity could one hope to recover a scriptural understanding of the Godhead. When writing about the fourth Gospel, Servetus reminded his reader, "This matter will turn out to be far easier if we do not overlook the Hebraisms here, seeing that John was a Hebrew."[33] And again, to drive home his central point that the original Christians were Jews writing in a Jewish intellectual milieu, Servetus wrote, "Reader, examine from the point of original causes what the first Christians understood by the term person."[34] In this vein Servetus explained, "This is a clear issue for the Hebrews; what we call *person*, they call *image*."[35] And in another place Servetus again turned to Jewish thought for a better concept with which to replace the Trinity: "Three *middoth*, three properties [or "attributes"] are said by the Hebrews to be in God; produced from God, not separate things."[36]

It is quite clear that Servetus identified with Jewish criticism of the Trinity and his writings indicates familiarity with traditional Jewish arguments against that important Christian dogma. Such criticism, however, did not help explain what Christians should believe, however effective these views might be in indicating what Christians should not accept. In attempting to determine "what the first Christians believed," Servetus turned to the earliest rabbinic literature and the Aramaic translations of

Scripture. Since Servetus assumed that Jesus and the apostles spoke Aramaic as well as Hebrew, turning to these sources had the advantage of not being corrupted by later rabbinic thought while reflecting the earliest Jewish opinion. Servetus noted, for instance, that "the rabbis called divinity *shechinah* from the very *shachan* which signifies inhabitation. Therefore, the divinity of Christ is an inhabitation within God."[37] Consequently, Servetus believed it was possible to draw together such diverse terms from varying sources as the "manifold aspects" of early Christian thought with the three "middoth" of rabbinic literature, and then use the notion of *shechinah* to explain that Jesus was an indwelling or attribute of the Father, which would bring us back to His being one of the three middoth or one of the manifold aspects. Using yet other rabbinic sources concerning the messiah, Servetus noted that the Son was "a sculpture within the divine essence itself."[38]

Attempting to bolster this notion of the Son as a divine sculpture within the stone of the divine essence, Servetus cited targumic literature.

"I will carve his figure," he says. In the Hebrew this is what it says: *Hinne tiftach pitcha*, that is, behold, I carving or laying bare His figure or image just as an artificer fashions a statue by carving stone and laying it bare. . . . With this the Chaldee interpreter agrees, who renders it, "Who turns his face to be revealed;" and thus the Targum of Jonathan has it, "*ha ana leyley haniyatha*," that is, "behold, I reveal or open his vision" . . . the words face, statue, hidden, concealed, habitation, shadow . . . were all written of Him in the Law.[39]

Having established that Jesus was an indwelling and not a separate being or person with an independent existence, Servetus followed his Jewish sources to the logical conclusion: "And apart from this consideration, to wish to apply the prophecies [of the OT] to Christ is to be wanting in good sense, in which matter the Jews accuse us with good sense."[40] Throughout his theological writings Servetus frequently cited both the Targum of Onkelos as well as the Targum of Jonathan as the authoritative voices of the Christian milieu of the apostles. In all cases, the Christian tradition was held up as deficient and erroneous whereas the Pharisaic position was usually accepted as the more authentically Christian view.

Servetus was also willing to accept later Jewish thought as authoritative, though it did not have the advantage of proximity to the time of the apostles. Servetus would have been the first to condemn the Jews for not seeing in Jesus the fulfillment of Jewish messianic expectation, and yet despite this grievous error he would write, "The Hebrews said in this sense, the messiah is from the beginning not because of some sophistical trinity but because his person and visible form subsisted in God."[41] And then, referring to a contemporary Jewish authority, Servetus continued, "Thus Rabbi Arama said concerning Genesis, that before the creation of the sun the name of the messiah was already seated on the throne of God."[42] Arama was not the only major Jewish authority cited by Servetus on theological matters, however, and one finds the name "Rabbi Moses" or "Moses the Egyptian" in many references to the medieval Jewish theologian and philosopher Moses Maimonides. When discussing the fullness of God's nature in a cosmic sense, Servetus maintained the same fluid views of God as when writing about progressive revelation through a series of names. Attempting to demonstrate the multiplicity of God's soul in the universe and the variety of His manifestations, Servetus used the concept *nishmat chayim*, the "soul of life," for which he cited Maimonides. In one location Servetus wrote that God was "one soul having many lives. The breath of God is called *nishmat chayim*, the soul of life."[43] To demonstrate how central this expansive notion of God was to Servetus's basic concept of God in a cosmic sense as well as in a trinitarian context, one would necessarily need to study the intricacies of Servetian cosmology. The following citation, however, makes amply clear how important and related Maimonides' concept of *nishmat chayim* was to Servetus's understanding of the relationship of Jewish thought to the Trinity. "God has on that account a thousand infinity of natures and a thousand infinity of essences, not divided metaphysically, but by ineffable modes. Therefore we conclude against those who teach the sophistical trinity."[44] Essentially, physical reality, like the names of God, reflected and expressed the nature of the Father. Servetus's cosmology and theology were divided only in terms of direction of focus, but both were heavily indebted to Jewish sources. Indeed, Servetus must have been very impressed with Maimonides' discussion of scriptural expressions of divine anthropomorphism in the first chapters of Genesis, for he noted with great approval, "Hence many of the Jews, as though dreaming of Christ, imagined there were bodily forms in God because *tzelem* ["image"] and *d'muth* ["form"] are attributed to Him in Scripture."[45]

Other issues in Servetus's religious writings also reflect Jewish influence, though to a lesser extent. Much of his very positive anthropology stressed the intimate connection between man and God. Within his religious system this has the effect of minimizing the effect of Original Sin upon subsequent generations and may reflect Servetus' intense interest in the views of Philo Judaeus, whom he used as a source in describing the composition of man. After citing a variety of ancient sources, including Plato, Pythagoras, and Hermes, regarding man's divine genealogy, Servetus turned to Philo in order to draw a religious conclusion: "Philo says in the book *Concerning Agriculture*, the soul of man was made and formed with the idea and image of the original word serving as a model. . . . Therefore, man was made after the example, form and figure of Christ, both in body and in soul."[46]

Exegesis was another area in which Servetus demonstrated great interest in Jewish thought. This area will be dealt with extensively in the next section of this book, but one citation can serve as an indication of the depth of Servetus's feeling. When discussing Psalm 2:7, "This day have I begotten thee," Servetus wrote, "I cannot refrain here from sighing when I see the replies that Rabbi David Kimchi made against the Christians on this point. I find the reasons with which they sought to convince him so obscure that I cannot but weep."[47] As we shall see later, Servetus's exegesis was an exercise on Kimchi's theme of a strict literal interpretation of Scripture along traditional Jewish lines of thought.

In attempting to assess Servetus's devotion to rabbinic literature, one cannot fail to be impressed with his steadfast assertion that Jewish tradition, especially early Jewish thought, was a reliable guide to primitive Christian thinking. Servetus's interest in rabbinic thought is a clear expression of Christian nostalgia for a pristine Christian past wherein Jewish thought constituted a most ancient testimony in reconstruction apostolic religion. Without this sense of nostalgia, reliance upon Jewish sources would make little sense. It is clear that one element in this commitment was Servetus's belief that Christian tradition was perverted by human imagination working hand in hand with the demonic influence of Satan. Viewed from this vantage point, Jewish thought, however erroneous, was still preferable to the devil's teachings. If the Jews did not accept Jesus, they dreamed of him; if they misunderstood salvation, Jews still retained a deep awareness of God.

In depending upon a Jewish monotheistic tradition both ancient and pure, Servetus did not believe the synthesis he hoped to create was at all problematic. Jews were nothing more than Christians who had not yet accepted Jesus as God. If they failed to appreciate this obvious fact, the reason was the offensive nature of trinitarianism. Whereas Servetus had nothing but scorn for the variety of Christians found in Europe during the

Reformation age, he could write about Jews, "We said above, with the Jews there was the shadow of faith in Christ. He spoke to them from the cloud and they believed Him."[48]

NOTES

1.   See my *Michael Servetus: A Case Study in Total Heresy*. For a different point of view, see A. Alcalá, *El Sistema de Servet* (Madrid, 1978), or C. Manzoni, *Umanesimo ed Eresia: M. Servet* (Naples, 1974).

2.   G. H. Williams, *The Radical Reformation* (Philadelphia, 1962), p. 3.

3.   Restitutionist ideas were fairly common during the sixteenth century, especially in radical circles. For a discussion of this tendency and a bibliography of other works on the subject, see F. H. Littel, *The Origins of Protestant Sectarianism* (New York, 1962). This volume was published previously in 1952 and 1956 under the title *The Anabaptist View of the Church*, but the new volume is enlarged and somewhat revised.

4.   Michael Servetus, *De Trinitatis Erroribus* (Hagenau, 1531), p.42b. (Hereafter cited as *Error.*)

5.   *Ibid.*, p.43a.

6.   *Ibid.*

7.   *Ibid.*

8.   M. Servetus, *De Restitutio Christianisme* (Vienne, 1553), p. 35. (Hereafter cited as *Rest.*)

9.   *Error.*, p.43.2.

10.   *Ibid.*, p.39a–b.

11.   *Rest.*, p. 399.

12.   *Error.*, p.37a.

13.   *Ibid.*, p.21b.

14.   *Ibid.*, pp.28b–29a.

15.   *Ibid.*, p.100b.

16.   *Ibid.*

17.   *Ibid.*, p.100a–b.

18.   *Ibid.*, p.96b.

19.   *Ibid.*, p.101b.

20.   *Ibid.*, p.102a.

21.   *Rest.*, p.325.

22.   *Ibid.*, pp.451 and 624.

23.   *Error.*, p.11b.

24.   *Ibid.*

25.   *Ibid.*, p.119a.

26.   *Ibid.*, p.119b.

27. *Ibid.*, p.20b and see p.111b.
28. *Ibid.*, p.13b.
29. *Ibid.*, p.15b.
30. *Ibid.*, p.42b.
31. *Ibid.*, p.37a.
32. *Rest.*, p.36.
33. *Error.*, p.117a.
34. *Rest.*, p.168.
35. *Ibid.*, p.108.
36. *Ibid.*, p.700.
37. *Ibid.*, p.74.
38. *Ibid.*, p.116.
39. *Error.*, p.113b.
40. *Ibid.*, pp.113b–114a.
41. *Rest.*, p.134.
42. *Rest.*, p.134. Concerning Rabbi Arama, see B. Heller Willenski, *Rabbi Yizhac Arama u-Mishnato* (Jerusalem, 1957); J. Bettan, "The Sermons of Isaac Arama," *Hebrew Union College Annual*, vols. 12–13 (1937–38).
43. *Rest.*, p.260.
44. *Ibid.*, p.128.
45. *Error.*, p.91b.
46. *Rest.*, p.104.
47. *Error.*, p.56b, and see *Rest.*, p.59.
48. *Rest.*, p.624.

Chapter Four

Johannes Reuchlin: The Discovery of the Secret Jesus

Historians of the Renaissance and the Reformation have found in Johannes Reuchlin a cultural hero, a giant of the northern Renaissance and a stalwart opponent of mindless censorship and religious unreason. We have had occasion to describe Reuchlin's pioneering role in advancing Hebrew study among Christians and his campaign for these studies against the conservative Dominican order in Cologne. In this chapter Reuchlin's significant contribution to the Christian-Cabbalah will be analyzed.[1]

The Christian-Cabbalah is at once the most enchanting, difficult, entertaining, and esoteric of the many types of Christian-Hebraica. Both in terms of method and ideas, Christian study of Cabbalah is also the most difficult form of Hebraica to appreciate today. Most orthodox Hebraists maintained that Hebrew and varying amounts and types of rabbinic literature could be beneficial to scriptural studies and might elucidate the inner core of rabbinic Judaism from which Christianity emerged. Additionally, and most importantly, most orthodox Hebraists maintained that Christian religious dogma and method were safely outside the scope and purview of their Jewish sources. But Reuchlin's interests were far different from those of most Hebraists, for unlike these other scholars, he was not primarily a translator of the word, nor was he an exegete on the word or even an exegete despite the word. Quite simply, Reuchlin believed that the branch of Jewish mysticism known as the Cabbalah was germane to Christian theological concept. Yet Reuchlin was not interested in the philosophical aspects of Cabbalistic mysticism. Ignoring those areas dealing with systematic exegesis, emanationist theosophy, theories of creation, and even God's relationship with the universe or man, Reuchlin was entranced by the technical and numerological methods used in such areas, which built upon the fact that Hebrew letters and numbers used the same symbols. Consequently, OT Scripture repesented a literary verbal elucidation of God's communication with man plus a more secret numerological code in which God's secrets and very identity were hidden and through which they might be deciphered. Whereas Jewish Cabbalists used a variety of numerological and acrostic techniques within the framework of normative Jewish exegetical and theological tradition or in conjunction with other acceptable modes of interpretation, Reuchlin essentially borrowed the techniques and methods but left behind the Jewish framework in which these techniques were developed. The result was a somewhat truncated method through which Reuchlin hoped to merge some Cabbalistic ideas with notions of Christianity.

Although such reasoning may seem strange to us today—indeed, it was strange even to many of Reuchlin's own contemporaries—the late fifteenth and sixteenth centuries abounded with thinkers convinced that conventional Christianity had to be added to or subtracted from to regain its authentic sense of doctrinal purity. Among sources commonly used for the reinterpretation of Christian dogma were Hermeticism, neo-Platonism, Orphism, the Druid experience, magic, and of course, the Cabbalah. D. P. Walker has studied this concentration on esoterica and ancient sources under the title of the "ancient theology."[2] Unlike Protestant and Catholic reformers who were essentially involved in the same process of cutting, adding, subtracting, and reinterpreting the Christian past, these Renaissance eclectics and syncretists attempted to discover the religious ideas of differing sources and traditions from what they assumed was a universal pattern of divine truth variously expressed in different cultures.

Reuchlin's importance in this context is derived from the fact that he pioneered the secret mystical Cabbalistic base of esoteric wisdom rather than use an Egyptian base as did Giordano Bruno. As such, Reuchlin was a prime example of Renaissance syncretism and curiosity into other religions and cultures and represents a case study in the innovative nonorthodox religious tendencies of his age. In short, Reuchlin was one of Europe's leading proponents of the ancient theology. The tie between the ancient theology and Jewish sources was the similarity between Pythagoreanism and Cabbalistic numerology. In turn, Reuchlin's "Pythagoreanism" was entirely based upon Jewish number codes that were in turn predicated upon a most exciting use of Hebrew. To a degree, his method obviated some of the importance of the NT since that corpus of writings existed in Greek. Reuchlin noted, "Therefore we generally call the language of the Jews holy and we say the sacred letters were written by God's finger and the sacred names [of God] were not invented by man but made by God Himself."[3] Reuchlin did not clarify whether NT names were included in the manmade category but felt that NT Greek would not have evoked the same reaction as the reading of Hebrew: "For when reading Hebrew I seem to see God Himself speaking when I think that this is the language in which God and the angels have told their minds to man from on high. And so I tremble in dread and in terror, not, however, without some unspeakable joy."[4] Consequently, whatever the value of mystical, religious, or other types of wisdom-literature written in other languages, Hebrew was in itself of importance because "God wished His secrets to be known to man through Hebrew."[5]

Reuchlin's enthusiasm for Hebrew was shared by other great linguists of the day, but unlike Sebastian Münster's fine grasp of Hebrew philological development or Paul Fagius's outstanding grasp of the rabbinic idiom in both Hebrew and Aramaic or even Servetus's enduring interest in religious and conceptual development mirrored in Hebrew-language expression, Reuchlin's interest was far more enthralling and esoteric and only he wrote of trembling in dread and terror. Additionally, Reuchlin's specific point of interest in Hebrew differed from that of other Hebraists, and he noted, "This alone is the field of true contemplation; the single words of which are single mysteries, and the single utterances, syllables, the apexes of the letters and the vowels are full of secret meanings."[6]

Unlike other Christian-Cabbalists who maintained that this esoteric system found its origin when God gave mankind both a written and an oral law on Mount Sinai, Reuchlin pioneered the more radical view that Adam too was taught the secrets of the Cabbalah.[7] Hence, Orpheus, Hermes, Plato, Pythagoras, and others all taught great wisdom of benefit to the Christian scholar, but Cabbalistically interpreted Hebrew was the oldest mystical system of all and could impart knowledge far more fundamental than any other system. If Hebrew was God's language and the Cabbalah His grammar, what was the message these divine tools might impart?

In his first major mystical work, *De Verbo Mirifico* (Basel, 1494), Reuchlin wrote that he hoped "to explain to our age (so far as history allows) almost all the names which in a former age wise men, endowed with miraculous operations, used in sacred matters. Accept therefore a disputation concerning the wonder-working word by three philosophers . . . so as to better elucidate the occult property of divine names [and enable] our finally choosing one supreme wonder-working and blessed name."[8] Some historians have incorrectly argued that Reuchlin was not referring to magic, though he made his meaning quite clear. Knowledge of such occult names would mean "that we ourselves are producers of marvelous works, above human power and although [we are] at the same time constituted in nature we hold dominion over it and work wonders, portents, and miracles which are signs of the divinity—by the one name which I have been eager to explain to you."[9]

Reuchlin was true to his word and devoted large sections of the work to discussions of many divine names from many ancient cultures and peoples. Reuchlin's conclusion was consistent with our discussion thus far: "The holy names of the Hebrews are more sacred than those of the Egyptians both because they are older and because they apply to the worship of the one supreme God."[10] Consequently, even though other names might bring man some insight into magical power, "no names . . . have the same power as those in Hebrew or those closely derived from Hebrew because of them all, they are the first formed by God."[11] In turn, Reuchlin devoted much space to discussion of the many different names of God mentioned in the OT and those discussed by Jewish Cabbalistic sources.[12]

Surely the need for accurate texts was fundamental to Reuchlin's purposes since only an exact rendering of the names would impart their magic and because numerological equations might be effective only if predicated upon knowledge of the exact number-letters. Unlike Protestant and Catholic scholars who labored to create good translations of Scripture for popular or scholarly use or for accurate bases of precisely defined concepts of dogma, Reuchlin's interest in the text's accuracy was for a purely mystical-magical purpose. He wrote that he hoped "to enter such great darkness and obscurities of sacred matters, the hiding places of secret words."[13] and that such matters were not for the populace at large, for "it is not proper to spread these veiled arcane and most secret symbols into the air, but to whisper them into the ear."[14]

Reuchlin's hesitation about spreading the Cabbalistic message far and wide was more than play-acting when we consider the interest with which his works were read by members of the Cologne Dominican order a few years later. Discovery of the wonder-working word would enable man to perform miracles such as curing the sick, raising the dead, freeing the soul from demons, and other acts of magic.[15]

The structure of the *De Verbo Mirifico* (hereafter *DVM*) was a three-way dialogue with spokesmen representing the different points of view the young Reuchlin wished to discuss. Each section made a specific point Reuchlin felt had bearing on the issue of magic with the first spokesman, Sidonius the Epicurean, presenting the fatalistic philosophy associated with that school of thought. Reuchlin disapproved of Epicurean fatalism and its resulting exhortation to passivity. Similarly, the idea of the universe as an uncaring mechanistic force over which man could exert no control contradicted all that Reuchlin wished to discover. Consequently, presenting this philosophy first and destroying its basic premises from both a Christian and Cabbalistic approach supplied the necessary groundwork for the remainder of the treatise.

In the second section the reader was presented with a discussion of the proper magical tools for the aspiring practitioner of the arcane. Baruch, the Jewish spokesman for the mystical Cabbalah, argued for that science. After presenting Reuchlin's ideas that all great wisdom originally came from the Hebrews with Plato and Pythagoras drawing their thoughts from a Jewish spring, Baruch emphasized the special importance of Hebrew as the original language of that original wisdom: "The language of the Hebrews is simple, pure, uncorrupted, holy, terse, and vigorous. In it, God spoke with man and men with angels, directly, face to face and not through interpreters."[16] Baruch next requested that the doors be bolted lest the uninitiated and uninformed overhear the discussion, and then he began his discussion of the names of God, the most important issue in this section.

Baruch explained that originally God had but one name. Because of the confusion resulting from Adam's sin in Eden, man could only understand God through a series of appellations describing different aspects of His being. The first series of names Baruch discussed was "Ehieh" ("I will be"), "Hū" ("He or Him") and "Esh" ("fire"), the *ignis* of many *prisca theologia* sources.[17] All three names, we are told, reflect the same single God in three different contexts of human understanding. "Ehieh" indicates that all that is, comes from God whereas "Hū" demonstrates His singleness and unity despite the variety of His manifestations. "Esh," the "fire," reflects God's appearance to Moses as a fire in the bush and the column of fire which led the children of Israel in the wilderness. Similarly, "Esh" is Orpheus's *ignis* and the same as the divine ether of yet other ancients.

A second series of divine names was also presented in Reuchlin's description of the ten *sefirot*, "emanations," through which the infinite and pure God related to the finite and mundane world of matter.[18] These *vestamenta dei* reflect His removal from the world and represent a stepladder or progression of diminishing divinity through which He relates to the world of matter. As we shall see later, Reuchlin had not acquired any expertise in understanding Jewish emanationist theosophy and did not understand the necessary dichotomy between emanationism and magic, systems that run at cross purposes.[19]

Scripture used the name "Elohim" to refer to the collective ten sefirot, and if one could concentrate the creative power of these emanations into a single expression, that name would be "YHVH," the Tetragrammaton, the four-letter name of God. "This is the most powerful name, worshipped by those above, obeyed by those below, cherished by earthly nature . . . it is said to bestow wonder-working powers on the human faculty."[20] This was the ineffable name consisting only of consonants whose secret pronunciation was known only to Moses.

There is a fundamental difference between the two series of names mentioned above and the Tetragrammaton. The former are human philosophical terms predicated upon human perception of divinity and reflect human understanding of His nature. To the extent that these names are necessary for man to comprehend God, they are not necessary for His own self-description and do not express, reflect, or manifest any truth essential to His being. The Tetragrammaton, on the other hand, is a secret code name whose pronunciation and use unlocks power from within the universe but does not present any greater intellectual insight into God. This name is the fundamental ground of all reality and existence which can be explained through this four-letter term. It reflects the four basic elements of natural existence, the four directions, the four qualities of tactile reality including the point, line, plane, and solid, the four tones of the musical scale, the four streams in Paradise, and yet many other unifying principles of being.[21]

Each of the letters in this four-letter name also reflects the totality of existence and possesses mystical significance.[22] The first letter, *y*, the *yod*, is numerically equivalent to *10* and is written as a point, the beginning and end of all reality. The second letter, *h*, the *hā*, is equal to the number *5* and thus represents the trinitarian unity of God plus the two levels of Plato's theory of reality where all things are reflected through the ideal and the real. The third letter, *v*, or *vau*, equals the number *6* and another great mystery. This third letter unites the monad (God) with the diad (two planes of reality) along with the triad (trinity) and constitutes the perfect expression of reality compounded on itself, within itself. The last letter, another *h*, together with the second letter, results in the *y* that is the beginning of the Tetragammaton and all reality. Taken together, the four letters of *Y-H-V-*

H (Hebrew does not distinguish between upper- and lower-case characters) are all there is to anything that can be.

Yet other names were described by Baruch including "Ish," "Yah," "Saboath," "Adonai," "El," "Shaddai," "Elion," and "Makom."[23] This set of names differs from the former series in that they were used in Scripture to describe specific divine activities on man's behalf and are thoroughly contextual in a literary sense. With this last discussion of divine names Reuchlin brought to a conclusion the second part of the *DVM*, not yet having revealed the ultimate wonder-working word.

To this point, each of Reuchlin's two spokesmen had made one essential point. In the first part, a Greek philosopher argued in favor of Epicurean passivity, a position rejected outright. A Jewish spokesman then argued for an ancient system of wisdom far older than Greek philosophy and far more acceptable. This wisdom discussed God's different names from different points of view with the magical rather than the scriptural or philosophical receiving primary emphasis. Much as the first section denied human passivity, the second section went on to argue in favor of the *possibility* of miraculous behavior on the part of humans. One of the names presented, the Tetragrammation, was demonstrated to be a code name tapping into God's power source, and in this sense it was substantially different from the names of the emanations or sefirot, or the names used in Scripture to describe God's activity in the realm of human behavior. The third section, then, was to be argued by Capnion, Reuchlin's alter ego, and would deal with the most important point of all—how the power of the Tetragrammaton might be harnassed for man's use.

It is in the third section of the DVM that we first come in contact with the Pentagrammaton, the five-letter name of God spelled *Y-H-S-V-H*. Capnion explained that the world went through three distinct ages. During the age of nature God was referred to as "the Almighty," in Hebrew expressed through the three-letter name of "Shaddai" that is, "SDY." During the subsequent age of the Law, the truth of God's being was expressed through the four-letter name "YHVH," the Tetragrammaton already discussed. During the age of grace, God was called "Y'hoshua" ("Deliverer"), another name for Jesus, and the power of this name is expressed through the five-letter Pentagrammaton that is the true, wonder-working word.[24]

The difference between "YHVH" and "YHSVH" was symbolically reflected in the addition of another consonant, for the added *s*, or *shin*, was of great magical and mystical significance. The shin was the essence of the third aspect of the original Trinity, Esh, or fire, and makes pronunciation of the Tetragrammaton possible: "When the Word descended into flesh, then the letters passed into voice."[25] Much as the Son assumed flesh and made God visible, so too did the Tetragrammaton assume an *s* in the middle and become pronounceable. Just as God became mundane in Jesus, the power of the Tetragrammaton passed from the transmundane to the mundane of the Pentagrammaton. Consequently, Jesus performed miracles including the curing of the sick, the quickening of the dead, and yet other miraculous acts and deeds. But if the name "YHSVH" was the wonder-working word and power behind Jesus' miracles, nowhere did Reuchlin explain how others might use this power. Moreover, a question arises whether Jesus performed miracles because He was a wise mortal and a Cabbalist and learned the power of the wonder-working word or because he was God. If Jesus' power found its origin in His being God, Reuchlin's discussion is fairly useless, for it was not given to man to join in God's power and Reuchlin pointed to no such avenue. If, on the other hand, Jesus' immense power was of Cabbalistic origin, the same wisdom Reuchlin hoped to pass on to his readers, Jesus was essentially converted into a very capable magician. The view that at base Jesus was a very good magician was not at all new. Early Jewish polemicists had argued that Jesus was a false messiah but a very good trickster.[26] To sum up, the *DVM* was a failure. After all is said and done, Reuchlin really did not tell us anything.

In attempting to understand this treatise, historians have often dismissed it as a secondary or minor, even unimportant, work.[27] Indeed, more than one author has treated Reuchlin without attempting to analyze this work at all. Other scholars are so imbued with the image of Reuchlin heroically doing battle against the Dominican dragon and so much a part of the legitimate humanist movement of his day that Reuchlin as magus proves embarrassing. Yet other analysts of the past have made Reuchlin into one of the original leaders of the free-speech movement but are irritated at what Reuchlin had to say. After all, it does seem a bit difficult to believe that Reuchlin fought against the Dominicans so long and so hard in order to advance the theories presented in the *DVM*.

Charles Zika has correctly understood the major significance of this early work and has written a very fine analysis of this treatise. In a fine piece entitled "Reuchlin's De Verbo Mirifico and the Magic Debates of the Late 15th-Century," Zika demonstrated Reuchlin's central importance in bringing together magic and the prisca theologia: "As is stated numerous times throughout the work [*DVM*] in what becomes almost a leitmotif—by this word man can perform wonderful works beyond human strength."[28] In assessing the historical significance of Reuchlin's first philosophical work, Zika wrote, "The historical significance of Reuchlin's DVM therefore lies in its attempt to give the range of occult ideas connected with the prisce theologia and magia contemporary significance."[29] Rather than place Reuchlin within the context of an orthodox Christian Humanism, Zika argued that this German scholar wished to "usher in the proliferation of works involving Hermetica, magia, and Kabbalah which marked the early 16th century."[30]

Aside from the obvious fact that Reuchlin himself performed no miracles, the *DVM* presented at least three major weaknesses that he attempted to overcome when writing the *De Arte Cabbalistica* (hereafter *DAC*) many years later. If there is weakness to Zika's argument, it is only that he has analyzed the *DVM* away from Reuchlin's later *DAC*. Before turning to this later work, however, let us look at some of the weak points in the *DVM*.

Reuchlin attempted to find in Cabbalah an intellectual system through which physical reality might be transcended. Thus, the wonder-working word was essentially a key with which to unlock and release mysterious forces not bound by the strictures of this physical world. His purpose was not to transform reality but to perform acts of magic. Reuchlin was a typical Renaissance neo-Platonist expressing the dualism of that philosophy rather than some maniacal Faust bent upon a scheme of self-indulgence. Consequently, Reuchlin combined his desire to transform nature with an ardent wish to express this power in religious terms. Hence, it was God's power Reuchlin wished to discover and God's power he wished to use, "via exemplum Christi." All three points of failure in the *DVM* relate to these faulty primary goals.

First, his understanding of Cabbalah was severely limited and flawed. Reuchlin mistook the Cabbalah's emanationist description of the mystical chain connecting man with God both for a vehicle through which God's power might be used by man and for an advocacy of magic. Attempting to use Cabbalah for his magical ends was similar to attempting to open a lock with a feather, for the magical acts he desired to perform did not come from some list contained in Cabbalistic literature but from the NT where similar acts were performed. Thus, if one makes the very curious assumption that physical reality might be altered through the use of an intellectual system or through the use of some magical word, a NT system of magic rather than Cabbalah would have been more consistent with Reuchlin's ends.

The system of transcendence taught by Cabbalah did indeed move from the mundane to the transmundane but only in application to God, not to man. Moreover, God communicated with physical reality from beyond the limits of existence through a series of emanations or sefirot and not through a magical term. We have already noted that Reuchlin did not present Cabbalistic emanationist theory coherently; indeed, some of the names were incorrect and in the wrong order. If Reuchlin wished to understand how God was translated into a finite world of corruption, he would have to have learned more about the ten sefirot. If Reuchlin wished to cross the border of physical reality, he would have needed to discover a system with that as its goal. If Reuchlin insisted upon using Cabbalah to alter physical reality, he would have required much more than a single wonder-working word to do so.

The second failure of the *DVM* was even worse than the first. Reuchlin never quite explained how the many OT names of God were used in conjunction with the performance of miracles when only the Tetragrammaton was subject to magical scrutiny. Thus, if "YHVH" was a magical agency, how were miracles performed in the name of "Shaddai" or "Elohim" or any one of a list of divine names? If it is assumed that the power of these names or just of "YHVH" originated from God's power, most of Reuchlin's argument was irrelevant. If, as Tertullian wrote, God might have saved mankind through the agency of a stone rather than through the incarnation of the Word, surely an examination of stones will yield little result. It is true that Cabbalistic sources spoke of divine names expressing transcendent power, but only in relation to God and because man and matter could not contain full divinity. Whereas Servetus understood that each divine name presented man with a measure of knowledge about God, Reuchlin believed that each name actually represented some objective magical potential that might be separated from God. Indeed, one implication of Reuchlin's understanding of magical power must be that God is powerful because He knows the secrets of the names rather than that the names have power because God makes them powerful. In either case, man cannot share this power.

The third systematic fault with Reuchlin's use and understanding of mystical magic must be considered the most serious of all. Very simply, his analysis of Jesus' name was not merely deficient but downright ignorant. This is very serious, if one considers that it was precisely such an analysis of "YHSVH" that led Reuchlin to conclude that this was the wonder-working word. It is philologically impossible to add an *s* to the middle of the Tetragrammaton much as it is not linguistically feasible to add a *q* to the middle of the word *Lord*. No less publicized a scholar than Lefèvre, whose Hebrew competence was far more limited than Reuchlin's, pointed this out in his Psalter of 1508 when he noted that Pico, Cusanus, and many others were in error when spelling Jesus' name in Hebrew. He noted, "The Jews, however, would take our savior's name Jesus spelled yod,sin,vau, ayin [i.e., Yeshua]. They would reject the other . . . yod, he,sin,vau,he as fictitious and too easily worked up by us."[31] And demonstrating his own inability to determine which view was correct since he knew no masoretic theory of voweling or punctuation, Lefèvre continued, "Either way, it is an august and venerable name." One might spell the word *fish* as "phish" but never "ghish" simply because the letter *g* and the letter *p* look alike. They only seem similar to those unfamiliar with English. Reuchlin's mistake did not speak well of his Hebrew learning in 1494 when the *DVM* was written. Curiously, Reuchlin believed he was competent to read and to study the Cabbalah even before he wrote his grammar in 1506. Perhaps this helps explain why he wrote his second Cabbalistic study some twenty-three years later, in 1517.

The *DVM* was unsophisticated, uneducated, and in the final analysis, un-Christian. It attempted to overcome the chasm of material reality and divine existence through a neat trick: magic. It converted Jesus from an eloquent moral teacher and source of divine grace in a sinful world to a magus whose abilities might be summed up in one word: magic. Finally, the treatise failed because Reuchlin could perform no miracles. Here, too, what failed can be summed up in one word: magic.

Over the intervening twenty-three years Reuchlin became a far more systematic and clear-sighted thinker. The *DAC*, the product of that twenty-three-year period, was what Reuchlin may have hoped the *DVM* to have been. Like his earlier work, the *DAC* was a three-way dialogue, this time among Philolaus the Pythagorean, Marranus the Mohammedan, and Simon the Cabbalist. This time Capnion did not directly participate in the discussions.

Reuchlin began with a description of the two levels of existence fundamental to the neo-Platonic view of the universe, and he differentiated that which was "lurid, sordid, and low" from that which was "pure, notable, and adorned with unbelievable beauty."[32] Rather than appeal to some magical formula to bridge the chasm between these levels of reality, he told the reader that Cabbalah "transforms external perceptions into internal perceptions, these into imagination, this into opinion, opinion into reason, reason into intelligence, intelligence into mind and mind into light which illuminates mankind."[33] The sefirot were presented as the bridge connecting these two planes, a Jacob's ladder across the limits of existence. No single-shot magical panacea was presented. In its place one finds instead a reasoned explanation for the necessity of these ten emanations precisely because the divine and the mundane cannot communicate directly. The universe is not the locus of innumerable divine and magical powers, as Reuchlin had argued in the *DVM*, but a patterned and structured framework through which divinity is manifest. The intercessors and intermediaries between the divine world of light and the human world of perception were the ten sefirot. The connection between man and God on a spiritual level, however, is numerology, the key to understanding God's word. In the *DVM* the few numerological arguments were more window-dressing than a functional part of a system, if only because Reuchlin had no greater understanding of numbers than he had of the sefirot. The argument in the *DAC* ran as follows: God communicates with the physical world through His ten sefirot because His purity and infinite nature demand removal from this lurid and transitory world of matter. Similarly, His spiritual message is shrouded in the secrecy of removal since the brilliance of His wisdom cannot be contained in mere words. Much as nature presents the *fact* of divine interference in the world of matter, the emanations explain how that fact came into being. Similarly, Scripture presents the objective *fact* of divine decree, injunction, and desire in terms of human behavior, but only a numerological explanation of Scripture explains the true wisdom of those decrees, injunctions, and desires. In both cases it is necessary to see behind the seemingly objective reality of Creation and Scripture in order to arrive at the true meaning of those phenomena. Thus, what sefirot are to creation, numerology is to Scripture. In turn, the sefirot can be reduced to numbers as well, as we shall see.

In and of themselves numbers are mere curiosities, but when applied to Scripture great spiritual meaning can be elicited from the text since all Hebrew letters are also numbers. Consequently, much as the verbal words of Scripture must be understood in terms of grammar, the numerical words of Scripture must be understood in terms of the mathematical equivalent of grammar. Reuchlin's so-called Pythagoreanism was in reality nothing more than the use of numerology for scriptural purposes. The system to be used, however, was not Greek but Cabbalistic. Thus, when Reuchlin wrote, "I will not speak on the meaning of the passage as a theologian but on the words as a grammarian,"[34] he was not avoiding theological controversy, as many of his analysts have maintained, but simply stating that from his orientation, grammar *was* theology. Hence he could write, "For now I clearly see that whatever Simon shows us corresponds exactly to the Italian philosophy of Pythagoreanism, so that I have decided for this reason that everything of both the Cabbalists and the Pythagoreans is of the same sort. For all our studies of both lead ultimately back to the salvation of mankind."[35] We have already noted how Reuchlin saw Hebrew as God's own language and spoke of trembling in dread and terror when reading Hebrew. Because God spoke in Hebrew but could be clearly understood only through numbers, Reuchlin wrote what must be obvious: "This alone is the field of true contemplation; the single words . . . and the single utterances, syllables, the apexes of letters and the vowels are all full of meaning."[36] In developing a true appreciation of sefirotic emanationism and the role of numerology as the key to understanding both the sefirot and Scripture, Reuchlin created a strong unity between his earlier views on the power of the Hebrew language and his later views that put Hebrew into an intellectual format. Rather than look for a wonder-working word, however, Reuchlin searched for unifying concepts and numbers through which the world, God, and even man might be explained. Reuchlin the would-be magus finally gave way to Reuchlin the serious thinker.

Before he could explain how numerology might elucidate the sefirot and their place within the Godhead, Reuchlin attempted to convert normative Platonic dualism into a Cabbalistic pattern so that the Jewish and the Greek systems might be mutually interchangeable. He accomplished this through a series of dualistic sets that built upon one another in progressive fashion. The very first set was the distinction between the *opus bereshith*, "work of creation," and the *opus mercava*, "work of the chariot or divine spirit."[37] Cabbalists distinguished between these two broad classifications, the first of which explained how God created the universe, or sefirotic emanationism, and the second of which dealt with his spiritual relationship with the world, as in the case of Ezekiel's chariot, or mystical numerology. Rather than present them as two broad but congruous classifications of how God enters the world through different channels, Reuchlin simply referred to the first as the science of physics and the second as metaphysics.

In turn a second dualistic set was built upon this first set with the physics of opus bereshith being made the equivalent of the study of *olam ha-zeh*, "the present physical world," while the metaphysics of opus mercava was equated with the study of *olam ha-bah*, "the spiritual world to come.''[38] Through these two sets of polarities, Platonic dualism was expressed in Cabbalistic language and converted into a religious system as well, since the spiritual world to come of olam ha-bah related to heaven.

The third set of dualisms followed logically enough. The world of the Talmud dealt with the religious dimension of the physical world (the opus bereshith and the olam ha-zeh) while Cabbalah dealt with the world of metaphysics (opus mercava, olam ha-bah, and spiritual reality).[39] This in turn gave way to the next set of dualisms which followed logically in Reuchlin's mind. Judaism was the religion of the physical world, opus bereshith, olam ha-zeh, and the Talmud, whereas Christianity was the religious expression of the spiritual opus mercava, olam ha-bah, and the Cabbalah. Judaism was the religion of this world and its practices, but Christianity was the spiritual religion of the Cabbalah and the world to come.[40] Again, compared with the immaturity of the *DVM*, the systematic and structured pattern of Reuchlin's thought in the *DAC* is impressive as is his thorough eclecticism.

Of course, it would always be possible to quibble with some of Reuchlin's distinctions. Surely Cabbalah was a Jewish science and not a Christian one, and one doubts that such distinctions as olam ha-zeh and olam ha-bah could have the Christian application Reuchlin discovered, considering the Jewish origin of all these terms and concepts. Still, the thinking is consistent and uniform and does provide a very firm basis for the very last set of dualisms. YHVH, the Tetragrammaton, is the God of Judaism, the work of creation, and the physical reality of this world whereas YHSVH, the Pentagrammaton, is the God of metaphysics, the spiritual world to come, and Cabbalah. We can again appreciate the great shift in Reuchlin's thought from the time of the *DVM*, over two decades earlier, when the Pentagrammaton was a magical term. The *DAC* provided the final point in a series of constructs which demonstrated the relationship of Cabbalah, Platonism, Pythagoreanism, and Judaism and made Jesus into the heir of Jewish and Greek wisdom and not simply a magician.

The remainder of the volume was devoted to numerological discussions, the true heart of the system. We are again reminded that such speculation was of Jewish origin since Cabbalah was the most fundamental layer of the prisca theologia.[41] This wisdom then was brought to the Greeks by Pythagoras, who learned it in Egypt from Moses, who learned it from God. The Greeks then spread this learning all over the world. Essentially, Reuchlin told the myth of the prisca theologia at this time in order to establish, yet again, the importance and religious significance of Cabbalistic numerology. Before beginning with Cabbalistic numbers, however, Reuchlin presented the reader with a few warm-up exercises of a more familiar Pythagorean nature.

We are told that *2* is the first number since *1* is the source of all numbers and hence not a number itself.[42] *Three* is the sum of the first number plus the source of numbers, and *4* is the square of the first number, *2*. When *1*, *2*, *3*, and *4* are added, the sum total is *10*, the perfect number because it expresses all the numbers composing it. These ideas were presented in the *DVM* and are generally considered the common knowledge of most number systems. Although it does not present a new feature to Reuchlin's discussion, the *DAC* made far more use of these numbers than the *DVM*. Much more important for Reuchlin's purposes, however, was his five-page discussion of the letters of the Hebrew alphabet.[43] After listing all twenty-two letters and presenting their numerical equivalents, Reuchlin also discussed each letter's theoretical and mystical meaning. Additionally, Reuchlin described several different numerological devices used by Cabbalists for the substitution and transposition of letters and several acrostic methods of interpreting Scripture.

Gematriah is the substitution of numbers for letters in which upper- or lower-case *a*, *b*, *c*, *d*, etc. are replaced by *1*, *2*, *3*, *4*, etc.[44] One example provided by Reuchlin was the word *b'cha*, "in you," used in reference to the fullness of God. Reuchlin argued that *b'* was equal to *2*, and *cha* was equivalent to *20*. The total, *22*, was equal to the number of letters in the Hebrew alphabet through which Creation was brought about. Another example is the Tetragrammaton, YHVH. According to gematriah this name is equivalent to *26* with *y–10*, *h–5*, *v–6*, and *h–5*. It is also possible to add these letters in progressive fashion rather than through simple addition. Through this method, each letter is equal to its numerical equivalent plus the total of previous letters. In the case of YHVH the process would be *y=10*, *h=15* (*10+5*), *v=21* (*15+6*), *h=26* (*21+5*), totaling *72* rather than *26*. We shall see Reuchlin making extensive use of this system.

Notarikon is more complicated and involves word contraction and acronyms. One example cited by Reuchlin was the word *amen*, in Hebrew consisting of the letters *a-m-n*, and usually translated as meaning "truly" or "verily." According to Reuchlin, this word was an acronym of the first letters of the Hebrew expression *Adonai Melech Ne'eman*, "God is a faithful king," equal to *91* when the letters were put into numbers: *a=1*, *m=40*, *n=50*. Thus, gematriah and notarikon might be used together or separately according to the given scriptural context. How valuable notarikon might prove to be often depended upon the third system used by Cabbalists, that of *themurah*.

Themurah is the system of letter, and more often word, substitution in which two words of the same numerical equivalent might be used interchangeably depending upon the context and concept of the original scriptural sentence. As an example, the name "[Judah] Maccabee" in Hebrew has four letters, *m-c-b-y*. The numerical analysis of this word, that is, the gematriah of the name, totals *72* when the letters *m–40, c–20, b–2,* and *y–10* are added together. If the name is deciphered according to notarikon, "MCBY" can be seen as a contraction for the first letters of the expression used in Scripture *Mi Comocha Be'aylim YHVH*, "Who among the mighty is like thee O Lord?" which was the rallying cry of the Maccabees against the Assyrians. In terms of themurah the Tetragrammaton might be used wherever the name "MCBY" is used since they have the same numerical equivalent *(72)* and because MCBY was also a divine contraction. Similarly, the name "Judah" is significant too, for in Hebrew it is spelled *y-h-v-d-h*, or the Tetragrammaton plus the letter *d* which is equal to *4*, the number of letters in the Tetragrammaton. In short, Judah Maccabee was able to win great victories over the better-equipped and larger Assyrian army because God himself fought along with the small band of troops Judah led.

The *atbash* method is the total reversal of numerical equivalents when the alphabet is put into reverse order. Thus, the last letter of the alphabet is equal to *1*, the next last equal to *2*, and so on. In turn, every Hebrew word would have a different gematriah, notarikon, and themurah through the atbash method. These in turn might be used when the normal order of letters to numbers did not present an adequate explanation of Scripture. Needless to say, literalists like Kimchi and Ibn Ezra had little use for such methods. But even devotees of these systems understood the need for consistent use of these methods rather than occasional utilization.

The most important part of the *DAC* was the last section in which Simon the Cabbalist introduced numerical theology. Simon had been absent from the previous day's discussion because of the sabbath and so he began his analysis with a description of the day of rest as a mystery of God according to Reuchlin's major source, Joseph Ibn Gikatilia.[45] Simon devoted some time to describing how the OT treats the sabbath day, pointing out that this was not merely a day of rest but, according to Exodus, the subject of a twofold injunction: "to keep it and to remember it." This double commandment reflects the two levels of existence in Plato's dualistic philosophy. In turn, the fifty-year jubilee is called a sabbath of sabbaths. It is also a mystery of God and furthermore has two dimensions as it is incumbent upon both the individual and society. Consequently, God's relationship with man and man's relationship with society are mirrored in the day of rest, which expresses the dualism inherent in the universe.[46]

In turn, the fifty years of the jubilee represent the fifty gates of understanding through which Creation was carried out, of which Moses mastered forty-nine and Solomon forty-eight.[47] We are told that there are two sets of fifty. First, the set representing the fifty years of the temporal jubilee, and second, the fifty gates of understanding in God's wisdom, in the ideal world. If the number *50* is multiplied by *2* and is further multiplied by *10* (representing the ten sefirot), the resulting number is *1,000*, which is the cube of Pythagoras' perfect number, *10*.[48]

If the number *1,000* is either increased or reduced to the nth power, we arrive at the *En-Sof*, the infinity that is God. Although this argument failed to make any conclusive point about God, it served to demonstrate the compatibility of Cabbalistic (sabbath) and Pythagorean (*10*-base) systems when predicated upon Platonic dualism.

Reuchlin then had Simon introduce the next set of important figures. Reuchlin said there are thirty-two paths of wisdom necessary for creation and he listed all of them and their translations.[49] These thirty-two paths represent the ten sefirot plus the twenty-two letters of the Hebrew alphabet. Thus there are fifty gates of wisdom, thirty-two paths of understanding, twenty-two mystical letters, and ten emanations. If *50* and *22* are added together, the resulting *72* accounts for the total number of God's names, the number of angels, and most importantly, a bridge connecting the power of numbers with the reality of the temporal world. Moses, we are told, was able to free the Hebrews from bondage in Egypt through the power of seventy names, with the two remaining names represented by the pillar of fire and the column of cloud that led the Hebrews in the Sinai wilderness.[50] Most important of all, *72* is also the numerical equivalent of the Tetragrammaton, YHVH, when the letters are added in progressive fashion:

$$
\begin{array}{r}
y-10 \\
yh-15 \\
yhv-21 \\
+\ yhvh-26 \\
\hline
72
\end{array}
$$

Essentially, Reuchlin thus far had succeeded in establishing a series of unities. First he demonstrated that Cabbalah, Platonism, and Pythagoreanism were all compatible conceptually and numerologically since all were predicated upon use of the number *10* as a base figure. From this foundation Reuchlin argued that God was infinite and that His being was expressed through a series of figures, one series of which added up to *72*, which was the numerical equivalent of the Tetragrammaton. In turn, this four-letter name of God was the square of the number *2* which was Pythagoras's first number. Having established the unity of all ancient wisdom both numerically and conceptually and demonstrated how these truths were reflected in the Tetragrammaton, Reuchlin proceeded to more technical Cabbalistic issues in order to arrive at an ultimate Christian numerological argument.

Since the Tetragrammaton is the complete expression of both the Jewish and the Greek number systems, it is not surprising that it served as the basis upon which Reuchlin built his next series of arguments. We noted that YHVH was equal to *72* when the letters were added in cumulative or progressive order. This name is also significant when the letters are added with simple number equivalents as follows:[51]

$$
\begin{array}{r}
y-10 \\
h-\ 5 \\
v-\ 6 \\
+\ h-\ 5 \\
\hline
26
\end{array}
$$

The number *26* then is also a base number along with *72* and other figures already discussed. Derivatives of YHVH all possess the power of the entire name, and Reuchlin cited but two examples of how Hebrew used God's name as a contraction in the form of *yehu-* or *yah-* in such names as "Adoniyah," "Eliyahu," and others mentioned in the OT text.[52] Reuchlin listed twelve possible combinations of the Tetragrammaton, all of which are divine appellations either in part or as a whole. The list includes *yhvh, yhhv, yvhh, hvhy, hvyh, hhyv, vhyh, vyhh, vhhy, hyhv, hyvh,* and *hhvy.*[53] To demonstrate the importance of even some of these permutations, Reuchlin cited a few examples of their inherent logic. If to the *26* of the Tetragrammaton, the number *4* is added (representing the number of letters in that name) plus *1* for God, the result is *31*, the numerical equivalent of the Hebrew divine name "EL."[54] In turn, if *EL* is added to the*—vh* of the Tetragrammaton, the result is *ELVH*, pronounced "Eloah," another OT name for God. If the same *EL* is added to the first two letters of the Tetragrammaton, plus a final grammatical *m* indicating plural, the result is *ELHYM*, or the "Elohim" used repeatedly in Scripture. Consequently, the many names of God used in the OT are really Tetragrammaton derivatives whose unity is numerological. Having demonstrated this unity, Reuchlin next turned to the Christian implications of these names.

We noted that the Tetragrammaton had twelve possible combinations of letters. Miraculously, twelve is also the number of letters in the composite name of God created by Reuchlin which reads thus: "AVBENRUACH-HAKODESH"; the name has twelve letters in Hebrew and means "Father, Son, Holy Spirit."[55] In this way, we are told, the Tetragrammaton gives expression to the truth of the Trinity. Lest the reader remain unconvinced, Reuchlin then argued that this twelve-letter name was the equivalent of the forty-two-letter construct of his own creation: "AVELOHIM, BENELO-HIM, RUACHHAKODESHELOHIM, SHELOSHABEACHAD, ACH-AD BESHELOSHA," which means "the Father is God, the Son is God, the Holy Spirit is God, three in one, one in three."[56]

Reuchlin believed he had demonstrated that the Jewish-Cabbalistic Tetragrammaton possessed within itself proof of the Trinity. Moreover, because all the ancient systems of numerology were in agreement, the Trinity was proved to be the absolute truth of all numerological systems.

The *DAC* has been heralded as the first major Cabbalistic work by a Christian author, and there can be doubt that this is true. Not only was Reuchlin conversant with many numerical devices, sefirotic emantionist theory, and some of the philosophical underpinnings of the Cabbalah, he also demonstrated some measure of cultural unity between the wisdom of the Greeks and that of the Hebrews which found their fulfillment in Christian thought. There are, alas, several problems with Reuchlin's arguments and his methods.

One area of improvement reflected in the *DAC* over the *DVM* was Reuchlin's ability to use numbers and his willingness to drop the Pentagrammaton as an important focal point of his system. Reuchlin did make use of the Pentagrammaton, but the degree to which he did so is inconsequential compared with earlier theories. Had Reuchlin been able to demonstrate in the *DVM* the numerological value of the Pentagrammaton, he might have been able to overcome the fact that *YHSVH* was not Hebrew. Unfortunately, Reuchlin did not have any real ability to use numbers in 1494, with the result that the linchpin of his *DVM* argument disintegrates under scrutiny. Since his wonder-working word rested on a foundation of sand, Reuchlin moved in a different direction in the *DAC*. Rather than prove the truth of Jesus Christ, Reuchlin attempted to prove the truth of the Trinity. After using traditional Jewish numerological codes and bases such as *10, 22, 50, 72,* and *26,* his proof of the Trinity rested upon none of these. Consequently, the methods Reuchlin had used to prove the viability of the Tetragrammaton were not those he used to prove the truth of the Trinity. In the latter case the only foundation for his trinitarian argument was that the Tetragrammaton had twelve possible combinations, all of which might possess divine power and significance. But the trinitarian formula developed by Reuchlin did not use any of the possible combinations of *Y-H-V-H.* Instead, it was the number *12* that interested Reuchlin because he could make up a trinitarian term with twelve letters, but with none of the base letters, which was the importance of this argument to begin with. Had he used some part of the Tetragrammaton in this trinitarian formula, Reuchlin's argument might have been much stronger, but there was no Cabbalistic formula proving the Trinity.

Actually, there was a very adequate basis for making a Christian argument from Cabbalistic numerology, and Reuchlin knew all the necessary components of this argument. Reuchlin also possessed the simple numerological skills required for this Christian proof, which eluded the *DAC* no less than the *DVM.* Had Reuchlin used his newly acquired numerology to prove the numerological viability of the Pentagrammaton, he might have developed a truly Christian and truly Cabbalistic proof of Christian thought. In short, had he used his new skills to prove his old point, Reuchlin would have demonstrated absolute mastery over Cabbalistic numerology.

The proof for Jesis based upon Cabbalistic numerology is as follows. One starts with the Tetragrammaton as a base, much as Reuchlin did; listed below are the direct and accumulated progressive additions of this name of God.

	direct				progressive		
direct addition	y=	*10*		progressive addition	y=	*10*
	h=	*5*			yh=	*15*
	v=	*6*			yhv=	*21*
+	h=	*5*		+	$yhvh$=	*26*
		26				*72*

Both *26* and *72* work very nicely in many OT contexts. If the same methods of addition are used for the Pentagrammaton, the results are as follows.

direct	$y=10$		progressive	$y=10$
addition	$h=5$		addition	$yh=15$
	$s=300$			$yhs=315$
	$v=6$			$yhsv=321$
+	$h=5$		+	$yhsvh=326$
	326			987

Reuchlin's problem was to demonstrate the religious numerological significance of either *326* or *987* much as he demonstrated the fundamental importance of *26* and *72*. This could have been accomplished easily through use of yet another number known to Reuchlin and used by him in other contexts. According to the rabbis, the number of commandments contained in the Law is 613, the *taryag mitzvot* upon which rabbinic Judaism is predicated.[57] Since Jesus fulfilled the Law, he is the equivalent of *613*. Had Reuchlin wished to express the idea of "God and His Word" in numbers, he could have added *26* to *613*, which yields *639*; or he could have added *72* to *613*, which would result in the number *685*. To summarize: by adding a good rabbinic number of *613* for the Law to the numerical equivalents of the Tetragrammaton, we arrive at two numbers, both of which come from Jewish foundations and both of which are the numerical equivalent of "God and His Word," a good Christian concept. In terms of numbers this is what we have accomplished thus far:

$$y=10$$
$$yh=15$$
$$yhs=315$$
$$yhsv=321$$
$$+ \quad yhsvh=326$$

987, which equals the Pentagrammaton

$$613 = \text{commandments of the Law}$$
$$+ \quad 72 = \text{Tetragrammaton}$$
$$685 = \text{Tetragrammaton plus Law, which equals God and His Word}$$

Since Jesus fulfilled the Law, Reuchlin would have to demonstrate that *987* and *685* are related. This could have been accomplished by subtracting *685* from *987*, which would yield *302*. This figure of *302* is truly a magical

number, for it represents the numerical equivalent of the *s* *(300)* for Jesus
with the remaining 2, Pythagoras's first real number, representing the Father and the Spirit. Through this proof, Reuchlin might have demonstrated the Trinity, the Pentagrammaton, and Jesus' fulfillment of the
Law—all through the use of rabbinic primary numbers and good Cabbalistic method.

Whatever the shortcomings of the *DAC*, its superiority to the *DVM* and
most other works by Christian Cabbalists is clear. One reason Reuchlin's
mature work was better than the *DVM* was the sources he used. He cited
most frequently works by Joseph Ibn Gikatilla (1248–1325), a major Spanish Cabbalist who was a pupil of Abraham Abulafia and a close friend of
Shem Tov de Leon, both major Jewish Cabbalists.[58] The two works used by
Reuchlin were the *Ginnat Egoz* ("Garden of Nuts") and the *Sha'are Orah*
("Paths of Illumination"). Both were written between 1274 and 1293, and
their influence on Reuchlin is apparent. The first book was a detailed discussion of the twenty-two letters of the alphabet, and the second was a complete discussion of the sefirot and emanationist theory, both areas of interest in the *DAC*.

The single most important source, however, was the *Sefer Yetzirah*, or
"Book of Creation."[59] The author of this volume is unknown, but it was
composed in Israel between the third and the sixth centuries. Although it
was fundamentally important to the development of later Cabbalistic mysticism, the *Book of Creation* is usually considered pre-Cabbalistic. From
Reuchlin's perspective this book was enormously important, for he believed it to have been known to Abraham and its content known even to
Adam. It expresses two basic trends of thought important to Reuchlin: the
importance of language as the medium of creation and the significance of
numbers and numerology in describing God's being. Indeed, the best opinion is that it was originally composed by an orthodox Palestinian Jew with
strong Pythagorean leanings. The book accounts for Creation as the product of a linguistic process whereby God spoke the world into existence
through the agency of the twenty-two letters of the Hebrew alphabet and
the ten sefirot. Taken together, the ten sefirot and the twenty-two letters of
the alphabet constitute the thirty-two paths of wisdom. The similarities
between these views and those expressed in the *DAC* speak for themselves.

Historians have had a difficult time assessing Reuchlin's ideas. All
sympathized with his struggle against the tyranny of orthodoxy but his
actual views left scholars nonplused and confused. Ludwig Geiger, Reuchlin's leading nineteenth-century biographer, considered Reuchlin's Cab-

balistic views nothing less than "the misbegotten progeny of a sick mind."[60] W. S. Lilly wrote, "It was but lost labor that he rose up early and late took rest, and ate the bread of carefulness in order to spin this cobweb."[61] Of course, such negative appraisals might reflect the general nineteenth-century impatience with all mysticism, but even more recent scholars of note have been dismayed by Reuchlin's preoccupation with numerology. David Daitches expressed the views of many other scholars when he wrote, "Thus it was that Hebrew scholarship in the Renaissance became entangled with the fantastic doctrine of the Cabbalah, an entanglement which had the unfortunate results in deflecting the attention of such a great scholar and otherwise clear thinker as Reuchlin from more profitable branches of Hebrew literature."[62]

Even Reuchlin's contemporaries shook their heads in dismay and wonder. The Englishman John Colet admired and praised Reuchlin's obvious erudition but added, "Sometimes the miraculous seemed to me more verbal than real."[63] Erasmus, who could not find it in his heart to defend Reuchlin against the Dominicans, found it possible to attack his claimed friend and colleague in *Praise of Folly*.

> I know of one notable fool—there I go again, I meant to say scholar—who was ready to expound the mystery of the Holy Trinity to a very distinguished assembly. . . . He expounded the mystery of the name of Jesus showing with admirable subtlety that the letters of the name seemed to explain all that could be understood about Him. . . . He amazed his audience even more when he treated the letters of the name mathematically. The name, "Jesus" was equally divided into two parts with the letter "s" left in the middle. He then proceeded to point out that . . . this connection showed that Jesus takes away the sins of the world. His listeners, especially the theologians, were so amazed at this new approach that some of them came near to being overtaken by that same mysterious force that transformed Niobe to stone.[64]

Even so radical a thinker and so severe a judaizer as Michael Servetus had little patience for the grammatical and numerological games Reuchlin and others played with the Godhead.

> O monsters of the world that God should be a jest to us because the endings of words requires it and that we should confess a plurality in God because one word requires it and not another, as though Hebrews, Greeks, and Barbarians ought to have nouns ending in——tia [*substantia, essentia, entia*] so that all languages may have a fixed rule for making sport of God.[65]

Only in recent years have some scholars come to understand the vital significance of Reuchlin's works as part of the prisca theologia and the religious
dimension to the Renaissance myth of the past. We have noted Zika's fine
work in the area of magic. Yet Reuchlin has yet to be discovered and placed
within the total context of Renaissance nostalgia.

Johannes Reuchlin's life and varied contributions defy easy classification. His struggles with the Dominicans, his pioneering work in Hebrew-
language instruction, and his enthusiasm for Cabbalistic mysticism, as
well as his ardent desire for church reform, all seem to be diverse tendencies.
For Reuchlin himself, his work with Cabbalah was by far his most important contribution to his age, and he must be ranked along with Pico, Giordano Bruno, Agrippa, and Ficino as one of the most seminal of late-
fifteenth/early-sixteenth-century thinkers. More than that, Reuchlin
must be ranked among the great mystics of his age, a designation no other
scholar has been willing to grant him. Reuchlin believed it was possible for
man and God to communicate directly, not through the agency of theology
and not by means of the Church, but through language, the same Hebrew
language used by Adam to speak to God.

Reuchlin believed Cabbalah might unlock all the secrets of the past,
all the secrets of Christianity, and all the wisdom of the classical world. The
key to Cabbalistic truth lay not in its logic but in the fact that God was its
author. Indeed, Reuchlin claimed for Cabbalah the same lineage Protestants claimed for Scripture and for the same reasons. Both maintained that
their corpus of writings was absolutely true because they were God's very
words. Consequently, if Reuchlin's logic often leaves something to be desired, surely the same might be said of Reformed predestinarian thought,
papal infallibility, and more than one point within the codex of Lutheran
principle. All of these thinkers reflected what I have been termed "nostalgia", the general longing and yearning for simple truths in a very confusing age of change. All such intellectual tendencies are essentially reaction-
ary, and it is a mistake to differentiate between the sense of nostalgia which
culminated in magic and Cabbalah and that which led to the Protestant
Reformation.

The Protestant search that leads to Scripture and Augustine is different
from the radical road back to Sinai or Pythagoras only in degree, not in
kind. Radical Cabbalistic thinkers made greater use of conceptual Jewish
sources than many Protestant thinkers because the former wished to circumvent and transcend that much more of the medieval Christian heritage
than the latter. It is futile to ask whether Reuchlin abused his sources in

demanding answers from them they were not created to deliver, for Reuchlin seems unaware that rabbinic mysticism did not develop over many centuries in order to add some element to a troubled Christianity. Similarly, it is futile to determine which parts of the Christian past might be rejected in the name of a "Scripture-pure-Christianity." For while Luther might have wanted to eclipse much of the work and decisions carried out at medieval church councils, it is also true that he considered cutting the Epistle of James from Scripture with the same knife. All such definitions are essentially self-serving and self-justifying.

Reuchlin opposed centuries of tradition in the name of a "new" truth—really an "old" truth from Sinai—which somehow ancient Greeks, Egyptians, and Druids also possessed but which was best expressed in the ancient wisdom of the Jews. Indeed, there must have been magic in the Renaissance, for then Jewish thought, while still anachronistic, was also antique and the embodiment of a lost tradition. The rabbis were still blind, of course, but they were also sources of mystical insight. Cabbalah may well have been the product of a God-rejected people, but it was also the intellectual awareness of an uncorrupted past. Insofar as Reuchlin was a Hebraist, he believed he was a witness to the most ancient testimony in an age of nostalgia, and he trembled in dread and terror.

NOTES

1. Concerning Reuchlin's Cabbalistic interests, the reader should consult the extensive bibliographical listings in chapter one, notes 17 and 19, and Blau, Secret, cited in note 1, introduction. The reader might also consult L. Spitz, *The Religious Renaissance of the German Humanists* (Cambridge: Massachusetts, 1963), chapter 4. Although the work as a whole is commendable, I believe Spitz has not always presented Reuchlin's Cabbalistic interests in their proper perspective. Spitz deemphasizes the magical-mystical element in Reuchlin's thought in order to present a more sanitized, almost Protestant, view of that scholar.
2. See works by Walter, Yates, Copenhaver, cited in note 8, introduction.
3. Johannes Reuchlin, *De Verbo Mirifico* (Basel, 1494), f.C8^v. This work and Reuchlin's *De Arte Cabbalistica* of 1517 were reprinted by Friedrich Frommann Verlag in Stuttgart-Bad Cannstatt in 1964. Henceforth these works will be referred to as *DVM* and *DAC*, respectively.
4. Johannes Reuchlin, letter of 19 March 1510 in *Briefwechsel* . . . ed. L. Geiger (Tubingen, 1875), no. 115, p. 123.
5. *Ibid.*, letter of 11 October 1508, no. 102., p. 105.

6. *DAC* (Basel, 1561), first published in 1517 in Hagenau, p. xx.

7. According to traditional Jewish literature, God gave Moses a written Law and an oral law to facilitate interpretation of the written one. According to rabbinic sources, the Talmud was the embodiment of that oral law, and consequently, the Word of God could hardly be studied away from the Talmud. Jewish Cabbalists presented a somewhat alternate view that the oral law given at Sinai was secret and was the Cabbalistic method of interpretation of Scripture. Christian scholars of the Cabbalah accepted this second version of a Jewish oral law and thereby justified their study of this esoteric Jewish source as a true and viable scriptural aid and not as a product of the rabbinic mind. The more radical notion that Adam too was taught the secret wisdom of the Cabbalah also had many adherents. These scholars noted that in giving all the animals their proper names according to their true natures, Adam was in fact expressing God's creative power in verbal form. Consequently, much as God spoke Creation into being and thereby associated the Hebrew language with divine creative potential, Adam was the first human being to comprehend the secret of divine creative principle in a verbal form, which accounts for his ability to name animals. Thus, through the medium of the Hebrew language and its Cabbalistic interpretation, both divine and human power are blended and expressed in a form acceptable to human intelligence. From this vantage point Cabbalah was the oldest wisdom-literature and the truest since it alone based itself upon Hebrew, which was God's language.

8. *DVM*, f.A2^r.

9. *Ibid.*, f.B4^r, *et al.*

10. *Ibid.*, f.C6^v–C7^r.

11. *Ibid.*, f.C8^v.

12. All of book two of the *DVM* deals with alternate names of God. These will be analyzed in greater detail later in this chapter.

13. *Ibid.*, f.Z2^r.

14. *Ibid.*, f.G8^r.

15. These many acts of magic seem derived from the apocryphal Acts of the Apostles, according to Zika, p. 133. See R. A. Lipsius, *Die Apokryphen Apostelgeschichten und Apostellegenden*, 1 (Braunschweig, 1883), pp. 380–83.

16. *DVM*, f.C5^v.

17. *Ibid.*, f.D3^r–D4^{r-v}.

18. *Ibid.*, f.E4^v–E6^r.

19. Blau, *Interpretation*, pp. 46–47, note 28, lists the correct order of the sephirot as well as Reuchlin's incorrect listing.

20. *Ibid.*, f.D6^v.

21. *Ibid.*, f.E4.

22. *Ibid.*, f.E4^v–E6^r.

23. *Ibid.*

24. *Ibid.*, f.G7^r.

25. *Ibid.*, f.G2^r–4^v.

26. See my article "The Reformation and Jewish Anti-Christian Polemics," *Bibliotheque D'Humanisme et Renaissance*, 41 (1979): 83–97.

27. Blau believed it was little more than "a pleasant little dialogue," p. 49; and Lynn Thorndike's evaluation of the work was even less positive, see *A History of Magic and Experimental Science*, 4 (New York, 1934): 517. Later in this chapter we shall have occasion to review other, even less favorable opinions of Reuchlin's work.

28. Zika, p. 107.

29. *Ibid.*, p. 137.

30. *Ibid.*

31. Lefèvre d'Etaples, *Quincuplex Psalterium: Gallicum, romanum, hebraicum, vetus, conciliatum* (Paris, 1509), f. 231. See Secret, p. 136; Zika, p. 133; Copenhaver, p. 198.

32. *DAC*, f.bil^v.

33. *Ibid.*

34. Reuchlin, *Rudimenta Hebraica*, p. 123.

35. *DAC*. The first dozen pages of book two present as many identifications of the two systems. See f.E4^v-ff.

36. *DAC*, p. xx.

37. *DAC*, f.Dii^v.

38. *Ibid.*, f.Diii^r.

39. *Ibid.*, F.Diii^{r-v}.

40. *Ibid.*

41. *Ibid.*, f.Fiii^r.

42. *Ibid.*, f.Fv^v.

43. *Ibid.*, f.Niii^r–Nv^v.

44. *Ibid.*, f.Mii^r–Miv^r.

45. *Ibid.*, f.Kii^r.

46. *Ibid.*, f.Kiv^r.

47. *Ibid.*, f.Kiv^v.

48. *Ibid.*, f.Kv^r.

49. *Ibid.*, f.Kvi^r–L^r.

50. *Ibid.*, f.L^{v-r}.

51. *Ibid.*

52. *Ibid.*, f.Mv^v.

53. *Ibid.*, f.N^r.

54. *Ibid.*, f.Mvi^v.

55. *Ibid.*, f.Oiii^r.

56. *Ibid.*

57. *Ibid.*, f.Nii^r.

58. Concerning this Jewish Cabbalist, see Gershom Scholem, *Major Trends in Jewish Mysticism* (New York and Jerusalem, 1941, 1954), lecture five.

59. *Ibid.*, lecture two.

60. L. Geiger, *Allgemeine Deutsche Biographie* (Leipzig, 1875-), 25: 793.
61. W. S. Lilly, *Renaissance Types* (London, 1901), p. 224.
62. David Daitches, *The King James Version of the English Bible* (Chicago, 1941), p. 127.
63. P. S. Allen, ed. *Opus Epistolarum Des. Erasmi Roterdami* . . . (Oxford, 1907–1947), II. letter 593.
64. Excerpt taken from Erasmus's *In Praise of Folly*, trans. J. P. Dolan, *Essential Erasmus* (New York, 1964), p. 151.
65. Servetus, *Error.*, p. 36a.

Chapter Five

Paul Fagius: The Emergence of the Christian Pharisee

We have looked at two different expressions of conceptual interest in rabbinic sources. Johannes Reuchlin, as we saw in chapter four, sought an ancient wisdom in Jewish mysticism and a key with which to open the numerical lock enclosing all reality. His sources, the Book of Creation and the writings of Joseph Ibn Gikatilla, were perfect for Reuchlin's goals since their purpose was the discovery of the ultimate expression of God's nature in numbers. Moreover, Reuchlin believed these views and writings to be very old—indeed, the oldest literature in existence. Reuchlin venerated many ancient sources, but Cabbalistic mysticism provided the very best expression of what he sought in the ancient theology, a reliable method for understanding God and the world.

Michael Servetus, as we saw in chapter three, walked a different route into the past. Unconcerned with Adam's truths and indifferent to Reuchlin's interest in numerology, Servetus sought to circumvent over one thousand years of church history and a theological system that culminated in the Trinity. Servetus wished to return to the age of the apostles when God was understood more clearly and God's message had not yet been perverted by the antichrist. Whatever else Jews were or were not, for Servetus this single people remained true to OT monotheism. If the NT was to be understood in its proper theological setting, an erroneous trinitarian church tradition would have to be replaced with an earlier Jewish theological setting through which the Word of God might be appreciated. Equipping himself with a wealth of Jewish terms, expressions, and concepts, Servetus rebuilt the Christian notion of the Godhead along lines more in keeping with his sources and his own views. In returning to Jewish sources, Servetus, like Reuchlin, was not attempting to return to Judaism or to demonstrate its superiority over Christianity. Both believed that their returning to the Jewish wellsprings of Christianity might enable them to restore some aspect of

that religion lost through the damage done by the passage of time, erroneous speculation, and ignorance of Hebrew.

Paul Fagius, a scholar who has been neglected to an unfortunate degree, laid a third foundation for the conceptual use of rabbinic sources and
the Christian return to a Jewish past.[1] Fagius's approach was necessarily
different from that of Reuchlin and Servetus, for unlike them he was an
orthodox scholar and minister. Fagius did not accept Reuchlin's presump-
tions regarding the antiquity of the Cabbalah, nor did he believe that an
arcane numerological system might shed light on Scripture where normative Christian method did not. Neither did Fagius assume that Christian
tradition had become filled with the satanic teachings of the antichrist. And
whatever the value of the Jewish monotheistic tradition, Fagius had few
doubts that Christian trinitarianism was the culmination and expression
of the belief in one God. Fagius's views, methods, and approaches to rabbinic literature were not intended to replace, supplant, circumvent, or up-
root orthodox Christian ideas. Whatever doubts Fagius harbored concerning scholastic method and medieval tradition, his misgivings were no more
radical than those he shared with Luther, Bucer, Calvin, and other major
Protestant thinkers. Paul Fagius's interest in Christian-Hebraica was in all
ways orthodox, but also a little unusual.

Paul Fagius searched rabbinic sources for descriptions of the Pharisaic
milieu from which Jesus and the apostles emerged. The return to Scripture
entailed a concentration upon the Word itself along with an awareness of
the cultural and intellectual milieu in which the Word was spoken, heard,
and written. Conceivably, understanding this background might help explain such pivotal issues as the faith-works controversy dividing not only
Protestants and Catholics but also Paul and James even earlier. Similarly,
many rituals described in the NT but confusing to subsequent Christian
tradition might find elucidation in the religious sources understood by
Jesus and the apostles but unknown to later Christians.

This innocent search for Christian origins, so very congruent with the
best of modern method, did in fact have an ideological base. The Reformed
Christianity Fagius espoused accepted the original OT covenant between
God and Israel as the premise and basis of the new covenant between God
and His church. Consequently, the OT retained a measure of importance
in Reformed circles that it did not command in Lutheran Protestant
thought. Indeed, despite his acceptance of the OT as the context from
which the NT emerged, for Luther, the OT social, economic, and religious
concept were the essence of anachronism. The political, economic, and

social regulations were considered part of an outdated ethnic code given to the Jews and valid only in the Holy Land. There was no validity at all for religious aspects of the old covenant for, as Paul had argued, the Law enslaved whereas the Gospel liberated. This notion of the "dichotomy of Law and Gospel" was fundamental to the differences between Lutheran and Reformed in many areas of thought and was similarly fundamental to their different approaches to the OT languages and idiom. If Luther saw the OT as the embodiment of the now-rejected old way, Reformed thinkers saw a blueprint for the heavenly society in its many regulations and stipulations. Rather than Lutheran dichotomy, Reformed thinkers understood continuity as the proper relationship between the old covenant and the new covenant. We shall have ample opportunity in the next section dealing with Scripture to observe how the Lutheran-Reformed split was reflected and expressed through the Christian-Hebraica of each. For the time being, however, it is sufficient to take note of this difference in conceptual terms to appreciate that Paul Fagius was more interested in the Pharisaic tradition of early rabbinic Judaism than any other Christian-Hebraist of the sixteenth century. Indeed, Fagius's contribution to Christian-Hebraica was less in the area of Hebrew sources than in Aramaic materials for the simple reason that he believed Jesus and the apostles spoke Aramaic and were conversant with religious literature in that language. For Fagius the reformer, discovery of the cultural and linguistic roots of the old covenant entailed a knowledge of Hebrew in order to read the OT. Aramaic was also necessary, however, in order to understand how Jesus and his Jewish contemporaries understood those Hebrew sources.

Paul Fagius was born in 1504 in Rheinzabern in the Palatinate. After receiving his early education from his father, a schoolmaster, Fagius moved to Strasbourg at the age of eighteen and became a student of Pellican's and a friend to Bucer and other reformers. In 1527 he accepted the post of schoolmaster in Isny in Swabia and became a pastor there ten years later. His steadfastness in the face of the plague of 1541 kept many wealthy town citizens from abandoning the area and earned him a fine reputation and much respect. With a generous grant from local patricians, Fagius was able to create a press in Isny and induced Elias Levita to join in this publishing venture. In the following year Fagius was invited by the senate in Strasbourg to replace the departed Capito as professor of Hebrew and was also asked to succeed the well-known pastor John Zwick in the city of Constance. The Landgrave of Hesse also honored Fagius with an offer to fill the chair of theology at the University of Marburg at this time.

After remaining in Constance for two years, Fagius returned to Strasbourg in 1544 but left for Heidelberg in 1546 at the invitation of Frederick II, elector of the Palatinate. Along with others who rejected the Interim agreement, Fagius felt it best to leave Germany; and with Bucer he traveled to England at the invitation of Bishop Cranmer. Unfortunately, soon after arriving in England in 1549, Fagius fell ill with a serious fever and died shortly thereafter. He was buried in St. Michael's Church in Cambridge, but during Queen Mary's reign his body was exhumed and publicly burned. Fagius's bones finally came to rest in 1558 when Queen Elizabeth had his remains publicly restored and buried.

Fagius the orthodox Protestant Hebraist was as removed from Reuchlin the Cabbalistic mystic as the latter was from Servetus the radical apocalyptic millenarian. Despite the enormous differences separating these three scholars, all shared a deep appreciation of rabbinic thought.

No work more clearly demonstrated Fagius's interest in rabbinic Judaism than his small treatise entitled *Hebrew Prayers*.[2] This short volume dealt with the blessings recited over wine, bread, and fruits and also presented the long grace recited after completion of the dinner. The title page stated why Fagius published material of importance seemingly only to Jews: "You have here, Christian reader, the customary table blessings of the Jewish people which are used to this very time on festive and celebration days . . . which Luke the evangelist describes when he makes mention of the cup both before and after the Lord's Supper." In point of fact, Fagius's interest in Jewish table blessings was only incidental to his greater concern with the proper celebration of this controversial Christian ritual. Not only were Catholics and Protestants deeply divided in their interpretations of this observance but Lutherans and Calvinists were equally at odds in attempting to define its significance and proper observance. Whereas different scholars representing the many differing churches and denominations and sects used a variety of sources and tools to determine the meaning of the Lord's Supper, Fagius noted what no other Protestant was aware of, that "such customs of blessings from that time have still endured among the Jews."[3]

Before presenting the simple blessing in Hebrew and Latin, Fagius observed, "Before all else, the head of the family—with all his family and servants at the table and holding a little cup of wine extended in his right hand—begins to recite as follows. . . . "[4] The similarity between Fagius's description and most pictorial presentations of Jesus officiating at the Last Supper is both clear and striking. The simple blessing, one of thanksgiving, was then presented without much debate but with the following comment: "This Jewish prayer is called *kiddush*, or the sanctification, which is very similar to the beginning of Christ's meal, as Luke writes."[5] Pressing home the similarity between the Jewish observance of this ritual and proper Christian practice, Fagius noted that among Jews the cup was then passed to all in attendance to share the wine. "Accept this wine of me, as he wrote, accept this and divide it between you."[6] If the observance was plain, the blessing itself was easier to understand, for it was a simple word of thanks: "Blessed art thou, Lord our God, King of the universe, who createth the fruit of the vine."[7]

Fagius also presented the blessings recited over bread along with his commentary indicating their relevance to the Christian world. After the simple prayer, identical to that for wine but this time thanking God who "createth the fruit of the earth," Fagius again pointed to "Christian" practice: "Having said this, he eats a small piece of bread and at the same time he divides a small portion [lit. "mouthful"] to each person sitting at the table."[8] We are once again reminded of the similarity between the pater familias and Jesus dividing the blessed bread and sharing the loaf that represents His body.

Fagius next turned to the long grace recited after completion of the meal. A complete Hebrew version was published along with a Latin translation, in addition to which Fagius presented his explanatory notes and comments throughout the text and in the margins.

The long grace is surely one of the loveliest expressions of Jewish thanksgiving liturgy. This prayer combines many agricultural themes with fervent hopes for a restoration of Israel to its land. More than most prayers, it reflects the close relationship Judaism envisions binding man to God. Fagius wrote at the outset of his translation, "This act of Jewish thanksgiving is called the *Birket ha-mazon*, or the blessing over food which in German is *das gros benedicite oder gratias*. And he who makes this blessing fills his cup with wine and extends his right arm."[9] Lest the reader assume this prayer has only Jewish significance, once again Fagius pointed to obvious Christian meaning, "Also, this is the cup which Christ commended to His disciples at His meal, along with the mysteries of His blood."[10] The next nine pages presented the full Hebrew body of the prayer in uninterrupted fashion. Fagius must have been terribly impressed with this prayer because at its conclusions, and in Hebrew, he presented his own variant of one paragraph along more Christian lines of thought. Essentially, Fagius used the Jewish prayer as his foundation and added Christian words and phrases to make it acceptably Christian. This short paragraph is presented below with Fagius's additions in italics.

> We thank thee, Lord our God, for *just as* you have given a lovely and spacious land to our fathers as a heritage, *so too have you given a spiritual land in heaven above on the merit and death of your first born son, the dear Jesus, messiah, our Lord, whom you sent to this world to forgive our sins, just as* you took your people Israel from the land of Egypt and redeemed us from the house of bondage, *similarly you took us from the power and slavery of Satan to whom we were in bondage through our sins according to his judgments and just as* your covenant which you have sealed in the flesh of your people Israel [i.e., circumcision] *so too have you sealed your covenant in our flesh that you gave us in place of circumcision which is baptism as a sign and witness for the forgiveness of our sins*, and for the *new* Law that you taught us, *through your son* and through your ordinances which you have made known to us *through your son*, and for the life, grace, and kindness you have bestowed upon us, *on account of your son, dear Jesus our Lord and messiah and redeemer, whose name will be blessed for countless generations and eternities, amen*.[11]

Fagius's message seems clear enough: Whatever the differences between Judaism and Christianity, it is possible to reach some accommodation between the two. Short of such agreement, however, Judaism has much to contribute to Christian observance.

The following eight pages of this treatise presented the Latin translation of the long grace. Once again Fagius took a Jewish prayer and amended it to present a Christian understanding of the original text. Significantly, the prayer was printed in Hebrew rather than in Latin.

> Have mercy, Lord our God, on Israel your people, *that is, on all the Christians who believe in the sent messiah, who are Jerusalem*, your spiritual city, in Zion, the spiritual abode of your majesty, on the royal house of David your chosen one, *who is your dear Jesus our Lord*, and on the great and holy temple in which your name will be invoked, blessed, and praised each and every day from the rising of the sun until its setting.[12]

Once again Fagius made abundantly clear that the old covenant and the new covenant could be brought together without either's undergoing radical change. One prayer might express the hopes of both religious expressions.

The Latin translation also presented textual and marginal notes on

Jewish points of interest. In the margin next to one prayer, Fagius noted, "This prayer is interposed at the beginning of the new moon which is called *Rosh Chodesh*."[13] And in another place, "This prayer is added on Sabbath."[14] Fagius also called attention to those prayers added on the special holidays of Chanukah and Purim, celebrations reflecting the national character of the Jewish people. Concerning the former, Fagius stated, "This prayer is added on the holiday which is called in Hebrew 'Chanukah' that is, dedication, which Judaeus Maccabeas instituted after the contamination of the sanctuary by Antiochus. Concerning this festival, see John 10."[15] John 10:22 speaks only of a "winter holiday" as a time reference, but I think it surprising that, considering Fagius's orientation he did not note that Chanukah is celebrated on the twenty-fifth day of the month of Kislev, December in the Latin calendar.

Purim is a festival commemorating the deliverance of Persian Jews under King Xerxes I (485–465 B.C.) as recorded in the Book of Esther. Fagius noted, "This prayer is added on the holiday of Purim, or 'Lots' from the time of Esther and Mordicai. . . . On this day the Jews make great merriment which Christians make in the bacchanalian festivals."[16]

In many locations Fagius added to Hebrew prayers through marginal notes rather than in the body of the text itself. Thus when the Jewish text read, "May the merciful one break the yoke from our necks; May He lead us securely into our land," Fagius added, "For this read: The yoke of Satan and the yoke of evil from our necks, and He will lead us from the life of this world to the life of the world to come."[17] A page later Fagius made another addition in the margin: to the text "May the merciful one grant us life in the days of the messiah and in the world to come," Fagius added in both Hebrew and Latin, "When He comes on the day of judgment to judge the living and the dead."

The remainder of the volume was devoted to a presentation of many occasional prayers and blessings such as those for fruits, spices, and lighter foods not requiring a full grace. In all cases the benedictions were presented in both Hebrew and Latin. Perhaps the clearest elucidation of Fagius's purpose came at the very end of this little book where he explained that all these many blessings, benedictions, and prayers were the fulfillment of the NT statement from I Timothy 4 and I Corinthians 10 where blessings are referred to. These Jewish prayers were the perfect fulfillment of the NT teaching: "Whatever therefore you eat or drink, or whatever you do, do all to the glory of God."[18]

The essence of Fagius's argument in this treatise on Jewish prayers was simply that Jewish ritual practice could illuminate many Christian practices and ritual requirements. Praising God for His bounty was a NT admonition, and Fagius's translation of Jewish benedictions demonstrated how Jews at the time of the apostles fulfilled this requirement. The theme of thanksgiving was also evident in the Jewish equivalent of the Christian Lord's Supper. Surely Fagius could not argue that the Jewish and the Christian practices were the same or should be the same, if only because such an argument would not prove very convincing to an audience unused to looking at Jewish practice for guidance. Yet, in constantly pointing out the similarity of the observances of the two religions, Fagius's point was clear. Similarly, his own partisan view of the Lord's Supper as a social celebration of thanksgiving was underscored in his interpretation of the Jewish antecedents of this Christian ritual.

Some observers would question Fagius's use of Jewish practice as a guide to proper Christian conduct, and this may explain why he did not attempt to argue his point more forcefully than he did in simply pointing out the obvious. But even if one is willing to concede this method and accept the validity of Jewish custom as an acceptable source, other questions must remain. Was it possible to accept this Jewish point of view without also accepting some aspect of the Jewish notion of good works? If Jewish sources could be accepted on this level of argument, where else might Jewish sources elucidate proper Christian practice? One might even wonder how Fagius differentiated between Judaism and Christianity since he was willing to draw strong parallels, such as he did when he converted Jewish prayers through the addition of a few phrases. Perhaps the most fundamental question a critical observer might have had about Fagius's treatise lay in understanding in what ways the NT was Jewish and in what ways it was recognizably Christian. Fagius's other works not only addressed some of these concepts but also intensified them even more.

Fagius's press at Isny published three other works we shall analyze in this section. All three works were published during 1541 and 1542, and all present a Christian understanding of the mature Pharisaic tradition. The three works are Fagius's translations of the Book of Tobit from the Apocrypha, *The Wisdom of Ben Sira*, and the minor talmudic treatise *The Ethics of the Fathers*.[19] Together they constitute a good focus for study of early Jewish concepts of piety and good works.

Rather than dismiss the Book of Tobit as yet another pietistic morality drama like the Books of Job or Jeremy, Fagius saw in this second-century-B.C. story of one Jew at the time of the Assyrian exile the perfect example of

Pharisaic piety. While everyone around Tobit was slowly assimilated into Assyrian culture and religion, this pious man quietly maintained the faith of his people and continued to observe what religious practices he could. Indeed, in his introduction Fagius noted that in the Book of Tobit "you have a most righteous example of correct and appropriate piety."[20] One good deed in particular captured Fagius's interest, however: the religious burial of the neglected dead. Tobit received no reward or compensation for this service, which included washing the corpse, dressing the body in a shroud, interring the body in the ground, and performing the proper rituals. Indeed, Tobit received no social recognition from his alienated brothers but continued to perform this religious duty out of deep faith and belief in the religion of his fathers. Tobit's life became complicated when he contracted a disease from a corpse and became blind. Tobit became bitter and miserable and developed a humiliating dependency upon his wife for even the most basic of human necessities. So miserable was Tobit that he prayed for death as the only possible release from his bondage to life. Fortunately, the story has a happy ending. Not only did the angel Raphael (Hebrew for "healer of God") eventually restore Tobit's vision and health but that same angel also vanquished the evil demon Ashmodai. As if that were not enough, Tobit also gained a daughter-in-law in the process; and the end of the book sees Tobit breaking into a song of praise for God in which Tobit predicts that Jerusalem will be rebuilt in great splendor.

The Book of Tobit has often been explained figuratively as a depiction of the temporary paralysis of the Jewish nation soon to be restored to its homeland. Tobit's NT counterpart in this sense is Joseph of Arimathea, who also buried the dead. For Fagius, however, the story had another level of importance. The peculiar form Tobit's piety took was not considered an act of charity by the rabbis since charity involved goodness toward the living, not toward the dead. Fagius was aware of this rabbinic distinction, and he noted that such gratuitous acts of righteousness are "truly works of piety . . . from which there is no hope of compensation whatever from the dead . . . which [kind of work] is called *g'miluth chasadim*."[21]

According to the Talmud, *g'miluth chesed*, "the bestowal of loving kindness," was considered superior to all forms of charity.[22] More magnanimity than charity or kindness, such activity was considered a divine attribute since God's actions on man's behalf were also acts of loving kindness for which there could be no reward, and Jewish prayer often speaks of God as a *gomeil chesed*, "He who acts out of pure goodness." The term *chesed* has another meaning, too, when used in relation to man, that of "grace." Much as God is truly gracious, Tobit's activity was also such. Consequently, the Book of Tobit was far from being a simple morality story for Fagius. Rather it was a prime discussion of the rabbinic concept of grace and the relationship of good works and faith. He noted about Tobit's g'miluth chesed, "For always, in a certain way, grace is a fruit which is gathered from its mother tree. And like pleasant wine, you draw it out of a jug in which it was first put."[23] Tobit's goodness was an act of grace finding its origin in God, not a good work finding its origin in the human personality. In short, Tobit was a good Protestant.

Much as Fagius hoped his work *Jewish Prayer* would elucidate the rabbinic notion of thanksgiving to enable better understanding of the Lord's Supper, he devoted this and other writings to the theme of explaining the relationship between faith and works. Despite his pegging of the concept of g'miluth chesed to the Protestant concept of grace, Fagius was also impressed by standard Jewish concepts of human goodness resulting from proper training and a righteous personality: "And it is generally so, the habits of the parents are passed to the children which the Hebrews eloquently describe in Hebrew *b'ma'aseh avot yasur banim*, that is, children imitate the actions of their parents."[24] Fagius then went on to discuss each of the story's personalities in terms of his or her indigenous and cultivated human piety: "Tobit comes from goodness, piety, excellence, from which the [son's name] Tobias also derives; the fatherly character admirably produced and expressed."[25] But much as Tobias received his knowledge of goodness from his father, his mother too made a strong contribution: "The name Hannah comes from grace and represents the good mother of the family,"[26] though "compassion" might have been a more accurate choice of word than grace.

Fagius also analyzed the names of the angels and the demons in this story: "Raphael, the angel of God, comes from *rapha*, to cure, to fix, as his name indicates, through whom God fixes all evil and misery and our affliction. Similarly, the [other] angel is called Azariah, in bringing divine aid."[27] It would appear that Fagius did see significance in these names since they indicated that help from "evil and misery and our affliction" (a reference to original sin?) and "divine aid" come from God, and not from man. A similar tendency might be observed from the name of the demon: "Ashmodeus is the name of a demon, originally from *shamad*, destruction, indicating devastation,"[28] perhaps indicating that both the evil poisoning man's soul and its cure come from outside man, from God.

Fagius's interest in Pharisaic morality might have been dismissed as an intellectual curiosity were it not for his publication of *The Wisdom of Ben Sira* at about the same time. This work also originated from the second century before Christ and consisted of a list of moral maxims and aphorisms not dissimilar to the Book of Proverbs. It also presented hymns, psalmlike poems and some prayers, all exhorting man toward piety and goodness. Fagius's edition of this work did not present any analysis of the text or a personal commentary, but the introduction made abundantly clear what value he saw in this minor work. Arguing in defense of Christian-Hebraica, Fagius noted that great value might be elicited "from the writings of the Hebrews, not only for the translation of language but for the cultivation of piety, the formation of morals in an institutionalized life —which must certainly be the proper goal of all our studies."[29] It is unfortunate that Fagius did not elaborate on the relationship between this early Jewish wisdom and Christian piety in the same fashion that he drew obvious similarities between Jewish prayer and apostolic Christianity. Without such an explanation or rationale, the study of Pharisaic morality would seem curious or unjustified from a Christian perspective. After noting that Ben Sira was "considered among the great early thinkers by the Hebrews," Fagius presented a far more telling reason for his unique studies: "[Jews] communicated the correct precepts of life and from these [precepts] it is possible to know the ancient wisdom of the ancient Jewish people who more than any other ancient people of the earth had precepts [of morality] known to them from God."[30]

The essence of Fagius's argument was not far removed from that of Reuchlin. Unlike Reuchlin, Fagius did not seek a secret source of wisdom or some method through which reality might be transcended. Like Reuchlin, Fagius believed the ancient Jews were closer to the true source of wisdom, in this case an ethical wisdom. Both scholars built their notions of a return to a Jewish past upon the same fundamental principle: God spoke to the ancient children of Israel. Reuchlin paid closer attention to God's grammar than did Fagius whereas the latter was more interested in the organization of daily piety developed by the Jews. Both agreed that the essential value of the message under consideration lay in its authorship and that this message was given to the Jews. Consequently, Fagius, no less than Reuchlin, expressed a variant on the ancient-theology theme and the sense of nostalgia permeating this tendency.

In stressing the religious value of Pharisaic formulations of human piety, Fagius surpassed the notion that Jewish sources were of value in elucidating the Gospel good news and may have placed value in Jewish

piety in and of itself. Surely those believing that the old covenant was outdated or that human limitations did not permit true piety would be very
distressed by Fagius's understanding of the value of Jewish literature.
There was an additional problem, too, for Fagius's views were dangerously
close to rabbinic justification of the Talmud. Like Fagius, the rabbis believed that OT ordinances and codes of behavior were of divine origin and
still constituted legitimate expressions of religious activity. The Talmud
was created so that these OT requirements might be instituted for specific
situations either not defined or not explicitly covered in the OT text itself.
Consequently, Fagius's Christian-Hebraica encountered two serious dangers, both involving the judaization of Christianity. Emphasizing a Jewish
understanding of OT piety entailed legitimizing a religious code and approach to human behavior which rejected original sin and the anthropology of human limitation resulting from that event in Eden. An individual
capable of acts of piety may also be able to please God in other religious
senses, thereby decreasing human dependency upon Jesus' vicarious
atonement. In a systematic sense, the insufficiency of the Law and the good
news of the Gospel are more than casually related. There would be little, if
any, need for Jesus' intercession between man and God if man were capable
of approaching God on his own. In turn, whether or not man can please
God depends largely upon one's reading of Adam's sin and whether or not
one accepts that this sin resulted in a state or condition of sin which makes
indigenous acts of piety and goodness impossible. Consequently, nothing
can signify the difference between Pharisaic Judaism and Protestant Christianity more clearly than the difference between the Talmud and Jesus'
vicarious atonement.

A second problem with Fagius's approach to Jewish sources was one
also affecting Servetus's approach. Both scholars assumed that ancient Hebrew writings, and even some not so ancient, constituted a bedrock of certainty that should have been accorded to Christian authority. Both scholars
were dangerously close to permitting the Jewish religion to provide pa-
rameters within which Christianity might find its definition. There was an
argument for the use of Jewish sources in helping define one basis of Christianity, but for both scholars there was also a danger that the basis would
determine the manner that future development of Christianity would be
perceived. Whereas Servetus permitted Jewish tradition a veto over subsequent separate Christian theological development, Fagius ran the risk of
denying Christianity a subsequent and separate soteriological development. How can one square the idea that the Law kills with the notion that

Jewish concepts of piety come from God? In short, if Fagius was correct, should Protestantism condemn the Pharisaic emphasis of salvation through good works?

It is usually difficult to know how a given Christian theologian would have appraised the Talmud since only an extremely small number of Christians were familiar with this corpus of writings. In general, however, Christian authorities were not well disposed toward these writings, if only because Christianity did not share Judaism's fervent belief that salvation, and not only sanctification, lay in the close bond between man and God which was expressed through piety and a system of good works. No group of writings more clearly reflected the good-works position of rabbinic justification than the multivolume code of Jewish law. Encompassing the totality of human and religious experience and discussing virtually every possible facet of human behavior, the Talmud was predicated upon the idea that every human activity might be carried out in a religiously valid manner pleasing to God. No group of writings was so detested in the Christian community as the Talmud; and though few could read the Aramaic in which it was written, it was held to be a vital hazard to the very existence of the Christian religion and Christian society. As a result, no group of Jewish writings was more frequently burned than the Talmud and none was as seriously castigated. One need only recall that the Reuchlin controversy originated when that scholar defended *Jewish* use of the Talmud. Had Reuchlin argued in favor of Christian use of this work, few if any would have defended him against his foes.

Hatred of the Talmud was not confined to the illiterate and the uneducated, however; and no less a scholar and Hebraist than Martin Bucer condemned this work. In his Cassel Advice of 1538 in which he drew up the first comprehensive Protestant plan for the treatment of Jews, Bucer specifically forbade Jews' referring to this code and prohibited them from following its stipulations.[31] Luther and others similarly condemned this work with a ferocity normally reserved for Anabaptists and other radicals perceived as the devil's offspring. This was not the case with Paul Fagius.

Considering Fagius's intense interest in rabbinic literature and Pharisaic morality, one should not be surprised that he was also interested in the Talmud. Of course, he had no patience with particularly legal sections or those parts devoted to a discussion of proper Jewish ritual observance, and he severely criticized the rabbis for their imaginative nonsense in these areas. Fagius's sole interest was in the treatise *The Ethics of the Fathers*, which was concerned with morality and ethics—that is, sanctification rather than justification. This minor piece of rabbinic literature was a compilation of maxims, aphorisms, and ethical statements, most of which would have pleased any Polonius. For Fagius this simple work reflected the very essence of the Pharisaic morality he esteemed; but more than that, it also provided a basis of apostolic morality as well. Fagius's volume *Sententiae vere elegantes, piae* . . . of 1541 consisted of a very good Latin translation of the ancient Hebrew and Aramaic along with the original text. Additionally, each maxim was followed by a commentary ranging in length from a few lines to several pages of serious discussion. In short, this was a major effort predicated upon a principal Fagius theme: the compatibility of rabbinic and apostolic thought.

Sensing a probable adverse reaction to this work among his orthodox colleagues, Fagius wrote a four-page introduction in which he attempted to justify this publication. Indeed, Fagius was wise to do so because even close friends such as Martin Bucer were upset by his interest in the Talmud.

Rather than attempt to justify this study on religious grounds, an almost impossible task, Fagius began his introduction in forthright humanistic fashion. His argument was simple: much as the Greeks and the Latins were considered great moral philosophers, the ancient Jews too were not deficient in this area. Fagius went on to point out that for these Jews moral philosophy was a religious concern rather than a mere intellectual or oratorical argument. In brief, if humanists were justified in studying classical sources for more than literary style, certainly an investigation of Pharisaic sources must be free from blame. Unlike the heathen sources, however, the Jewish rules for life contained in *The Ethics of the Fathers* were inspired by the OT. Moreover, Fagius noted, moral philosophy did not suffer from the passage of time and as such retained its validity. He ended his introduction by stating that salvation could come only through Jesus, and he wished his reader well in the standard literary fashion of such prefatory chapters.

Unlike classical maxims and aphorisms, Fagius found Christian meaning in the moral statements of the *Ethics*. And if he failed to point this out in his introduction, he made it apparent in the body of the work itself. In some places Fagius merely noted a small similarity between the *Ethics* and the NT: When the Jewish text read, "Yose ben Yo'ezer of Zeredah said, 'Let your house be a meeting place for scholars. Sit at their feet in the dust and thirstingly drink in their words,' " Fagius noted that Luke 10:39 used the words, "Mary, sitting at Christ's feet, heard His words."[32] The very next precept read, "Yose ben Yohanan of Jerusalem said, 'Let your house be wide open [to strangers]. Treat the poor as members of your own family.' "

Fagius in turn wrote, "The practice of hospitality is recommended even more for strangers, a virtue always and admirably practiced by the Patriarchs . . . as the Epistle to the Hebrews 13:1–3 relates."[33] Thus, on virtually every page Fagius noted the similarity between the moral assertions of Jews and the Christians of the apostolic age. Time after time we read, "This sentence clearly agrees with the sayings of Christ. . . ."[34]

Other rabbinic maxims elucidated concepts more clearly Christian. When the Jewish text read, "When ten people sit together and occupy themselves with the Torah, the Shekinah [i.e., the "divine presence"] abides among them . . . whence we know that the same applies to three [for] . . . it is said, 'In every place where my name is mentioned, I will come to you and bless you,' " Fagius in turn noted, "And Christ said in the Gospel that wherever two or three gather in my name, I will be in their midst."[35] Fagius also noted that both religions admonished their followers to pray for the welfare of government and to make blessings for food eaten.[36]

In yet other places the same congruity between the NT and the *Ethics* was demonstrated. When the text read, "Any assembly which is not for the sake of heaven will not be of permanent value," Fagius's comment was, "This sentence agrees with the words of Christ in Matthew 15:13. Every plant which my heavenly father has not planted shall be uprooted."[37] And to demonstrate this compatibility even further, Fagius noted how the Pharisee leader Gamliel was also in agreement: "Similarly, [it agrees] with Gamliel's speech for the freeing of the apostles. Acts 5 . . . for if this counsel or work be of men, it will come to naught. But if it be of God, you cannot overthrow it lest by chance you be found to fight against God. Thus said Gamliel."[38]

Had Fagius's interest in the *Ethics* concentrated solely and only on ethics and morality, as the introduction would indicate, Christian critics might have been chagrined by the effort, but certainly they would have gone no further because ethics is not theology. In point of fact, Fagius did attempt to draw theological implications from this work. Indeed, Fagius's interest in ethics and morality was actually secondary to his desire to draw a conceptual similarity between the two religions. An investigation of the amount of discussion accorded different rabbinic assertions would appear to support the notion that Fagius was primarily interested in conceptual issues and only discussed ethical assertions in a more casual fashion. More than that, Fagius was quite willing to read Christian content into the Jewish text where none was necessarily there. When the Jewish text read, "Be

not like servants who serve the master for the sake of receiving a reward,''
Fagius wrote, "This sentence makes clear to what extent it [*Ethics*] agrees
with the doctrine of the apostles and Christianity."[39] No doubt the main
doctrine Fagius was referring to was the notion that grace is an unmerited
gift of God, and it is possible to interpret this rabbinic statement in that
fashion. It is also unlikely that that was the intent of a religion that stressed
human capability in pleasing God. It is far more likely that this assertion
was meant to emphasize human character and integrity and the ability to
act out of genuine belief rather than from mercenary motives. In other locations Fagius was willing to go to even greater lengths to make a Christian
point from a statement not warranting that conclusion. When the Jewish
text told about man's likeness to God, it asserted, "Beloved is man for he
was created in the image of God. It is by special divine love that he is informed that he was created in the image of God." Fagius reinterpreted the
entire motive and context of the statement to apply to Jesus: "The dignity
of the first man is recommended, who was the most outstanding of all His
creatures, who was made in His imagination, clearly greatest in innocence,
justice, and sanctity and about whom the Evangelical writings explain to
us."[40] The words used by Fagius might apply only to Jesus, first created
within God's mind, whereas the Jewish text referred to man in general and
Adam in particular. Certainly it is less likely that these rabbinic authors
were referring to Jesus "about whom the Evangelical writings explain to
us."

No amount of poetic license can excuse a misreading of the text in
which concepts from one religion are read back into another religion with
complete disregard for what the latter really believed. But if Servetus believed Jews dreamed of God, possibly Fagius was partner to the same interpretation of that dream. In one instance, however, no dream could possibly
account for Fagius's conclusion. Whatever else Judaism believed and however else that religion is understood, the free-will position espoused by Judaism has never been misunderstood—except by Fagius. The Jewish text
read, "Everything is foreseen [by God] yet free-will is granted to man; the
world is ruled with divine goodness and all is according to the amount of
man's deeds," yet Fagius attempted to turn this statement 180 degrees to
favor a Protestant position: "The Hebrews explain this sentence in this
way. First, it is an affirmation of divine providence, without the distinction
of which it is impossible to carry out or undertake human activity."[41] Even
were Fagius correct in this evaluation, the second part of the statement, "all
is according to the amount of man's deeds," was not so easily explained

away. Nonetheless, Fagius explained this ultrapositive assessment of human capability by stating that "all is according to the amount of one's deeds, but not according to the greatness of the deeds," which not only misrepresented the original statement but failed to make logical sense as well.

Considering the ease with which Fagius was able to make the rabbis speak a Christian dialect, one finds it surprising that he found it necessary to condemn the rabbis and the Talmud. When the text of the *Ethics* read, "Rabbi Judah said, 'Be careful in teaching for an error in teaching amounts to intentional sin,' " rather than explain his verse as a simple attempt at the intellectual and religious uniformity demanded by orthodoxy, Fagius wrote, "This sentence appraises what the Hebrews teach; the unfruitfulness and foolishness of the rabbis. The openly acknowledged dogma of the Talmud, which, because of the emptiness and stupidity, they teach incorrectly . . . in like manner, if blindly, they teach false doctrine."[42]

It is probable that Fagius believed that Christian interpretation of the Talmud, even if out of context, was better than a Jewish interpretation in much the same way that Christian interpretation of Scripture was better than Jewish explanations. If so, one must seriously wonder whether Christian-Hebraists demonstrated interest in Jewish opinion or in what they could turn Jewish opinion to mean. Fagius, after all, was not alone in his reinterpretation of Jewish sources. Servetus used Jewish tradition against trinitarianism without considering that the very same Jewish tradition would have condemned his own views. Reuchlin looked for wonder-working words and proofs of the Trinity from a mystical source with far different interests and concerns. Similarly, Fagius read Jewish books dealing with good works and piety only to gut them of their essential beliefs in favor of Christian concepts at best unknown to these rabbis or at least rejected by them outright. Then again, non-Hebraists demonstrated the same intellectual integrity: Luther wished to base his understanding of Christianity upon Scripture alone but went on to wonder whether the Epistle of James should be part of Scripture since it disagreed with his own beliefs.

There can be no question about Fagius's belief that certain Jewish sources might illuminate early Christian practice and belief. Since the overwhelming percentage of early Christians during the first two generations of the Christian era were Jewish and no doubt reflected many religious concepts inherited from their contemporaries and fathers, some rabbinic opinion *might* be seen as a help in clarifying some early Christian attitudes. Even so, this method could be of value only to the extent that ancient Judaism and ancient Christianity were understood and honestly appraised. In point of fact, Fagius, Servetus, and Reuchlin were more interested in advancing a specific understanding of their religion which found its origin in their own times and used ancient sources, both Jewish and Christian, merely as building blocks in an argument. The one quality that all three Hebraists shared was an inability to see in Hebraica more than a foundation for their own views. It was as if the rabbis all said but one thing, the content of which depended upon which Hebraist was consulted. Consequently, Christian-Hebraica must be understood within the context of a Europe-wide desire to bolster contemporary belief through what was perceived to be a strong ancient base. Were this not so, none of these scholars would have appealed to Jewish sources since those sources were not traditionally used, not traditionally well thought of and respected, and not generally accepted as authoritative. All three scholars sought in Jewish sources some quality that they could not find in Christian sources, for surely they would have used them had they provided that quality. This quality, access to an uncorrupted source of truth, was essentially the same as that sought by secular humanists using ancient Greek and Latin materials. In all cases sixteenth-century scholars were imbued with a vision of the past which was untroubled by all the many intellectual factors that made them distrust their own roots and sources and made necessary the search for better, more truthful roots. Essentially, all were intellectually nostalgic. Moreover, all three scholars used the terminology of nostalgia. Servetus sought for "what the first Christians believed" and wished to reject what "was added later by people in later times." Fagius defended his pursuit of ancient Jewish piety, a concept he claimed "was not corrupted by the passage of time." Reuchlin was the most extreme of all, for he would be satisfied only with a wisdom that went back to Adam in the Garden of Eden. The widespread popularity of Christian-Hebraica can be explained by a great many factors, but surely one stands out above the rest: It was the study of Hebrew in an age of nostalgia, the pursuit of the most ancient testimony. But if this assessment would appear to apply more to the Renaissance than to the Reformation, let us turn to yet another branch of sixteenth-century nostalgia, Protestant scripturalism, and examine its relationship to Christian-Hebraica.

NOTES

1. It is unfortunate that Fagius has attracted so little scholarly attention. For a

complete list of his publications, see R. Raubenheimer, *Paul Fagius* (Grunstadt, 1957).

2. Paul Fagius, *Precationes Hebraicae quibus in Solemnioribus Festis Iudaei* . . . (Isny, 1542).

3. Prefatory letter to the above.

4. *Ibid.*, p. A2.

5. *Ibid.*

6. *Ibid.*

7. *Ibid.*

8. *Ibid.*

9. *Ibid.*, p. A3.

10. *Ibid.*

11. *Ibid.*, pp. B3–B4.

12. *Ibid.*, p. B6.

13. *Ibid.*, p. C.

14. *Ibid.*

15. *Ibid.*, p. C1.

16. *Ibid.*, pp. C1–2.

17. *Ibid.*, p. C2b.

18. *Ibid.*, p. C5.

19. Paul Fagius, *Tobias Hebraice* . . . (Isny, 1542), hereafter *Tobias*; *idem*, *Sententiae morales Ben Syrae, Vetustissimi authris Hebraei.* (Isny, 1542) (hereafter *Ben Syrae*); *idem*, *Sententiae Vere Elegentes Piae* . . . (Isny, 1541) (hereafter *Sententiae* . . . *Elegentes*).

20. *Tobias*, p. A1.

21. *Ibid.*, pp. A1–2.

22. *The Babylonian Talmud*, trans. and ed. I. Epstein (London, 1948–). Tractate on Peah 4:19.

23. *Tobias*, p. A1–2.

24. *Ibid.*, p. A2.

25. *Ibid.*

26. *Ibid.*

27. *Ibid.*, p. A3.

28. *Ibid.*, p. A2.

29. *Ben Syrae*, p. A1.

30. *Ibid.*

31. Bucer's attitude in this regard will be analyzed in a later chapter where his treatise concerning Jews will be discussed.

32. *Sententiae* . . . *Elegentes*, pp. 4–5.

33. *Ibid.*, p. 6.

34. *Ibid.*, p. 27.

35. *Ibid.*, p. 51.

36. *Ibid.*, pp. 42, 45.

37. *Ibid.*, p. 78.
38. *Ibid.*
39. *Ibid.*, p. 4.
40. *Ibid.*, p. 58.
41. *Ibid.*, p. 59.
42. *Ibid.*, p. 80.

PART III

Scripture and the Myth of the Past

Chapter Six

Overview: Contours and Variety of Scriptural Study

Throughout the Middle Ages the Roman Catholic church depended upon Jerome's fifth-century translation of Scripture into Latin. Whether in the areas of exegesis, pastoral care, political precedent, or social and legal concerns, Jerome's words were used by priests, scholars, lawyers, and those wielding political authority. Indeed, this text enjoyed such great esteem that in many ways it was not thought of as a translation but as the Latin voice of God, the very embodiment of Holy Writ. Without his translation it is possible that Christianity might have been confined to Greek-speaking areas of the empire, for Scripture existed heretofore only in Hebrew and Greek. With Jerome's translation Christianity was able to spread the Gospel to all people reading, speaking, or having familiarity with Latin in western Europe. One unfortunate result of Jerome's successful Latin work was that the Greek and Hebrew versions received little attention. Of course, much the same might be said of all good translations; they are created to fill a need and do so at the expense of the original. Since little Greek and no Hebrew had been part of the barbarian cultural life and since the Bible existed in Latin, the original languages were not so much forgotten as never learned in the west.

Translating important works is always difficult, but unlike philosophical, political, or literary creations, Scripture was not the product of human imagination or the result of an individual genius. Scripture represented God's revealed truth coined in Hebrew and perhaps in Greek, but certainly not in the Latin idiom. Sophocles and Polybius might be translated by those who understood them, but God's Word was another matter altogether.

Jerome was a scholar of great psychological depth, cultural breadth, and sincere religious devotion. In creating his translation, he consulted Jewish linguists and textual experts to gain the greatest possible insight into the meaning of the text. Despite the inherent difficulties in presenting the literature of a rich religious tradition over two thousand years old as well as a new corpus of writings expressing a somewhat different awareness of God, Jerome did a remarkable job. Indeed, the Vulgate must be considered one of the most significant works, if not the single greatest literary accomplishment, ever produced in western civilization.

During the Reformation age Jerome's work was found increasingly wanting. It was condemned as either too Jewish or too Hellenistic, too inaccurate, and too Catholic. However, even those most severely condemning the Vulgate still accorded Jerome great honor and respect. Even if greater facility in Hebrew and Greek justified the Vulgate from a scholarly point of view, which was not the case, it had one limitation that could not be overcome—it was in Latin. Latin was no longer the vulgate or common language of Europe's growing population, and to the degree that different corners of Europe spoke a variety of vernacular languages and dialects, western Christians were increasingly removed from God's Word. If the Reformation would mark a return to Scripture, it would have to be translated into these vernacular tongues. If each and every person was to read Scripture, it must first be available to be read. In short, Jerome's intellectual and religious accomplishments would need repeating.

The need for vernacular translations of Scripture was apparent before the Reformation when incomplete or poor-quality renditions of the text appeared, such texts as the Lollard Bible or that used by the Waldensians even earlier. Either out of fear of the effect of poor-quality translation or because it saw these works as a challenge to its own authority, the Church was critical of these efforts and insisted upon its sole right to interpret God's Word. In either event, the advent of printing made the Church's desires somewhat academic, for it was difficult, if not impossible, to control press production. Increasing numbers of literate town dwellers expressed diminished faith in a church whose responses to the age of the plagues were increased taxation, multiple papacies, intense papal-episcopal conflict, and escalating hostility toward secular power and authority. Consequently, the existence of a disillusioned and educated laity, the difficulties in the Church, and the viability of printing contributed to, some say necessitated, the creation of new religious institutions and new translations of Scripture to serve those institutions.

The number of Bible translations during the Reformation age was very large indeed, with some exerting enormous influence in both a religious and cultural sense. Both Luther's German Bible and the King James

Bible enjoyed a popularity and respect that transcended religious concerns, and both were equally important in influencing the development of the languages in which they were written. Consequently, the need for a better translation of the OT into the vernacular can be added to the list of many factors making a knowledge of Hebrew important during the Renaissance and Reformation ages. We have already noted such factors as the ancient theology, restitutionism, and the elucidation of the NT as causes for the study of Hebrew. No less important was the need for a better translation of Scripture on the one hand as well as a different understanding of the OT to support the new Protestant religions on the other. For much as God's Word would be put into German, English, French, and a variety of other languages, it would also be given a Protestant rather than a Catholic interpretation.

Translation and exegesis are the two forms of scriptural study we must deal with in this section. Though they are inextricably related and demand the same understanding of Scripture, translation is directed toward the reading laity whereas exegesis finds its audience among scholars and others devoted to a critical evaluation of the text. This difference in audience is very significant, for exegesis, even if influential, will necessarily reach a smaller readership. Translation, even if extremely poor, can conceivably influence a vast number of people.

This section will deal with problems involving both exegesis and translation, and as in previous sections, note will be taken of the incredible diversity in the use and understanding of Jewish sources. There is one fundamental difference between use of rabbinic ideas in a conceptual sense and use of Jewish sources for scriptural purposes. Whereas Christian-Hebraists of a conceptual bent all found important but different ideas from a Jewish past, Hebraists dealing with Scripture had the Word as a fundamental basis and principle. Most Christian students of the Bible used the very same Jewish sources, but their interpretation of these sources differed enormously. Whereas critics might condemn Servetus's understanding of Christian history, Reuchlin's sanity, or Fagius's motives, students of Scripture used the same Hebrew OT text and the same Jewish authorities to develop vastly different interpretations of the text. Before dealing with these different approaches, tendencies, and interpretations of the Bible text and the uses made of Jewish sources toward these ends, we must first consider a few technical problems as well as the nature of Jewish scriptural literature.

It is very important to appreciate that both exegesis and translation were openly confessional pursuits and were not conducted for objective scholarly ends. All maintained that without a knowledge of Hebrew, the OT, at the very least, was incomprehensible. When writing about Psalm 133, Luther noted how the Hebrew text "reflected conditions unknown to the Gentiles and so sound barbaric and absurd. On the other hand, the words of the Gentiles also sound barbaric to the Holy Spirit and the Holy Spirit sounds barbaric to the Gentiles. . . . He is barbaric to us and we are to Him."[1] More clearly perhaps, Servetus noted that "the Hebrew tongue, when translated into any other language is defective and the spirit is almost lost,"[2] and yet none of these scholars who were so critical of the Vulgate's inaccuracies attempted to produce an objective translation. Although one may normally consider the literal accuracy of a translation, the goal desired by the translator, and the basis upon which such work is judged, many Reformation-age translators were of a different mind. Bucer argued that translations were primarily pastoral, that is, for laymen who could not read the original text; and a purely literal translation would present the reader with strange and unfamiliar terms that might actually inhibit proper Christian understanding. He wrote, for instance, "For it is against all common sense that what ought above all to be made clear to everyone should be so translated as to be intelligible to none."[3] Accordingly, Bucer was perfectly willing to accept the name "paraphrast" rather than "transla-tor." Luther too wrote, "I am no Hebraist as regards grammar and rules for I let myself not be bound but [let the spirit] pass freely through."[4] Many other Hebraists differed with Luther and Bucer and others preparing texts for pastoral purposes. They attempted to produce accurate renditions of the text along strict linguistic lines. However, if one standard of a translation's worth was its pastoral, emotional, or moral edification or gratification, the extent to which linguistic tools and sources might be beneficial could be limited.

The same is certainly true of Bible glosses. Although technically eluci-dations upon the text, both exegesis and isogesis are primarily interpreta-tions of the text in question. If exegesis explains the text, it does so in order to advance a more general view of Scripture and religion. To an extent, both exegesis and isogesis may be considered the rationalization of reli-gious ideology by use of the text upon which that religion is built. Conse-quently, exegesis is often apologetic, often polemical, but is never a simple explanation of the text. As an example we might consider the fourfold meth-od of scriptural exposition so common before and after the Reformation.[5] Certainly a literal interpretation would have been sufficient for an under-standing of the text itself, but the three remaining methods, the allegorical, tropological, and anagogical interpretations, added the ideological super-structure and rationalization through which the text was approached, conceived, and even integrated within the body of that religion's thought. In short, the literal presentation of the text can tell us what it says, but the other methods are necessary to tell us what the text means. It would appear that most Reformation translators and exegetes were more interested in explaining Scripture's meaning to the reader than in simply presenting the text for an honest appraisal by any who would read God's Word.

One should not think that the Jewish sources in question were any more objective or expressed an intellectual attitude more free of confessionalism than the Christian scholars using them. For example, the most popular Jewish scriptural sources were the grammars and works of exegesis of Rabbi David Kimchi, not only the leading medieval Jewish linguist but also one of Judaism's most accomplished anti-Christian polemicists.[6] Even those sources that were not polemical or anti-Christian still used a historical-literal method of scriptural exposition which assured a Jewish understanding of the text and diminished a Christian spiritual interpretation that might lead to Christ. Consequently, scholars might argue about choice of methods and sources, but they could not possibly avoid Christian denominational confessionalism and were hard pressed to avoid being influenced by Jewish confessionalism.

One of the most fundamental problems of Christian use of Jewish scriptural sources involved the concept of prophecy. Unlike the NT, the OT does not speak of Jesus explicitly. Indeed, He can be located in the OT only by making Him the center of messianic prophecies written hundreds of years before Jesus' birth. Jews have always argued that such messianic prophets like Isaiah or Jeremiah must be understood within the context of their own times to account for their popularity and acceptance. Had the prophetic messages applied to the Incarnation many lifetimes in the future, no one would have understood them and they would have been forgotten. Consequently, Jewish scholarship has argued that Jesus could not have fulfilled prophecies written about contemporaries. Yet, these same Jewish authors also maintained that there was some future vision of a national redeemer and so a prophetic sense did exist, but not one that might apply to Christ.

Christian scholarship moved in a different direction altogether and tended to view the OT as a preamble to the NT whose primary message was messianic and Christian. The strict historical sense applied to ancient Jews alone and was "dead" in that it had no current application, and by definition God's eternal word was eternally meaningful. We shall have an opportunity to return to these problems later in this section, for the time being it is important that we understand that Christian-Hebraists were aware of these problems. We shall soon note how Bucer maintained that Kimchi and Ibn Ezra were beneficial in all but prophetic passages. Other Hebraists made similar disavowals while defending their overall use of Jewish sources.

Most Christian-Hebraists interested in rabbinic sources were Protestant exegetes rather than Catholic students of Scripture. Indeed, the desire to use Jewish sources for the interpretation of Scripture seems entirely related to almost universal Protestant rejection of the fourfold method of scriptural interpretation in favor of a more literal method. Within the fourfold method, the literal aspect might remain simply that, with more conceptual interpretation easily relegated to the other three forms of exegesis. In utilizing a literal approach only, Protestant scholars were forced to bolster and strengthen mere linguistic literalism into a more complete method that included both philological and historical appreciation of the text along with a tacit acceptance of its dogmatic significance. In the development of this new method, Jewish exegesis took on importance, for Jews had long insisted upon a heightened or developed literal interpretation. Regarding the Psalms, for instance, the words were applied to David, thereby eliminating the need for a Christo-centric interpretation. This Jewish method stood diametrically opposed to most medieval Christian exegesis that made Jesus so very central in an understanding of the Psalms that David was removed from the picture and there was little awareness that the Psalms had been written in a specific time and place and under certain circumstances from an individual point of view. One way to correct this overly spiritual and imaginative tendency was to learn Hebrew, and learning Hebrew meant becoming familiar with Kimchi. Michael Servetus, always an astute observer, was quick to see the problem. When commenting upon the difference between traditional Christian approaches to the Psalms and Kimchi's arguments, he noted, "They argue against him that the literal meaning did not refer to David; he argued against them that the spiritual meaning did not refer to Christ."[7]

The problem was a simple one: to create a literal interpretation of the text which was not bound by Jewish literalism, that is, a literal method that still accepted prophecy as the context of that literalism rather than the historical context presented by Jewish scholars. To one extent or another, all the scholars dealt with in this section were forced to grapple with these problems of method. Their solutions were as different as their general religious orientations.

Servetus's work is illustrative of the ease with which it was possible to move from acceptable to unacceptable historical method. Making extensive use of Kimchi, Servetus not only interpreted the Psalms in reference to David but also reinterpreted all the prophets along historical lines. Isaiah, Jeremiah, and others referred not to Christ but to Cyrus, Hezekiah, Zerubabel, and other redeemers of Israel. When treating Psalm 2:7, "Thou art my son, this day have I begotten thee," Servetus wrote, "I cannot refrain here from sighing when I see the replies that Rabbi David Kimchi made against the Christians on this point. I find the reasons with which they sought to convince him so obscure that I cannot but weep."[8] The essence of Kimchi's argument here, so admired by Servetus, was simple: The Psalms presented no prophecy of Christ and possessed no specifically Christian meaning. Widespread rejection of Servetus's views coupled with universal praise for Kimchi pointed toward the difficulty of setting standards for acceptable use of Jewish sources because the proper literal interpretation of Scripture was neither safe nor simple. If the fourfold method entailed excesses of one sort, the new literal approach was prone to its own sort of abuse.

One need not have been a Servetian radical to make extensive use of Kimchi. No less sober and orthodox a thinker than Martin Bucer also used this authority when interpreting the Psalms. When writing about Jewish sources, Bucer thoughtfully noted:

> Amongst them are two others, Abraham son of Ezra and David Kimchi, who have with great endeavor pursued the true significance of the words and natural word order. . . . These men interpret scarcely anything without the warrant of parallel texts which they cite with great attention to the proper sense well beyond the practice of other Jewish scholars. I confess to the glory of God, who gives all things useful, that I have been greatly aided in the commentary of the Psalms by these men, as I have indicated throughout the work.[9]

Bucer made extensive use of these two sources, for they enabled him to reconstruct the historical and philological literal meaning of the text. Both Kimchi and Ibn Ezra were outstanding examples of the twelfth- and thirteenth-century Jewish Hispano-Provençal school of *p'shat*, "literal exegesis." And while Bucer also made significant usage of Rashi's *d'rash*, "mildly anagogical commentary," he rejected the premises of this method and chided his Jewish source for fantasizing. Essentially, Kimchi and Ibn Ezra represented the Jewish version of a method Bucer hoped would become universally accepted in Christian circles. In many locations Bucer advanced the idea of following the *historia* of the text: "In this, I have strained all the powers of my nature to this end, that I should expound the individual points truly and above all according to the historia."[10] Bucer's use of Kimchi was no less extensive than Servetus's, but he was more aware of the possible pitfalls in using this source. He wrote that he would follow their lead "except where they are hemmed in by prophecies of the spiritual kingdom of Christ and true inner righteousness, which rests upon the faith of the savior."[11]

Other scholars of the Strasbourg-Basel-Zurich school of Hebraica also sought and found a historical guide in Jewish scholarship. Oecolampadius wrote, "For my part I am compelled to confess that I have been unable to grasp the mind of the prophet . . . except that I had the ability to read Hebrew and consult the commentaries of the Hebrews, I would not have dared to undertake this [scriptural study]."[12] In his preface to his commentary on all of Scripture, Pellican noted that use of allegory was most often the result of poor linguistic skills and an inability to understand the literal sense; we have already noted his willingness to follow Jewish authorities.[13] Wolfgang Capito, another great Hebraist and leader in the Strasbourg church who has only recently begun to receive the attention he deserves, noted, "Unless the historical, with the aid of the spirit, have faithfully laid the foundation, whatever reflection is built upon them will collapse in ruins, wandering about in unsure passages, making itself a laughing stock with its allegories."[14]

Other than Servetus's radical approach and the more moderate path taken by the Strasbourg-Basel-Zurich school of Hebraica, there was yet a third variant of the Hebraica method which was developed in Wittenberg and to a great extend reflected Luther's own understanding of the value and use of Jewish sources.

Like so many other theologians and scriptural scholars of the Reformation age, Luther's appreciation for the value of Hebrew increased as his distaste for the traditional fourfold method of scriptural exposition intensified. Looking back at his earlier exegetical approach, Luther could write in 1532, "When I was a monk I was a master in the use of allegories. I allegorized everything. Afterwards . . . I recognized that allegories are nothing. . . . Before I allegorized everything, even a chamber pot, but afterwards I reflected on the histories and thought how difficult it must have been for

Gideon to fight with his enemies in the manner reported."[15] Luther's sentiments were those of an increasing number of scholars exhibiting renewed interest in the literal and historical sense of Scripture. In this case, Luther saw Gideon as a man with a mission, and although God may have stood at Gideon's side, he could appreciate both the fear and the anxiety that ancient leader must have felt. Believing that the younger Luther may have missed the point, the older Luther noted, "At that time I dealt with allegories, typologies, and analogies and did nothing but clever tricks with them."[16] And affirming what so many other students of Scripture also believed, the older Luther felt he had found a far better approach to God's Word: "Now I have let them go and this is my last and best art, to translate the Scriptures in their plain sense. The literal sense does it . . . the other is tomfoolery, however brilliant the impression it makes."[17]

Like so many other theologians of his age, Luther also appreciated the value of Hebrew in discerning the Jewish background from which Jesus and the apostles had emerged: "The NT, though written in Greek, is full of Hebraisms and full of Hebraic expression."[18] And again, the names of Moses and David Kimchi, the finest Jewish grammarians to his time, evoked in Luther, as in so many others of his age, respect and interest: "If, however, I would study Hebrew, I would take as guides the purest and best grammars of David Kimchi and Moses Kimchi who are most excellent grammarians." But, perhaps wistfully, Luther noted, "If I were younger I would want to learn this tongue [Hebrew] because without it one can never rightly understand the sacred Scriptures."

The views expressed above were so very common among scholars running from extreme radical to orthodox that one must be surprised that in actual fact Luther's knowledge of Hebrew remained very limited throughout his life. Although he spoke with great pride of the circle of Hebrew scholars at Wittenberg, a group he referred to as his "sanhedrin of the best people possible," Luther himself never progressed past rudimentary familiarity with Hebrew grammar. Had Luther been a lesser scholar and had his interest in the OT been less intense, one might overlook Luther's lack of skill with Hebrew. Yet, it is possible that Luther's sincere desire for Hebrew was in fact offset by his entire approach to Scripture and the method of exposition developed in Wittenberg. In essence, it is my contention that Lutheran notions of the dichotomy of the Law and the Gospel on the one hand and the *loci* method of exposition and argument on the other made it either unnecessary or even undesirable for Hebrew studies to develop in Wittenberg in as rich a fashion as they did in other religious centers in Europe.

No theologian of the Reformation age propounded hermeneutical views more clearly of the loci school of thought in keeping with the Lutheran notion of the distinction and opposition of the Law and Gospel than did Philip Melanchthon. In his *Ratio Discendae Theologiae*, Melanchthon described the proper theological approach to the study of Scripture in which Paul's Epistle to the Romans was to be read first and then the other Pauline letters.[19] After this, the student was to read the rest of the Gospels, and only after mastering the NT was the student to approach the OT. In turn, the Psalms and Genesis were to be read first and the historical sections last. There was nothing necessarily unusual about this procedure, and many Protestant authorities would have agreed with the wisdom of a scriptural method predicated upon theological concept and belief. In terms of historical development and critical method, however, Melanchthon essentially turned the Bible upside down in order to reach NT conclusions from the OT. In assessing this method, Peter Fraenkel has written, "They should read the OT, into which they are to read back the common places that they have collected out of the New (not, Melanchthon thinks, in an artificial way, but because the books of the whole covenant do in fact contain the same teaching and can be conveniently understood in this way)."[20] It should be clear, however, that reading Scripture in reverse order of composition involves much more than Christian convenience. It is not at all clear why it should be necessary to read Scripture backwards and why it should be necessary to read NT themes back into the OT if indeed both covenants present the same ideas and teachings. If Scripture is uniform, would it not make more sense to read the Bible from the point of true development and begin with Genesis and end with Revelation?

The unresolved, and unstated, problem was that the OT, understood in its own historical context away from the NT, did not give strong support for the christological positions and formulations Christians drew from the NT. In other words, if the OT was understood as possessing its own integrity and autonomy and was interpreted within its own conceptual context and not that of the NT, it is possible that large parts of the OT would oppose much of the NT. Melanchthon simply rejected the autonomy of the OT and made its message dependent upon the Gospels and Paul's theological formulations. Heinrich Bornkamm identified the vital issue when he wrote that "any research which thinks historically will have to give up, without hesitation or reservation, Luther's scheme of Christological prediction in the OT."[21] In fact, not only Luther's scheme but all systems that consistently read NT themes back into the OT would suffer. The problem was a severe yet simple one for Bornkamm: "How can the OT be understood in a Christo-centric sense, how can the OT be substantially directed toward Christ if historical exegesis no longer understands Christological prophecy . . . ?"[22] Though Bornkamm was assessing Luther's message to a modern world, his appraisal of modern historical exegesis applies to any system of interpretation based upon historical-contextual development. Bornkamm's conclusion, written some four hundred years after Melanchthon's *Ratio*, has a familiar ring to it. He concludes by noting that "the Christological prophetic interpretation is forced to carry the concepts of the NT revelation into the OT and put them into the mouths of the patriarchs and writer."[23]

Since the proper interpretation of Scripture was to be determined on a thematic basis rather than according to other principles such as historical development or cultural context, discovery of the best themes and adequate categories of thought was of prime importance. Indeed, without such categories and themes Scripture might be reduced to a jumble of statements, assertions, proscriptions, warnings, and promises. Significantly, Luther wrote about the proper translation of Scripture in the following way:

> First, if some passage is obscure I consider whether it treats of grace or of the law, whether wrath or the forgiveness of sin and with which of these it better agrees . . . for God divides His teaching into Law and Gospel. The Law, moreover, has to do with civil government or with economic life or with the church. . . . In theology [too] there are Law and Gospel and it must be one or the other. . . . So every prophet either threatens or teaches, terrifies and judges things or makes a promise.[24]

Consequently, although Luther predicated his thoughts on the Psalmist's sense of God's wrath and mercy, stern judgment and steadfast love, this categorical approach could be applied to the entire OT. All of the OT might be understood along lines of thought determined on the basis of NT concepts and through categories of religious concept determined on the basis of post-OT Christian intellectual development.

The notion that Christian scholarship must read concepts back into the OT in order to guarantee uniformity of ideas between the two covenants certainly runs against the grain of modern theories of scholarship, be they biblical, exegetical, or otherwise. Similarly, the loci method, however beneficial to organized thematic study of Scripture, does little to aid in understanding the historical development of scriptural dogma. From the Lutheran perspective, however, the application of an *a priori* method was not an issue of convenience but a fundamental principle of scriptural study. Paul's Epistles were to be read before the remainder of the NT, which in turn was to be studied before the OT. This method was a direct outgrowth of Paul's concept of the dichotomy of Law and Gospel in which the former enslaved while the latter liberated. Not only was the OT the flip side of its more positive foil, the NT, but even those beneficial parts of the OT could only take on meaning given them by the subsequent NT message. Consequently, rather than speak of an a priori method, Lutheranism would speak of a pattern of conceptual primacy of greater importance than the historical development of those concepts.

From the orientation of this belief-centered method of scriptural study, good language tools or critical philological methods are of secondary importance, and it is thus debatable whether so conceptual an approach to Holy Writ would benefit from a knowledge of Hebrew. To put this matter in Luther's words: "Languages themselves do not make a theologian but they are of assistance for it is necessary to know the subject matter before it can be expressed through languages."[25] If the internal logic of the OT, its thematic unity, and its conceptual development must be predicated upon the NT, to what extent might the language used by the OT have greater relevance or importance than that which the NT concept imparted to it?

One can sympathize with Luther's wish to learn Hebrew yet understand why in fact he never mastered that language. Similarly, one can sympathize with Luther's rejection of the fourfold method, what he regarded as the allegorization of chamber pots, and yet comprehend why he opposed its replacement with a strict historical-literal approach to scriptural interpretation. Conversely, it is possible to condemn Luther's method as inconsistent, too. If he could appreciate Gideon's difficulties and fears, should he not also appreciate that Isaiah, albeit in ignorance, yearned for a national redeemer when he called Cyrus the Great a messiah [Isaiah 44:28 and 45:1] and wrote of the coming liberator because he was caught in the depression of the Babylonian exile? In essence, the loci method was trapped between what it viewed as two extremes. On the one hand the historical-literal-philological approach deemphasized the spiritual message of the OT and made more difficult its predication upon the NT. This might lead to the judaization of Christianity but short of that, to a lessened sense of the dichotomy of Law and Gospel. On the other hand, avoiding the use of Hebrew altogether and refusing to understand Gideon's plight might lead to the allegorization of all OT events and could result in a new form of the fourfold method. Consequently, the Law-Gospel dichotomy and the loci method on the one hand and exegetical use of Hebrew philology on the other might conceivably run in opposing directions.

If seminal Hebraists such as Paul Fagius and Sebastian Münster could embrace Hebrew and the rabbinic idiom, it was because they, unlike Luther, did not categorically distinguish between Law and Gospel. If an ingenious radical like Michael Servetus could use rabbinic thought to bolster his antitrinitarian emanationism, this was because he did not distinguish between Judaism and Christianity as did Luther. But given his predispositions, how might Luther truly appreciate Hebrew study? "If," as Luther wrote in 1521, "I know what I believe in, then I know what is written in Scripture, for Scripture contains nothing but Christ and Christian faith,"[26] did he not then have to accept the allegorization of the OT or reject it out of hand in a Law-Gospel dichotomy? In either event, the literalist work of David Kimchi, for whom Luther expressed such admiration, would be of little value.

Clearly, Luther wished to avoid the pitfalls of both the fourfold method and an overly strict historical interpretation. At the same time he wished to respect the literal sense of the OT text in a christological setting and yet maintain the dichotomy of the Law and Gospel. In attempting to unravel this Gordian knot, Luther was influenced by the great French humanist Jacque Lefèvre d'Etaples, who seems to have had a similar knot to unravel and whose edition of the Psalms of 1509 was of great value to Luther.[27]

Luther filled the margins of Lefèvre's psalter with his own notes in preparation for his lectures on the Psalms. This may represent a turning point in Luther's exegetical development. Lefèvre's preface rejected the import of any strictly historical meaning to the proper understanding of the "literal sense" of Scripture. "Far be it from us to believe that this is the real content of the term 'literal sense' (the so-called sense of the letter) and to make David an historian rather than a prophet." Discovering the true literal sense, Lefèvre continued, involved "the retention of the prophet and of the Holy Spirit speaking in him." Consequently, rather than the literal sense referring to what was literally written, Lefèvre wrote, "We call the literal sense that which agrees with the spirit and which is revealed by the Holy Spirit . . . and is infused by the Holy Spirit." Thus, in reality the literal sense and the spiritual sense were the same, leaving the reader to ponder what the opposite of either might conceivably be. Both Lefèvre and Luther believed that only a prophet, that is, one able to understand the Holy Spirit, could understand the prophets: "Nobody can understand God or God's Word unless he receives it directly from the Holy Spirit."[28] But did one need to know Hebrew to understand the Holy Spirit?

It would appear that both Lefèvre and Luther confused the literal *sense* of the words with a deeper subsequent spiritual *meaning* of the text. This point can hardly be in dispute when one considers that at the time of composition of his psalter Lefèvre knew no Hebrew at all. Similarly, when he composed his seminal and important lectures on the Psalms, Luther knew little, if any, Hebrew. Indeed, during these early years in his development, Luther was suspicious of mere use of the Hebrew text altogether and condemned those who spoke of the "literal truth," especially Nicholas of Lyra and Paul of Burgos, upon whom he would eventually become very dependent. He noted how such literalism "seems to be said according to the Jewish conjecture, for in their carnal understanding they adjust the text of Scripture as it seems good to their minds."[29] At this point in his development, Luther considered those using the simple wording of the text as conjecturalists whereas those like himself who used spiritual meaning as a guide were to be considered literalists.

When writing about the differences between the scriptural methods of Erasmus and Luther, W. Schwartz noted that Erasmus "based his interpretation of the text on grammar and knowledge of philology," or in plainer words, Erasmus hoped to base his views on what the text actually said. On the other hand, "for Luther it was theology which governed grammar. Therefore the proof of his own word-by-word explanation lay in its agreement with his theological principles even though this might mean a forced interpretation."[30] Luther accommodated such critical assessment when, as we observed earlier, he noted, "I am no Hebraist as regards grammar and rules for I let myself not be bound, but [let the spirit] pass freely through."[31]

It is not surprising that many Christian scholars, when first reading the original Hebrew OT text, found many discrepancies between the actual wording of the text and what had traditionally been read into that wording. One routine explanation for this discrepancy was to blame the Jews for adjusting the Hebrew text for their own purposes. It is indeed amazing that in the Reformation age those who knew little or no Hebrew were adept enough in that language to determine that Jews had tampered with the text. This charge was one made fairly frequently in both Catholic and Protestant communities but nowhere with more frequency than in Wittenberg.[32] However absurd this accusation appears in light of modern scriptural studies, the fact that Lutheran scholars in particular were convinced of its truth may help to explain why the quality of Lutheran Hebrew studies trailed woefully behind the study of Hebrew in Reformed centers. Given Lutheran distrust of the Hebrew text and its disparaging attitude toward the Law—which could at best only corroborate NT truth in any event—it is not surprising that Wittenberg never developed a single truly competent Hebraist.

Essentially there were three different Protestant attitudes toward use of Jewish sources in the study of the OT. There were strict historical literalists like Servetus who identified the spiritual meaning of the text with the historical background and context that produced it. Jewish sources might be utilized with great confidence here, for there would be considerable agreement between Jews and Christians using this method. In turn, the NT would be understood on the basis of concepts drawn out of the earlier OT. We have already noted how Servetus predicated his understanding of the Godhead upon rabbinic thought.

The second tendency would include scholars from Strasbourg, Basel, and Zurich who depended upon Jewish sources but maintained a strong understanding of those sources' limitations. Aside from clearly prophetic areas of the text, this group would use Jewish sources with full confidence. The OT would be explained within the context of its own historical development, much as the NT would be explained in terms of its own development. This school, primarily Reformed in orientation, tended to view the two covenants as separate and therefore deserving of separate treatment even though all conceded the primacy of the new covenant for purposes of salvation.

The third tendency found its most vocal spokesmen in Lutheran circles, which recognized a dichotomy between Law and Gospel and subjugated the interpretation of the former to that of the latter. Jewish sources were not considered particularly beneficial since Jews were the embodiment of the Law-mentality, which was reflected in their approach to Scripture. Consequently, adherents to this approach would learn Hebrew but not rabbinic sources since interpretation of the text involved reading NT themes back into the OT. Therefore, to the degree that a passage was spiritual or prophetic, Jewish sources become increasingly meaningless. As we shall note, there were occasions in which even the Hebrew text itself was disregarded in favor of a NT concept.

It would appear that the extent to which a scholar was willing to use Jewish sources was the degree to which those Jewish sources would be permitted to contribute to the conceptual understanding of the text. Thus, Servetus made use of over a dozen different rabbinic sources whereas Bucer used many fewer and Wittenberg scholars still fewer, if any. In this sense scriptural Hebraica differs from conceptual Hebraica, for in the latter case the degree of Jewish influence was less dependent upon the number of sources used than on the initial philosophical desires of the author making use of the sources.

There was yet a fourth type of Christian-Hebraica exegesis: the use of Jewish sources and materials to elucidate the NT. This last category was quite controversial since it entailed bringing Jewish views and literature into the Christian house of Scripture at a time when increasing numbers of Christians came to believe that Scripture was the Christian's only true home. This approach found its justification in the hesitant concession of most scholars that much of the NT represented a Hebrew mentality and must be understood in that context. Fears of judaization of the OT were so strong, however, that this important approach to the NT was stillborn, with Sebastian Münster's edition of the Gospel of Matthew in Hebrew as its only representative. Although the work was presented as a missionary work and camouflaged as such, it was in reality an ethnographic study of the NT in terms of Jewish concepts and practices. This important work will be treated in a later section of this volume.

NOTES

1. Martin Luther, *Lectures on the 15 Gradual Psalms, 1523–1533*, in *D. Martin Luthers Werke*, Kritische Gesamtausgabe (Weimarer Ausgabe), 40^{III}, 459:2, 463:8. (Hereafter referred to as *WA*.)
2. Michael Servetus, *Biblia Sacra ex Santis Pagnini tralatione* . . . (Lyon, 1542), introduction.
3. The best treatment of Bucer's views on translation, use of Jewish sources, exegetical method, and interpretation of the Psalms is Hobbs's "Introduction to the Psalms Commentary of Martin Bucer" cited in the introduction. This citation appears on p. 310 of that work. The reader should also consult other articles by Hobbs listed in the introduction and works by Bernard Roussel also previously listed. Also, J. Müller, *Martin Bucers Hermeneutik* (Gütersloch, 1965).
4. M. Luther, *Tischgespräche*, in *Samtliche Werke*, ed. Irmischer (Erlangen, 1830–), pp. 314, 112.
5. For additional sources on medieval scriptural study, the reader should consult B. Smalley, *The Study of the Bible in the Middle Ages*, 2nd ed. (London, 1952); Henri De Lubac, *Exegese Médiévale: Les Quatre Sens de l'Ecriture*, 4 vols. (Paris, 1959–); C. Spicq, *Esquisse d' une histoire de l' exégèse latine au moyen age* (Paris,

1944); J. S. Preus, *From Shadow to Promise* (Cambridge, Massachusetts, 1969). Concerning Reformation scriptural Hebraica, see my article "Sixteenth-Century Christian-Hebraica; Scripture and the Renaissance Myth of the Past," *Sixteenth-Century Journal*, 11 (1980): 67–85.

6.   Concerning Rabbi David Kimchi, the reader might consult the following: Frank Talmadge, *David Kimchi* (Cambridge, Massachusetts, 1976), and two articles by Talmadge: "David Kimchi as Polemicist," *Hebrew Union College Annual*, vol. 38 (1967) and "David Kimchi and the Rationalist Tradition," in vol. 34 of that same journal. R. G. Finch, ed., *The Longer Commentary of R. David Kimchi on the First Book of Psalms* (New York, 1919); A. W. Greenup, ed., *The Commentary of Rabbi David Kimchi on the Book of Psalms* (London, 1918); Baker and Nicholson, *The Commentary of Rabbi David Kimchi on Psalms CXX–CL* (Cambridge, 1973).

7.   Servetus, *Error.*, p. 56b.

8.   *Ibid.*, and see his *Rest.*, p. 59.

9.   Hobbs, "Introduction . . . Bucer," p. 227, citing Bucer's *Sacrorum Psalmorum Libri Quinque* (Basel, 1547). In "Ratio Explanationis" following the two introductory prefaces.

10.   *Ibid.*, sig. 5V.

11.   *Ibid.*, "Ratio Explanationis."

12.   J. Oecolampadius, *In Iesaiam Prophetam Hypomnematon* (Basel, 1525), f. *a*3 v°.

13.   K. Pellican, *Commentaria Bibliorum* (Zurich, 1532–), 7 vols., volume 1, sig. a2–b4; concerning Pellican, see Zürcher, *Konrad Pellicans Werken*.

14.   Wolfgang Capito, *In Habakuk Prophetam . . . enerrationes* (Strasbourg, 1526), f.5ʳ; concerning Capito, see James Kittelson's *Wolfgang Capito: From Humanist to Reformer* (Leiden, 1975).

15.   Luther, *LW*, 54:46.

16.   *Ibid.*, p. 406.

17.   *Ibid.*

18.   M. Luther, *Tischgespräche*, Erlangen edition, 62:314, 112. The following citations also from this source.

19.   This work can be found in the *Corpus Reformatorum: Philippi Melancthonis Opera quae supersunt omnia*, ed. Bretschneider, Bindseil (Halle and Brunswick, 1834), vol. 2.

20.   Peter Fraenkel, *Testimonia Patrum: The Function of the Patristic Argument in the Theology of Philip Melanchthon* (Geneva, 1961), p. 357.

21.   Heinrich Bornkamm, *Luther and the Old Testament* (Philadelphia, 1969), p. 262.

22.   *Ibid.*, p. 121.

23.   *Ibid.*, p. 263.

24.   Luther, *LW*, 54:42.

25.   Luther, *WA*, vol. 2, no. 2,758 (1532).

26.   *Ibid.*, 8:236.

27.   Lefèvre d'Etaples, *Quincuplex Psalterium*. For a discussion of this work's importance, see Heiko Oberman, *Forerunners of the Reformation* (New York, Chicago, San Francisco, 1966), pp. 279–307. The following citations are from f.a^{v-r} of the Paris edition.

28.   *Ibid.*, for Lefèvre; and *WA*, 8:546 for Luther.

29.   Luther, *WA.*, 3:518.

30.   W. Schwarz, *Principles and Problems of Biblical Translation* (Cambridge, England, 1955), p. 192.

31.   Luther, *Tischgespräche*, Erlangen edition, 62:314, 112.

32.   Luther, *WA*, "Tischreden," vol. 1, no. 1,040; vol. 2, no. 2,758 a,b, of 28 Sept. to 23 Nov. 1532; vol. 3, no. 3,271, a,b, of 9 Aug. 1532; vol. 5, no. 5,327 of 5 Nov. 1540, and preface to the OT of 1523.

Chapter Seven

Unacceptable Historical-Literal Interpretation

Normative theological systems may be influenced by philosophical considerations but must be based upon scriptural authority. Although different Christian denominations place varying degrees of emphasis upon the primacy of the Bible or suggest contrasting methods of interpretation, Scripture remains the criterion of theological formulations. If one alters normative thinking, one must necessarily change the existing relationship with Scripture through reinterpretation of at least key passages relevant to those modifications. We have already noted the radical changes Servetus made in normative theological speculation, for he not only rejected the orthodox Trinity but also substituted in its place a modalistic concept of the Godhead which denied Jesus any independent role or activity. In this chapter we shall have the opportunity to observe the exegetical method Servetus developed in order to support his theological beliefs.

Michael Servetus was but one of many Reformation-age radicals concerned with hermeneutics, though few in the sixteenth-century community of scholars created a method of analysis so radical.[1] His system was predicated upon a diminished sense of OT prophecy of Christ coupled with a heightened awareness of the historical context as the proper agency of scriptural interpretation. By developing a historical-contextual approach to the exegesis of each book of Scripture, Servetus may have laid a foundation for modern biblical scholarship. However, in his own day this method was easily misconstrued. Servetus's ideas were not understood as advanced method so much as blasphemous heresy intent upon the destruction of Christian prophecy and God's Holy Writ. Nowhere were Servetus's ideas and method more consistently applied than in his exegesis on the Psalms, and nowhere were the results more dramatic. Before turning to Servetus's Psalms scholia, however, a few points might be clarified regarding his approach to Scripture and his distaste for conventional Christian method.

Servetus's main disagreement with traditional Christian OT exegesis was based upon the latter's traditional approach of reading NT concepts back into the OT in order to guarantee a uniformity of theses between the two covenants. He believed Scripture could be understood only when the historical background of the Bible provided the main ground of interpretation. OT support of NT theological concepts, as proposed by Melanchthon and others, was totally unacceptable.

In attempting to determine the specific contemporary historical background for different books of the OT while utilizing this material as the context of explanation, Servetus came face to face with the entire problem of whether this body of writings possessed prophetic truths of the coming Christ. Certainly if each book of the Bible was given purely historical interpretation and meaning, there seemed no basis upon which to understand any prophet speaking of a future event. Each prophet would become the spokesman for his own time and explicator of its understanding of God. When writing about the inner systematic truth of the prophets, Servetus observed, "For each of the prophets pursued, according to the letter, their history . . . as the course of their history led them."[2] But before one could assess the historical background, one had to learn the Hebrew language, for "the Hebrew tongue when translated into any other language is defective and the spirit is almost lost [and] cannot be exactly rendered in our translations." Second, rather than apply a NT context as Melanchthon advised, the reader, Servetus admonished, should learn Jewish history, "especially since they who are ignorant of the affairs and customs of the Hebrews very easily give in to the contempt of the historical and literal sense . . . from where it comes to pass that they ridiculously and in no manner of purpose pursue the mystical sense everywhere." Rather than learn theology, the reader is directed by Servetus "to get a knowledge of Hebrew in the first place and after that to diligently apply yourself to the study of Jewish history before you begin reading the prophets." These prerequisites were so important that in the introduction to his edition of the Pagninus Polyglot Bible Servetus wrote, "This is submitted to the judgment of those, and of those alone (for no others can be judges) who are well versed in the Hebrew tongue and Jewish ecclesiastical history." Servetus made no mention of NT concepts illuminating the meaning of the OT; indeed, he clearly argued that the very opposite approach was to be taken. He departed from conventional formulae in stressing that the OT was to be understood in a Jewish, not Christian, framework.

The application of this approach could only have had controversial results. Isaiah, Jeremiah, and others were discussed only in terms of a setting they would have recognized in their own time. Where Isaiah wrote, "Behold a virgin shall conceive and bring forth a son," Servetus commented, "This was true, according to the letter of Abias then with child and about to bring forth Hezekiah who was called the strength of God and Immanuel, and just before whose reign the two kings who were in hostility in Judea were both defeated."[3] And when the same prophet wrote, "And He will send a savior to them," Servetus again saw no allusion to Christ, claiming instead, "That is Hezekiah; for the Egyptians, having been oppressed by the Assyrians, when they saw him have so great a victory over the Assyrians praised the Lord and entered into a treaty with them at the same time."[4] Even when Isaiah proclaimed this savior to be of God, Servetus continued in his line of argument, "Because, 'Immanuel,' God is with us, is meant for Hezekiah against the Assyrians."[5]

Although King Hezekiah was of major importance to Servetus in understanding Isaiah, other historical personalities were also cited by this Spanish radical. When Isaiah wrote, "For the Law shall go forth from me," Servetus responded with, "The Law from Cyrus . . . predicting the rebuilding of the New Jerusalem."[6] In yet other places Servetus again detected Cyrus as the source of Isaiah's inspiration, noting on one occasion, "The righteous man Cyrus was going to execute the justice of God in the destruction of Babylon."[7]

Another prophet of great importance to Servetus was Jeremiah, and here too the Bible text was explained along historical lines. When Jeremiah wrote, "I will raise to David a righteous branch," rather than see any allusion to Christ, Servetus wrote, "This was meant literally of Zerubabel and it is plain from Zachariah that he had the government in his hands."[8] In yet another passage this same prophet again referred to the savior of that generation: "For behold, I will bring forth my servant, the branch," and again Servetus wrote, "Behold, I will make Zerubabel my servant, the branch to come, who is the true branch of David."[9]

There appear to have been places where Servetus was at a loss to find the proper historical personality to link to the passage at hand. In such situations he was willing to use a mild figurative method that did not concede any prophetic meaning to the text. When Hosea wrote, "Out of Egypt have I called my son," Servetus commented, "The people of Israel . . . even as it is said of Solomon, 'I will be unto him a father and he shall be unto me a son.' "[10]

Needless to say, Servetus's views did not go unnoticed. Erasmus responded, "We fancy we see heralds of the far bolder and more original exegetical annotations with which Servetus, under the assumed name of Villanovanus, accompanied his reprint of the Pagninus Bible."[11] Calvin, however, reacted far differently. Seeing the serious theological implications of Servetus's interpretations, he wrote, "The perfidious scamp wrenches the passage [of Isaiah 53] so as to apply it to Cyrus. . . . Everyone will agree that I was right when I told him that no author had so boldly corrupted this signal prophecy."[12]

The essential point was not whether Servetus corrupted this signal prophecy of Christ, but all prophecy of the Son of God. If relevant passages of Scripture were consistently interpreted from a national Jewish point of view rather than from a Christian framework, in what sense could there be any true Christian concept of prophecy? In what sense could Christ fulfill prophecies not truly written about Him? Servetus dealt with this issue in forthright fashion: "Perchance you object; 'do the prophets not see the future?' I respond. They have visions under the covering of a shadow. That which they predict is not clear [to them] in the sense that we understand it. As Daniel said, 'I hear and do not understand.' Similarly, Habakuk preached from ignorance."[13] Thus far Servetus simply reiterated traditional blindness of "vision through a glass darkly," but then he continued, "There is no enigmatic vision of the future then so much as a view of present things." The prophets wrote of contemporary events, "as the course of their history led them." If Bornkamm lamented the contradiction between the historical and the prophetic interpretations of Scripture, Servetus exhibited no such difficulty, for he was far less concerned about the prophetic than about the historical. Yet Servetus did not destroy all Christian use and interpretation of the OT and was even willing to accept a modified form of typology. Though he understood that each prophet was writing to, for, and from the context of his own times, there was some intimation of the future. He would not subscribe to traditional typology in which Christ's actions were foreshadowed in the specific behavior of earlier personages—though he did write, "The purpose of God is concealed in historical types as if under a kind of covering, even as Christ Himself is covered under types."[14] However, Servetus added, "And to wish to apply the prophecies to Christ is to be wanting in good sense, in which matter the Jews accuse us with good reason." Consequently, Servetus's typology was primarily literary and perhaps analytical but certainly not prophetic. That is, OT types of Christ fulfilled the same redemptive function as Christ but were not dependent upon the later Son of God for any sense of their own definition and completion. If Christ was the true messiah and Cyrus a true deliverer of Israel, Cyrus was not so much a type for Christ but both were types of redeemers.

What were David's Psalms and what was their significance? This book was for Servetus primarily an autobiographical work by Israel's most important king. Because David was God's elect and chosen for kingship, much of what appeared to be descriptions of Christ were actually only descriptions of David's own election.

Servetus's historical-contextual understanding of the text is apparent from his gloss on the opening verse of Psalm 1. When David wrote, "Happy is the man that hath walked not in the council of the wicked," Servetus noted that David was referring specifically to the wicked advice of Achitophel.[15] And when David wrote in the second Psalm, "Let us break their bands asunder and cast away their cords from us," Servetus wrote that this was an obvious reference to Absalom's rebellion.[16] Psalm 5 referred to "the man of blood and deceit" and again Servetus saw this as a reference to Achitophel.[17] Indeed, David was so caught up in contemporary events that when he wrote in Psalm 4:5, "Tremble and sin not," Servetus did not note David's general desire for righteousness but explained that the king meant, "tremble before the Lord as when Absalom chased you."[18]

More meaningful passages, usually taken as references to Christ, were similarly given historical interpretation. When the text read, "They gave me gall for meat and vinegar for drink," Servetus noted, "This Nabal did literally [I Samuel 25] when he gave sneers and curses to David's messengers instead of proper refreshment in return for all his favors to him."[19] Significant here is that Servetus explained David's words on the basis of earlier historical material rather than upon later theological concepts. Indeed, the marginalia to the text present dozens of citations to the Books of Samuel and Kings by way of elucidating David's meaning. Thus far, however, Servetus only highlighted David's historical circumstances and would no doubt have earned the praise of his contemporaries had he stopped at this point. He did not, however. Servetus used this same method in interpreting possible theological passages as well. When commenting upon Psalm 110, "Sit thou at my right hand," for instance, Servetus saw no theological meaning and instead understood this as a reference to David's establishment of his capital in Jerusalem, the seat of a great empire and future seat of the Temple.[20] He concluded by asserting that Solomon too sat at God's right hand and verse 4 of Psalm 110 implied that it was Solomon and not Christ to whom the text applied since, like Melchizedek, David's biological son was both king and priest.

Even more significant were Servetus's observations regarding Psalm 2:7, "The Lord said unto me; thou art my son. This day have I begotten thee." We have already noted Servetus's chagrin and disappointment at Christian responses to David Kimchi's work on this passage normally understood as an allusion to Christ's relationship to the Father. Servetus, however, understood this passage in quite different fashion: "David, when he escaped from his enemies, is said to be born this day and at length to be made king this day."[21] The same sort of explanation was advanced to interpret Psalm 22:17, "They have pierced my hands and feet." Here again Servetus wrote, "David, in making his escape [from his enemies] with difficulties like that of a wild beast getting through thorns, had his hands and feet pierced through."[22]

Servetus's theological works give further elucidation of his historical-contextual approach to Scripture and provide an elaboration upon the views expressed in his Pagninus scholia on the Psalms. When writing about Psalm 2:7 in his early work, Servetus noted "that he [David] was rescued from perils and then he says, 'today I have been begotten.' And this too we say when we escape from great peril, 'today I have been born.' And the most correct explanation is this: This day have I begotten thee as king, as clearly appears when David says of the same day, 'I know that I have this day been made king over Israel' [II Samuel 19] and to this meaning he adds his escape from the hand of Saul [II Samuel 22]."[23] Once again we notice Servetus's use of previous historical writings, the Second Book of Samuel rather than later Pauline or evangelical writings, to give the contextual meaning to this important Psalm.

Not content to present his own view and leave the matter to rest, Servetus pointed out why Christian exegetes were so mistaken concerning this verse of Scripture: "They [Christian exegetes] said it [Psalm 2:7, "this day"] was understood as speaking of the mathematical [i.e., conceptual] Son; *this day*, that is, before all worlds, *have I begotten thee*. They most foolishly make an aeon out of *this day* although in the Hebrew the demonstrative pronoun is used indicating *this* [*very*] *day*."[24] In correcting this error born of ignorance of Hebrew, Servetus noted the correct views of the Targum. "And so the Chaldean paraphrast reads; 'as if I had created thee on that day' . . . hence, he is understood to have been born because he was born again as it were, with full authority, a new man newly created king."[25] So much for the spiritual prophetic interpretation of Scripture.

One can easily understand the point of contention involved here, for the difference between Servetus's understanding of Scripture and that of his orthodox contemporaries was the same as that which separated Jewish and Christian understanding of Scripture and prophecy. If the Psalms referred only to David, no case of Christian prophecy might be made and there would be no scriptural verification of Christ's eternality. On the other hand, Jewish rejection of Christ's assumption of the messianic mantle must fall to the ground if indeed the Psalms referred to him. Consequently, Jewish insistence upon a literal-historical rendering of the text is as logical as Christian insistence upon the spiritual meaning of the prophet's words. For both Jews and Servetus there was another issue involved, however. Psalmic prophecy of Christ's mission would nicely support the eternal division of the Godhead along trinitarian lines, a point discussed by Kimchi in his commentary on the Psalms. In an opening paragraph of his provocative editorial work *Responses to Christians,* an abbreviated commentary on the Psalms, Kimchi wrote, "Answer them [regarding Psalm 2:7] that the divinity of both Father and Son is not probable for the divine is not separable, not being a body subject to separation. Rather He is one, unified in all ways, not to be increased, decreased, or divided."[26] Were Christ truly the Son of God, there must have been an unequal sequential relationship between them "for if both always existed, they would be called twins, not father and son." However one chooses to describe the relationship between Jesus and the Father after the Incarnation, before His birth He could only be a son, or any person different from the Father, if there was some qualitative or sequential difference between them. When writing his magnum opus, *The Restitution of Christianity,* Servetus discussed this very point when dealing with Psalm 2:7. Using Kimchi's language, Servetus argued that if indeed Christ was born *this day,* that is, before all Creation and all time, Christ would be eternal "to which they [Jews] respond: 'if so, then for eternity there have been two distinct beings, similar and equal, who were twins and not father and son.' "[27] Taking aim directly at the Trinity, Servetus continued, "If there [was] a third being there, added to the two equal beings, [there would be] triplets like Geryones."[28] Accepting Jewish criticism of the Trinity as essentially valid, Servetus argued that Psalm 2:7 could not refer to Christ or to any divine being since this would necessitate equality of divinity with the Father—the state of twinship—which the anti-trinitarian Servetus rejected. This rejection permitted Servetus to use Jewish sources, indeed *any* Jewish source, in interpreting the Psalms and the rest of Scripture. It is significant that Servetus used not only Kimchi's Psalms commentary but even the wording used by that Jewish authority in his anti-Christian polemic.

Viewed in the light of his antitrinitarianism, the rest of Servetus's exegesis on the Psalms takes on consistent meaning. When commenting upon another important verse, "The Lord said unto my Lord," Servetus again departed from a long tradition of Christian interpretation which understood this verse as corroboration of the equality of the Father and Son. Servetus, however, wrote, "Some [theologians] argue from an equality of natures because it says, using the same word, 'The *Lord* said unto my '*Lord.'* But they should be pardoned for in not knowing the original language of the holy Scripture they do not know their own selves. Yet you, if you know Hebrew, will find the prophet saying, *YHVH na'am l-adonai* [that is, "Jehova said unto my Lord"].[29] The term *adon*, "lord," was applicable to David or any other temporal ruler, and it was used only once in that sentence, not twice.

Servetus accomplished two things through this argument. First, he denied the reference to Christ, for the only divine name used in that verse was "YHVH." Second, even if *adon*, "lord," was a reference to Christ, the use of a different word for the Father, "YHVH," clearly demonstrated some difference between the Father and the Son. The only possible relationship might then be one of subordination of the Son to the Father since the latter used a divine name while Jesus used a name that might apply to David or any other mortal ruler. The only way this verse might substantiate an orthodox position would be if the reference to the Father and the Son was the same with both using the same name, "YHVH." Regarding this possibility, Servetus wrote, "Nor does He [Christ] make a point of applying the name *YHVH* to Himself for in that case it would have been easy for the Jews to reply to Him."[30]

There was a limit to what use Servetus might make of Jewish sources since he did believe Jesus was the messiah while they did not. Attempting to argue that there were some slight indications of things to come, Servetus interpreted Psalm 68:5, which reads, "Sing unto God [i.e., Father] . . . whose name is the Lord [i.e., "Yah"]" in the following manner: "Exalt by His name *yah* he says and because He [Christ] is called *yah* the Father is called Jehova, that is, He will give being to Him that exists or will make Him to be Christ."[31] The notion that *yah* was an inhabitation within God was an idea we encountered in a different form in Reuchlin's delineation of the twelve alternates of YHVH and was a commonplace in rabbinic thought. Along the same lines of thought we find Servetus, as we saw in chapter three, referring to Christ as the "shechinah," an indwelling within God, a concept he also borrowed from rabbinic sources we had occasion to discuss earlier. Thus we find Servetus commenting upon Psalm 17:5 where David said to God, "I shall be satisfied when I awake with thy likeness," in the same subordinationist fashion, "And in that passage *temunah* ["picture"] denotes the form, figure, likeness, and image of Jesus Christ as he appears in the 16th Psalm which the Hebrews call the 17th."[32] Christ was a *temunah*, "representation," of the Father, and David referred to him not as a savior but as a function of the Father's being and power.

Continuing a historical-contextual analysis to serve his own theological purposes, Servetus attempted to discredit the notion that OT references to Elohim were invariably references to Christ. Servetus cited Psalm 45, in which Solomon was called "Elohim," and other locations where this term referred to mighty and powerful human beings.[33]

It must come as no surprise that Servetus' antitrinitarianism provided the impetus for his exegesis of the Psalms as well as the basis for his historical-contextual biblical criticism. The use of rabbinical exegetical writings was an integral element in this argument, for through use of these sources Servetus was able to argue against the Trinity, Christ's eternality, and His alleged role in human history before the Incarnation. Through a rejection of prophecy in the Psalms, Christ was reduced to a temporal aspect of the Father's self-expression and mode of the Father's being. Critics continually drew attention to Servetus' use of Jewish sources as if the act of condemning him as a severe judaizer might explain his heretical views.[34] Such a simplistic Jewish explanation for all of Servetus's heretical views is too limited, for it does not take into account his equally interesting use of Patristic and Hellenistic sources. Moreover, most of Servetus's sources were used by most orthodox Christian-Hebraists as well. Yet, Servetus must be distinguished from all other Christian-Hebraists of the Reformation age, for he used these Jewish sources not merely to elucidate Scripture or to gain greater insight into the text but for theological purposes as well. But then, these Jewish sources did constitute the most ancient testimony in an age of nostalgia.

NOTES

1. See my article "Michael Servetus: Exegete of Divine History," pp. 460–69.
2. Michael Servetus, *Biblia Sacra ex Sanctis Pagnini tralatione* . . . (Lyon, 1542). Because there are several different editions of this work, all citations will be based upon scriptural passage number rather than the page number of this specific edition. In the case of Psalm references, however, page number has also been in-

cluded since Servetus did not list Psalm number according to a traditional or consistent numbering pattern. This citation was taken from the introduction as were the next following quotations. (Hereafter cited as *Biblia.* . . .)

3. *Ibid.*, Isaiah 7:14.
4. *Ibid.*, Isaiah 19:20.
5. *Ibid.*, Isaiah 8:10.
6. *Ibid.*, Isaiah 51:4.
7. *Ibid.*, Isaiah 41:2.
8. *Ibid.*, Jeremiah 23:5.
9. *Ibid.*, Jeremiah 3:8.
10. *Ibid.*, Hosea 11:1.
11. L. I. Newman, *Jewish Influences on Christian Reform Movements* (New York, 1925; reprint 1966), p. 519, citing Erasmus's Psalm scholia added to his Greek NT.
12. Calvin, *Opera*, ed. Baum et al. (Braunschweig, 1863–1900) 8:496–97. (Hereafter cited as *C.O.*)
13. Servetus, *Rest.*, p. 318.
14. Servetus, *Error.*, f.114a.
15. Servetus, *Biblia* . . . , Psalm 1, f.116b, Col. A.
16. *Ibid.*
17. *Ibid.*, Col. B.
18. *Ibid.*
19. *Ibid.*, f.122b, Col. A. Servetus lists this as Psalm 68.
20. *Ibid.*, f.126b, Col. B. Servetus lists this as Psalm 109.
21. *Ibid.*, f.116b, Col. A.
22. *Ibid.*, f.118a, Col. B. Servetus lists this as Psalm 21.
23. Servetus, *Error.*, f.56a.
24. *Ibid.*, f.56b.
25. *Ibid.*, f.55b.
26. D. Kimchi, *Kitvei Radak* (Tel Aviv, 1949), p. 91.
27. Servetus, *Rest.*, p. 59.
28. *Ibid.*, p. 60. Geryones was a mythical Spanish king with three bodies but one head.
29. Servetus, *Error.*, f.20b.
30. Servetus, *Rest.*, p. 65.
31. Servetus, *Error.*, f.115b.
32. *Ibid.*, f.87a.
33. *Ibid.*, f.14b.
34. Oecolampadius observed, "Proinde satis video quantum tu a nobis recedes et magis judaisas quam gloriam Christi praedicas," in *C.O.*, 8:860. Similarly, the ministers of the Genevan Company of Pastors were very upset by Servetus's use of Jewish sources. See Robert M. Kingdon, Jean-François Bergier, eds., *Registres de la Compagnie des Pasteurs de Genève au temps de Calvin* (Geneva, 1962). And also *C.O.*, 8:505, 515.

Chapter Eight

Acceptable Cultural-Ethnographic Interpretation

Fagius's exegetical treatise *Perush ha-milot al derech ha-p'shat* . . . , or *The Interpretation of the Words According to the Literal Translation*, was unique in that it dealt with only the first four chapters of Genesis.[1] The first 155 pages consisted of 208 word or phrase entries each of which presented the original Hebrew under discussion, a Latin translation, and an in-depth commentary concerning grammatical or conceptual points of interest. Despite its limitation to only four chapters of Scripture, Fagius's treatise focused on a rich unit of the Bible dealing with such important concepts as the nature of Creation, the formation of man, the tree-of-wisdom episode in the Garden of Eden, and Cain's slaying of Abel. The remaining 20 pages of the work presented Genesis 1–4 in Aramaic along with its Latin translation.

The extensive commentary indicates that Fagius's purpose was not simply to present a better translation of the text. Rather, he hoped to elucidate upon the nature of Hebrew expression in these cornerstone chapters of God's Word, present a distillation of Jewish opinion regarding the pivotal events in Eden, and build a fundamentally Jewish argument for the Christian interpretation of Scripture. In carrying out this serious task, Fagius made extensive use of standard Jewish authors familiar to Christian-Hebraists. David Kimchi was cited 42 times; Rashi, 43 times; and Ibn Ezra, 65 times. Both the Targum of Jonathan and the Targum of Onkelos were referred to over 40 times, but Fagius's most critically used Jewish source was Rabbi Moses ben Nachman, or Nachmanides, cited 43 times, often in central locations. Other Jewish sources cited less frequently were Saadia, Rabbi Tanchuma, and Rabbi Joshua, among others. Altogether, Fagius consulted Jewish authorities over 258 times, making this a most important example of Protestant use of Jewish exegetical sources.

Like other works of this type, its purpose was to present the Christian scholar with as much divergent Jewish opinion as possible. The earlier entries dealing with Creation concentrated primarily upon philological and grammatical points whereas later items, especially those treating Adam and Eve, were more heavily conceptual and intellectual to demonstrate the compatibility between Protestant and Jewish exegesis.

From his first entry it was obvious that Fagius was not committed to Neo-Platonism or other ancient philosophies as were a great many other Christian-Hebraists. Fagius explained that there were many Hebrew expressions for creation, but Scripture used the term *barah* since it alone implied *creatio ex nihilo*. Other terms such as *asah*, "made," or *yahtzar*, "formed," were also discussed.[2] When explaining the plural name of God, "Elohim," used in the first verse of Scripture, Fagius explained that it was the plural of *Elah*, "deity," rather than the more traditional *El*, "God." Fagius noted Nachmanides' view that the plural referred to the so-called royal we and Ibn Ezra's view that the plural included God and His angels, but he did not mention any Cabbalistic notions involving emanationism or numerology and concluded that this divine name was best interpreted in trinitarian terms. More acceptable to Fagius was the Jewish distinction between "Elohim" as *mi'dat ha-din*, "attribute of authority," characterizing God's relationship with the universe, and "YHVH," the *mi'dat ha-rachamim*, "attribute of mercy or grace," describing His relationship with humanity. Creation was a function of the more formal "Elohim," which explained its use in the first verse of Scripture. Fagius returned to this distinction in divine nomenclature several times in order to highlight the significance of different divine names in different contexts.

Thus far Fagius had demonstrated little he could not have found or deduced from Jerome's Vulgate or any other translation of Scripture accepting the distinction of Lord-God. The preoccupation with divine names characterized virtually all Christian-Hebraists, as we have noted with such different thinkers as Servetus and Reuchlin. When dealing with the actual definition of creation, however, Fagius demonstrated greater specific use of the views of his Jewish sources. He explained, for instance, that the seemingly simple expression "heaven and earth" could be misleading.[3] Citing a variety of sources, Fagius argued that these terms refer to conditions of creation rather than geographic locations. The word *shamayim*, "heaven," was a contraction of the two-word phrase *sham-mayim*, literally "water-there," which is to say a region of moisture and mist. In turn, the word for "earth," *ahretz*, we are told, derived from the root verb *rootz*, "to run," indicating a tractable area upon which one might run or walk. This opinion was heightened when Fagius explained the word for insects used later in the text. The word the Bible used was *sheretz*, or "that which runs quickly." Consequently, God first created a condition of moisture or water and a condition of land or a tractable area. Other terms such as *tehvel* and *adamah* were also discussed since they, too, could mean "earth" but were not used there.

To highlight his discussion of scriptural creation of conditions of existence, Fagius devoted considerable space to the phrase "the earth was empty and void." The text used *tohu va-vohu*, and Fagius noted that far from meaning "void," *vohu* was a derivative of *bo-hu*, literally "in-it," implying fullness and content rather than its absence, though Scripture did not elucidate upon the content of the fullness.[4] Similarly, the term *tohu* does not mean or imply "emptiness" or "a lack of substance" but "a fullness or depth of matter," and Fagius compared it with the word *t'hom*, "the depths," used in a later verse, "the spirit of God was on the face of the depths." As a result, God's first activity involved the creation of the conditions of moisture, solidity, and an undifferentiated, unformed mass.

The fourth element of creation was the divine spirit that enlivens and exists in the form of a great wind. The text spoke of "the spirit of God which hovered upon the face of the depths," and Fagius explained that the term "spirit" was misleading here because of its more usual religious connotation.[5] He far preferred Nachmanides' explanation that the *ruach*, "spirit," was also the word for "wind" and although *ruach Elohim* might be understood in this context as meaning "the spirit of God," it actually meant "a great or powerful wind." Fagius's position was predicated upon Nachmanides' assertion that the name "Elohim" acted as an adjectival amplifier when used in conjunction with a noun. This construction is quite common in the OT as when Jonah was sent to preach to the "mighty city"—and certainly not the divine city—of Nineveh (Jonah 3:3). To emphasize that Scripture spoke in nonspiritual and natural terms, Fagius argued that the word "hovered," *merachephet* in Hebrew, implied a state of extreme excitement and frantic movement more in keeping with a mighty wind than with the Spirit of God. Indeed, the accepted translation of "hovered" was the opposite of the wording and meaning of Scripture. This discussion of the first two verses of Scripture, here simplified, consumed twelve pages of commentary.

It would appear that Fagius attempted to avoid overt philosophical discussion of platonic or Cabbalistic concepts of creation. Indeed, even the legitimate Christian concept of the word from verse 3, "And God *said*, Let there be light," evoked no response from Fagius. For Cabbalists and other mystics like Reuchlin, creation through the spoken word was intriguing and fundamental to their approach to Scripture. Even nonmystical sources like Rashi and Ibn Ezra found this language significant as did the author of the fourth Gospel who wrote that "In the beginning there was the word." Fagius did not discuss this phrase at all, nor did he allude to any of the traditions of interpretation surrounding the concept, though the words "and God said" were important to Fagius in other contexts, as we shall see.

Another example of Fagius's determination to avoid the philosophical (and nonliteral) was his discussion of the phrase of verse 5, "there was evening and morning, one day."[6] The words were not complicated, but in fact neither the sun, the moon, nor the stars had been created and yet Genesis spoke of a morning, an evening, and a day. Surely this curious phrase might have been a philosopher's sandbox, but Fagius avoided all complexity in arguing that the etymology of these terms also indicated conditions of existence rather than temporal zones. The word *erev* meant "evening," but it derived from the verb "to mix," whereas the term *bo'ker* meant "morning" but derived from the verb "to explore or discover," and these words described the creation of darkness and light. Consequently, in addition to the previous conditions of existence created by God out of nothingness, He also created a condition of discernment (light, morning) and a condition of mixture or confusion (darkness, evening). The term "one day" referred not to the temporal day consisting of twenty-four hours or one rotation about the sun but marked the completion of all fundamental conditions of existence. And once again, following Nachmanides, Fagius argued that the first of several orders of creation had been completed.

None could fault Fagius in faithfully following his Jewish guides through the etymological thicket of Genesis 1. If his commentary shed little light on any religious themes of significance, Fagius's work reflected a deep appreciation of the Hebrew language and constituted a fine demonstration of how limiting the use of a translation might be if one knew no Hebrew. Surely there was nothing controversial in the use of Jewish sources for etymological elucidation, for essentially, Fagius was doing what his title indicated: describing the meaning of the words according to the literal interpretation.

Fagius departed from his literal interpretation when dealing with those verses of Genesis 1–4 which had more direct theological or Christian conceptual meaning. When treating the creation of man, Fagius attempted to use his Jewish sources as guides for the spiritual interpretation of the concept as well as the words involved. When Scripture read, "And God said: Let us make man in our image, after our likeness . . . ," Fagius was willing to accept the view that this similitude was reflected in man's dominion over all creation much as God held dominion over all existence.[7] Not insignificant was Fagius's rejection of any of the more usual Jewish views that described this similitude in terms of human potential and intelligence. He also explained that there might be merit to the notion that "let us," the plural *na'aseh* in Hebrew, might be understood as a royal we, but he strongly emphasized the obvious trinitarian allusion. As when explaining the plural *Elohim* in trinitarian terms in a previous verse, Fagius noted his disagreement with Jewish authorities and simply went on to other issues where his sources might prove more helpful. Indeed, because Genesis presented two different accounts of the creation of man, Fagius succeeded in turning disagreement with his sources into compatibility. Verse 7 of chapter 2 read, "Then the Lord formed [*yahtzar*] man of the dust of the ground and breathed into his nostrils the breath of life, and man became a living soul."[8] Devoting six pages to this sentence, Fagius made significant Christian use of Jewish concepts to reach a Christian goal for the first time. Of the two different statements describing man's creation, the former, "Let us create," might possess greater Christian trinitarian significance since God used the plural form when He said, "Let us [*na'aseh*] make." In the second account, the plural *Elohim* was used to refer to God but the verb indicating "formation" was in the singular person and thus constituted a weaker trinitarian argument. Rather than build upon the former, more trinitarian foundation, Fagius pointed out the significance of the plural "Let us" and moved on to the second account where a specific Rashi commentary provided the basis for a fruitful Christian argument. Rashi noted that *yahtzar*, "formed," usually spelled with one *yod* at the beginning of the word, was spelled with a double *yod* in this instance. According to Fagius, Rashi argued that this double construction indicated that the verb might be interpreted in the present tense as well as in the future tense. Though Rashi did not make this point at all, Fagius felt free to develop his own spiritul interpretation for this curious construction. He argued that there were two creations, as Rashi supposedly taught, and then used the Jewish distinction between *olam ha-zeh*, "the temporal world," and *olam ha-bah*, "the future spiritual world," to account for these parallel acts of creation. Going far past Rashi, Fagius then elaborated, "For our transformation, which we expect from salvation, is in heaven when Jesus Christ transforms our humble body to conform to His glorious body. And on that day, man will not be resurrected as a brute animal, as Rabbi Solomon also says. The verb *yahtzar* is written with one *yod* not two, where it concerns the creation of animals."[9] This Christian interpretation of *yahtzar* was acceptable from a Christian systematic standpoint but was problematic from an exegetical point of view. Fagius left unsaid that Rashi was not committed to a literal interpretation of Scripture and that his *d'rash*, "spiritual method," was no less objectionable from the literal viewpoint than the most removed and mystical of Christian interpretations. Also left unsaid was what in fact Rashi did claim was created twice, but we shall return to this point.

Fagius, like Servetus and many other Christian-Hebraists, felt comfortable giving a spiritual interpretation of the text only when the Jewish source indicated the same tendency. Of course, the spiritual interpretation given tended to be Christian rather than Jewish. The problem was that Christian scholars often could not or did not adequately distinguish between the different schools of Jewish interpretation though they would never permit themselves the same freedom with various Christian schools of exegesis. As a result, after making innovative use of Rashi's point of the double *yod*, Fagius turned to a different exegete, Nachmanides, to continue his argument as if the two exegetes were in agreement with each other and with his own development of this verse. Noting his own pleasure with his double-creation theory, Fagius wrote that Nachmanides also noted that Creation was now complete and perfect and the text used the full name of God, "YHVH Elohim," as an indication. And noting that two names of God (Nachmanides' perfection) were used with a twofold creation (Rashi's double *yod*), to which Fagius had added the explanation of olam ha-zeh and olam ha-bah to account for the concept of the Resurrection, he then concluded, "Surely this was done because use of the full name [indicates] the excellence and dignity of man. For surely this is the work of the merciful God [i.e., *midat ha-rachamim*]."[10] In this way Fagius was able to tie together almost every concept used when describing creation of the conditions of existence to the creation of man, which in turn was given a Christian orientation.

When discussing the phrase "He breathed into his nostrils," Fagius noted Ibn Ezra's view that this was the spirit of vitality given to all life forms, but he preferred Nachmanides' position that this was a special spirit given only to man since it consisted of "a divine air which proceeds from the mouth of God . . . that is, it comes from His substance."[11] Once again Fagius had accepted Nachmanides' nonliteral view over Ibn Ezra's simple literal explanation because of its compatibility with his own Christian ideas, and Fagius concluded, "Undoubtedly, this is what our savior said to the apostles in communicating His holy Spirit, inflating them with it, 'Accept this spirit of me.' "[12] Thus the creation of man consisted of parallel acts of creation as well as parallel spirits given to man. Also, creation of this world was carried out by Elohim (attribute of authority) whereas creation of man was a product of YHVH (attribute of mercy). In turn, man's vitality was a product of the Spirit, and hence, a trinity.

The Christian-cum-Jewish argument continued in Fagius's discussion of that which was blown into man's nostrils. Scripture speaks of *nishmat chayim*, a rather complicated term that has provided much material for philosophers to ponder.[13] *Chayim* means "life," but *nishmat* is more complicated and can conceivably possess two different meanings. On the one hand there is the Hebrew word for breath, *neshēēma*, and Scripture might be interpreted as speaking of a simple breath of life. But the Hebrew word for soul is *neshama*, and if this is the origin of *nishmat* in Scripture, then the Bible is speaking in far more spiritual terms of some spirit of the soul. Literalists such as Kimchi considered this a simple breath of air much as they claimed that the ruach Elohim of Genesis 1 referred to a strong wind rather than to the Spirit of God, a position accepted, as we have seen, by Fagius. In this instance, however, Fagius the former literalist continued to find spiritual figurative meaning in the text. Without citing his source, he argued, "And many Hebrews believe that *neshama* ["soul"] and *shamayim* ["heaven"] are related."[14] Though the etymological connection of the two terms is dubious at best, especially for Fagius who earlier had argued that *shamayim* was a contraction of *sham-mayim*, "water-there," as a condition of existence, Fagius accepted this interpretation here since it fit into his double-creation and resurrection themes.[15]

Thus far Fagius's attempt to use Jewish sources to build a Christian argument was successful for several reasons. The two traditions were similar enough to permit cross-influence, and the text lent itself to a measure of nonliteral interpretation. Moreover, Fagius could pick and choose those sources whose ideas on any given phrase, or even word, best suited his purposes. Exegetes often blend a variety of ideas from various sources, but from a Jewish point of view there was an erratic quality in using Kimchi's *p'shat*, "literal," along with Rashi's more figurative *d'rash* method, which was combined with Nachmanides' far more spiritual approach to textual analysis. Fagius could bend and borrow with such ease because the Christian thematic unity that Fagius provided came from outside the conceptual framework from which these sources wrote. To an extent, Fagius used rab-

binic opinion within a preconceived pattern in which each source was selected to fill a given slot, here grammar and there concept, toward a greater
end to which the sources themselves did not lead. Consequently, it is not
surprising that in many locations tension and inconsistency existed between his various sources themselves or between his sources and the overall
pattern into which they were fit.

When discussing the significance of the tree of life, Fagius accepted
Nachmanides' simple interpretation that the fruit of that tree granted man
extended life.[16] When discussing the tree of wisdom, Fagius again followed
Nachmanides' view that stressed that willfulness rather than wisdom or
knowledge resulted from the eating of that tree's fruit.[17] Indeed, Fagius
rejected the literalist view advanced by the Targum that wisdom was imparted by that tree. For Nachmanides it was important to stress the issue of
willfulness because this was the major distinguishing feature separating
man from the animal world and upon which that rabbi would build a very
strident view of man's ability to perform acts of goodness and righteousness. Fagius followed a different route, however, and after stressing his acceptance of Nachmanides' willfulness, he discussed several related terms
such as *da'at*, "wisdom," *bechirah*, "choice," *chayfetz*, "desire," and *rat-
zon*, "will." Rather than stress the righteousness potential implicit in this
discussion adapted from Nachmanides, Fagius concluded, "From the eating of the fruit, a depraved nature came about," which would have troubled
Nachmanides but fit into Protestant systematic quite nicely. Fagius was
unwilling to concede that man might add to his own knowledge, understanding, and wisdom through any act of human activity and flatly stated,
"A knowledge of good and evil is not possible without divine revelation."
If one considers the direct nature of Adam's communication with God, his
ability to speak with God, and even his desire to hide from God, it is difficult to understand why Fagius would stress the post-expulsion-from-Eden
concept of revelation. It would appear that Fagius simply read post-Eden
conditions back into man's pre-sin existence when he wrote, "God is the
only good and He alone can alter that which is bad." According to Fagius's
logic, it followed that if man had no free will after the Fall and no access to
divine wisdom after being thrown out of Eden, the same must have been
true before the Fall. The fact of the matter is, of course, that no less reliable a
source than Scripture itself speaks of a tree of wisdom granting a knowledge of good and evil and tells that God seems to have given the tree its
name and could have called it something else had he wanted to and that
man is nowhere considered bad but is clearly called good. If Fagius's view

of willfulness was exactly the opposite of Nachmanides', he liked this view because it was the only position that permitted him to build a Christian argument. "If Adam had persisted in his original justification, with the exception of his sin everything man did was no different from other animals of heaven and earth for all his impulses were natural." Consequently, man sinned and became willful but demonstrated this depraved quality even before eating the fruit. Had man not been depraved even before sinning, "all his impulses were natural" would place responsibility for sin squarely upon God or would lead to diminishing the importance of that act as Jewish authorities claimed. Surely if it is axiomatic that only God is good but that man is evil and in possession of no wisdom, total human responsibility for sin might be difficult to defend.

The problem of responsibility is evident in Fagius's treatment of the snake's role as well. Was the snake Satan in the form of a reptile, or was this a simple animal? Explaining that Satan took on reptilian form might diminish human culpability, for surely no one—especially an innocent like Adam—could spar with the devil. Moreover, Fagius would then be forced to explain how Satan existed in Eden. On the other hand, if Fagius argued that the reptile was an ordinary garden snake, he might have to explain how this ordinary creature could reason and persuade Adam and Eve to sin, since in the long run culpability would fall on their shoulders. Given this choice, Fagius chose the anticipated position: "Truly, we teach according to the simple meaning of the words and we must first of all say that Scripture speaks about the natural animal whose venom kills."[18] A sentence later, however, Fagius conceded, in less literal fashion, that Satan can speak through "the guise of animals as the angels can speak in the form of asses," no doubt referring to Bilam's talking donkey.

Fagius's use of Nachmanides' willfulness rather than wisdom was somewhat contradicted by his treatment of a related verse where Scripture stated, "And Lord God took the man and placed him in the Garden of Eden." Following Rashi's interpretation, Fagius asserted that not physical removal from one place to another was involved here but an "intellectual attraction and persuasion of man."[19] Rashi could argue that man was intellectually persuaded in conjunction with the intellectual awareness and wisdom he would acquire in eating of the tree of wisdom. Fagius's position, however, was that man had to be persuaded because he was innocent and ignorant and, like mankind in general, depended upon God to do good things for him since he could do nothing good on his own. Yet Fagius did not believe that the same innocent and ignorant Adam might be persuaded by the snake in similar fashion. Fagius used Rashi when he chose and Nachmanides when his views were better suited to the overall pattern imposed upon the text. Overall, Fagius's orientation is very clear: Reject any independent positive action on Adam's part as inconsistent with God's being the sole source of goodness but accept human culpability for all actions that might damn man and use those Jewish sources which would support these views.

Fagius found himself in a difficult position since he accepted various "Pelagian" Jewish views to fit into a non-Pelagian Christian pattern. His solution was to reject, temporarily, the literal interpretation and present a blatant and uncalled-for spiritualization of the text. Once again Fagius extricated himself from his difficulties by appealing to the Resurrection: "So too, God, through His eternal word who is Christ . . . transfers us from this world to the eternal beauty of paradise because we have faith in Him."[20] Fagius's argument was an evasion of the reality of the text in question especially since he had earlier rejected any discussion of the so-called word as Christ.

The general run of Fagius's argument is intellectually inconsistent if religiously acceptable. He stressed man's intellectual attraction to Eden, but not man's equal ability to be persuaded by sin. Man could not gain an understanding of good and evil or acquire any measure of wisdom but might be indicted for willfulness. The snake was not Satan but a normal creature that could speak and reason, and if the entire structure seems clouded and inconsistent, Fagius avoided it all by arguing that much of the story was essentially an allegory of our own removal from Paradise. The views in question are not the problem, nor is it difficult to appreciate Fagius's defense of the central concepts he elicited from the text. It is, however, quite doubtful that rabbinic sources or a Hebrew text was really necessary at any point in his argument. Moreover, he made the most salient argument through a spiritual allegorical interpretation of the text and not through the literal method advocated in his title and advanced throughout his commentary.

In some places the tension between Fagius the Christian-Hebraist and Fagius the Christian exegete is very apparent. When warning man against eating the fruit of the forbidden trees, God tells man that the punishment will be "surely thou shalt die." The Hebrew text uses a peculiar expression for death, for rather than simply state "you will die," the word "death" is compounded in the double construction *mōt ta-mūt*, with death repeated twice. Fagius had an interesting explanation: "If I am permitted to philosophize a little, the double verb indicates the death of both the body and the soul."[21] This position was certainly consistent with Christian systematics and indicated why Jesus was necessary to atone for a mankind unable to atone for itself. It was also an argument that ran against the grain of Hebrew linguistics as well as a literal interpretation of the text, and Fagius himself conceded, "The duplication of verbs signifies vehemence and certainty . . . that is, certainly you will die."[22] Fagius also noted that Jewish authorities would not accept his Christian interpretation, for "according to the *derech ha-p'shat* ["literal interpretation"] or simple sense, this property of the holy tongue signifies only vehemence and certainty."[23] Moreover, Fagius indicated other scriptural passages where the same double construction was used and could not possibly mean death of the body and the soul as in I Kings 2:42 where Solomon offers this punishment for disobedience to himself. Attempting to justify a position predicated upon "philosophizing a little" and running counter to Hebrew linguistics, Fagius simply shifted responsibility: "But further, not all Hebrews deny the double experience of Adam's death, who teach not dissimilar things and who wonder about man's sin, whether the soul and the body were both punished."[24] Unfortunately, Fagius did not indicate who these authors were and what their not-too-dissimilar positions were. Moreover, Fagius did not indicate whether these Jewish sources saw the soul simply laboring under a heavy load easily lightened by rabbinic good works or whether the soul was totally impoverished by depravity. What followed was a long Hebrew citation indicating that it was the nature of sin to affect both the body and the soul of man. Rather than an exegetical reference, this paragraph was a philosophical statement directed against the separation of the body from the soul, common to Greek and Christian thought but rejected by Judaism. But even if this citation was a direct exegetical comment from some leading rabbinic authority, it was no more acceptable for Fagius's literal interpretation of the text than other Jewish allegorical or mystical glosses. Perhaps because he was treading on thin ice, Fagius did not cite his source or its author or address the question of why this Jewish departure from literal exposition was acceptable to him in this instance.

Fagius's attempt to bolster Christian anthropology with Jewish thought does not ring true. But even if one considers the content of Fagius's other works treated earlier, it is not clear whether he understood the implications in anthropology and soteriology separating Jewish and Christian religious thought. For each place in which Fagius chided his sources for advancing too optimistic an appraisal of human potential, there are other instances in which he sought to find Jewish support for the more radical Christian anthropology.

Fagius's misinterpretation or erroneous reading of Jewish anthropological intention is very common throughout this volume. When in chapter 3, verse 7, Scripture described the most immediate effect of eating of the fruit of tree of wisdom, it used the expression "and their eyes were opened." Rather than imply a simple opening of the eyes, Scripture used the Hebrew expression *tipakachna* and not the simple verb for opening, *tipatachna*. In explaining this more rarified term, Fagius turned to Rashi: "Agreeably, Rabbi Solomon says the verb *tipakachna* refers more to the soul and the mind than to the keenness of physical vision."[25] Indeed this was true, for Rashi claimed Adam and Eve had acquired a measure of wisdom hitherto not possessed by them, and we have already discussed Rashi's views concerning the tree of wisdom. Fagius drew a different conclusion from Rashi's words: "They emphatically experienced a spiritual and physical death . . . a clear destruction of the spirit." And continuing a line of Christian reasoning, Fagius added, "They saw and understood, according to what God showed them, how many generations were lost because of them." This conclusion, allegedly built upon Rashi's view of the act of sin, actually misrepresented that rabbi's ideas. Moreover, this conclusion was then added to the notion of a spiritual and physical death which Fagius also attempted to graft onto a Jewish interpretation. But even if Fagius's argument had been completely built upon Jewish sources, it would not have been a foundation predicated upon a literal interpretation of the text. Fagius also glossed over important differences separating Jewish and Christian anthropology when he commented upon verse 9 of chapter 3, where God called to man but man hid from God. Scripture used the expression *va-yikra*, "He called." Fagius noted, "Hebrews observe that what is written is not without significance, 'And He called' rather than 'And He said' for significantly, through their sin the first humans were alienated from God."[26] Indeed, Jewish exegetes had taken notice of this more formal relationship between man and God indicated by this term, yet they also pointed out that the very next words indicated that God's anger was short lived, for the complete verse read, "And Lord God called to man and He said. . . . " Moreover, Jewish scholars noted that God referred to himself in this instance with his full name, including YHVH, the attribute of mercy. Fagius's treatment of this verse, allegedly with Jewish agreement, stressed the alienation of the verse but neglected to mention the second part of the verse where the tone was considerably changed, for God did not damn man outright but asked, "Where art thou?"

The desire to read a strong measure of alienation of man from God was consistent with Fagius's overall Christian orientation to the text and to the meaning of Eden. His desire to support this orientation through a use of Jewish sources continued when he analyzed verse 24 of chapter 3 where Scripture told that God placed the cherubs at the gate of Eden "to guard the way to the tree of life." Fagius's commentary read, "It is significant that no one can reach eternal life without his attempting through Christ . . . the Hebrews correctly say that none will enter Eden except the just, as it is written, 'This is the gate of the Lord, the righteous will go through it' [Psalm 118]. But they are blind in this for they do not understand that this speaks of justification through faith in Christ."[27] Although Jesus' importance could not be disputed, his presence within the text itself would have been difficult to support through a literal interpretation of Scripture.

Fagius cannot be faulted for carefully picking and choosing those rabbinic opinions on important passages of Scripture which were amenable to Christian ends. Fagius was, after all, a Christian theologian writing about Christian themes for a Christian audience. Yet one cannot help but feel dismayed when Fagius attempted to demonstrate the Jewish basis for this Christian position and presented a picture of Jewish and Christian exegesis running along close parallel lines. Although he never blatantly misquoted his sources, Fagius was guilty of not presenting that side of Jewish thought which ran counter to his overall thesis of the compatibility of Jewish and Christian thought and the consistent transition between the two.

The misreading of Jewish concept, so common a characteristic of Christian-Hebraica, was very clearly reflected in Fagius's discussion of the Jewish concept of the *yetzer ha-rah*, the "evil inclination within man." Fagius understood this concept as essentially the same as the Christian notion of a depraved human nature resulting from Original Sin. Indeed, Fagius even wrote, "And [Rabbi Menahem] Recanati wrote that Adam's sin was passed on to all mankind,"[28] further identifying Christian Original Sin with Jewish anthropology. This is an extremely important point, for if humanity was in fact depraved or possessed such limited capability for righteousness that man was unable to please God through his own efforts, the entire edifice of rabbinic Judaism would crash to the ground. Moreover, the need for Jesus' atonement for mankind would be apparent, much as the Protestant position condemning all good works in favor of faith would be justified. In short, if Fagius's contention is correct and if the two concepts were interchangeable or even similar, he would have proved the truth of Christianity from a Jewish foundation. In point of fact, there were some very important differences between the two concepts, and Fagius should have been aware of them since the sources he used for this exegetical work discussed them at length. If we recall, Fagius was terribly impressed with Rashi's discussion of the spelling of *yahtzar* formed with two *yods* rather than one. Fagius indicated that this meant there were two creations, one in the temporal world and one in Paradise which man will inherit in the Resurrection. Fagius did not tell the reader that Rashi had a somewhat different notion of the double creation, one that was decidedly not compatible with Christianity. Rashi wrote that the double *yod* indicated the creation within man of two distinct capacities or inclinations. These were the *yetzer ha-tov*, the "good inclination" that led man toward righteousness and goodness, and the *yetzer ha-rah*, the "evil inclination" that through temptation led man toward purely selfish and evil goals. Because man was created with both capacities, he was neither evil nor good but possessed the free will to act on his inner impulses, proper education, and a pattern of good works which constitutes rabbinic Judaism. Unlike the depraved human nature that resulted from Original Sin, the Jewish "evil inclination" was a concomitant part of human creation along with the opposite tendency toward righteousness and goodness. There can be no question about Fagius's familiarity with this concept if only because Rashi's gloss on *yahtzar* discussed both inclinations at length. Similarly, *The Ethics of the Fathers*, which Fagius edited, translated, and annotated from a Christian perspective, also discussed these concepts at great length and in detail. Considering his misreading of this basic concept of man, one must wonder to what extent Fagius misrepresented Nachmanides' willfulness or other central points in his Jewish-Christian argument.

Quite possibly, Fagius's concept of the continuity of the two covenants led him to draw conclusions equating the continuity of the Jewish and Christian traditions as well. Essentially, Fagius's approach was the exact flip side of Luther's notion of the dichotomy of Law and Gospel. Fagius's argument in attempting to draw a Jewish base for Christian understanding of Genesis 1–4 was substantially the same as the one he advanced in his other works, dealt with earlier in this volume. We have had ample opportunity to observe the extent to which Fagius attempted to build his understanding of Christianity upon a Jewish foundation. Jewish ritual, we were told, would tell us much about the proper celebration of the Lord's Supper, much as Jewish apocryphal writings would present the positive side of Pharisaic ethics. *The Ethics of the Fathers* would elucidate the basic similarity between Jewish and Christian ethical, moral, and social concepts. We noted earlier that most of Fagius's edition of the *Ethics* dealt with hard religious concept and not ethical or moral concerns. In a similar vein Fagius's exegetical writings presented the compatibility of the two religious traditions and the similarity between their exegetical orientations.

If the significant degree of compatibility Fagius discovered between Jewish and Christian thought was more the result of his own reading of these sources and was perhaps unwarranted by the basic ideas of the writings themselves, few of his readers were in a position to realize this fact. His arguments seemed convincing and all the citations from Jewish sources Fagius brought as support did indeed appear to bolster the Christian view Fagius wished to demonstrate. Indeed, open-minded readers might have wondered why the Jewish religion had been so maligned since it was obviously so similar to Protestant Christianity. One implication of Fagius's work may well have been that a reevaluation of Judaism was in order, and no less a scholar than Martin Luther wrote as much in 1523 when composing his short missionary piece *Jesus Christ was Born a Jew*.

Though Fagius and Servetus disagreed about Christian belief, their understanding of Jewish sources was very similar. Both essentially used their sources quite selectively to bolster specific views in specific intellectual contexts. Both argued that their specific religious orientation might be supported and demonstrated as an authentic expression of OT Jewish religious thought. Whereas the OT text itself did not adequately reflect their orientation, some Jewish source could be found to present the text in such a fashion that the desired result would be attained. Neither scholar believed he was misrepresenting Jewish opinion, but then neither explained why Jews found their positions no more acceptable than other Christian expressions.

Both scholars shared one additional characteristic: the desire to prove Christian truth on the basis of Jewish rabbinic thought. Indeed, had this not been the case, there would have been no justification for citing rabbinic arguments or going past the original Hebrew text at all. The two scholars differed regarding *why* they sought to demonstrate their NT religion on the basis of a different OT religion. For Servetus, as we have seen, so much Christian history and tradition was tainted that only a most radical return to basic sources could be used to rebuild a true Christianity. Although Fagius accepted the tradition Servetus rejected, he believed the NT tradition should be more securely anchored to the original OT tradition. Nothing could express the continuity from the old covenant into the new more completely than a demonstration of scriptural affinity, but as Bornkamm and many, many others have demonstrated, such continuity is difficult to prove. Fagius accepted the next best thing: a continuity of exegetical and conceptual understanding of the text. If Servetus searched Jewish theology for some formulation he could accept in a Christian setting, Fagius sought a Jewish anthropology that would demonstrate the authenticity of Protestant systematics.

Both scholars shared one additional characteristic: Both were considered severe judaizers. One can imagine how the Dominicans in Cologne felt about their works and presuppositions, but even other Christian-Hebraists were increasingly skeptical and fearful about the strange product of these Hebraists. Nowhere was the opposition to this more creative Christian-Hebraica more fully expressed than in Wittenberg where there was outright condemnation of such open-ended Christian use of Jewish sources and great disagreement about the nature of the continuity between the covenants. And nowhere was the defense of Jewish studies more fully and completely expressed than in Basel, a center of covenantal thought where the OT and the NT were conceived as a continuum that denied and rejected the dialectical approach taken by Luther in his concept of the dichotomy of Law and Gospel. In short, much as Switzerland and Germany differed in their basic orientations to Scripture, so too they differed in their conception of the proper use of Jewish sources.

NOTES

1. Paul Fagius, *Exegesis sive expositiones Dictionum Hebraicarum literalis et simplex in quatuor capita Geneseos pro studiosis linguae Hebraicae* (Isny, 1542). Latin title follows full Hebrew title.
2. *Ibid.*, pp. 1–3.
3. *Ibid.*, pp. 5–8.
4. *Ibid.*, pp. 8–10.
5. *Ibid.*, pp. 10–12.
6. *Ibid.*, pp. 13–14.
7. *Ibid.*, pp. 26–29.
8. *Ibid.*, pp. 41–42.
9. *Ibid.*, p. 42.
10. *Ibid.*, pp. 41–42.

11. *Ibid.*, pp. 43–45.
12. *Ibid.*, p. 44.
13. *Ibid.*, pp. 44–47.
14. *Ibid.*, p. 44.
15. *Ibid.*, p. 42.
16. *Ibid.*, p. 50.
17. *Ibid.*, pp. 50–51, and the next four citations are also taken from these pages.
18. *Ibid.*, p. 71, listed incorrectly as 17.
19. *Ibid.*, p. 53.
20. *Ibid.*
21. *Ibid.*, p. 57.
22. *Ibid.*, p. 55.
23. *Ibid.*, p. 57.
24. *Ibid.*, pp. 57–58.
25. *Ibid.*, p. 79, plus the next two citations.
26. *Ibid.*, p. 83.
27. *Ibid.*, pp. 114–15.
28. *Ibid.*, pp. 102, 103.

Chapter Nine

The Basel-Wittenberg Conflict

The decade of the 1540s witnessed the production of a great number of OT translations from the original Hebrew and many exegetical works involving use of Jewish sources. In the previous decade there was great emphasis placed upon the production of good texts, but during the following years increased competence and additional time produced more ambitious results. Servetus, Fagius, Münster all did their best work during the 1540s and laid the foundation for subsequent Christian-Hebraica for the remainder of the century. The 1540s also witnessed another development: a climate of tension within the ranks of Christian-Hebraists. Perhaps in recognition of Servetus's revolutionary hermenuetics and Fagius's strident rabbinism, increasing opposition and resistance to such use of Jewish sources resulted in growing tension between Lutheran and Reformed Hebraists. Unlike the previous conflict surrounding Reuchlin, both parties to this conflict were Christian-Hebraists. Consequently, the conflict was not whether a Hebrew OT was to be used or the importance of Hebrew for exegetical purposes but what place and role *medieval* Jewish sources would occupy within the process of scriptural study.

Sebastian Münster took upon himself the task of defending Hebraists from the charge of judaization and improper use of Jewish sources. In 1546 he produced a second and enlarged edition of his fine 1534 translation of the twenty-four books of the OT.[1] In this edition as in the earlier, both Latin and Hebrew texts appeared in facing columns and each chapter was followed by Münster's annotations. The later edition retained the same translation, but the quantity and quality of material presented in his gloss were substantially better. In the 1546 edition everything from grammar to subtle theological issues was raised, and the number of Jewish sources cited was far greater than in the earlier edition. Most important for our purposes, however, Münster included a new introduction entitled "Hebrew Commentaries Are Not to Be Condemned" in which he provided the first systematic defense of Christian-Hebraist reliance upon Jewish exegesis. In retrospect one cannot be very surprised by Münster's defense. He was the most respected Hebraist of the day and certainly the best known. His was the first new translation of the OT from Jewish sources, and he was the Christian scholar who most openly admitted his reliance upon Jewish teachers when he wrote about his relationship with Elias Levita. With Münster's guidance, Froben of Basel had published vast quantities of rabbinic material and soon replaced Bomberg as the major provider of Hebraica to a Christian audience. If Münster was not defending other Hebraists of the day, he was certainly defending himself.

The opposite point of view found its clearest expression in Johannes Forster's lexicon, published posthumously in 1558, in which the introduction was devoted to arguing against Münster and other judaizing Hebraists. The view that judaizing Hebraists were responsible for much Protestant dissension was an important charge made by Forster and even earlier by his mentor, Martin Luther, as we have observed. Indeed, Forster's accusations seem to have been taken directly from Luther's mouth. Though his introduction mentioned neither Münster nor Fagius by name, it is clear that Forster had both in mind in writing his broadside against all Hebraica outside Wittenberg. The immediate response to Forster by Hebraists critical of his position would seem to indicate that contemporaries were of the opinion that Forster lost this debate to Münster. As will be apparent by the end of this chapter, the passage of over four centuries has done little to change this assessment, though Forster must be credited with presenting a point of view several decades in the making and one that remains prevalent within some Christian circles to the present day.

For Münster all theoretical considerations regarding the use of Jewish sources were meaningless since "many places in Scripture are obscure and perplexing and they cannot be easily understood without the Hebrew tradition—whatever the smart ones growl today."[2] Perhaps directing his first point to a Catholic audience, Münster based his argument on the precedent set by an earlier student of Scripture: "The work of St. Jerome teaches us that not all the writings of the Hebrews are to be condemned by someone trying to render the Holy Hebrew into Latin." Turning to other critics, possibly Lutheran, whose most strident charge was that Jews could not understand Scripture since they rejected Jesus as the messiah, thereby demonstrating their inability to understand God, Münster wrote, "If this were true, that the Jews could not interpret Scripture . . . from whom, I ask, did Jerome learn the interpretation of the Law and the Prophets? Not from the Jews?" Other critics argued that since Jerome's work made use of the best Jewish scholarship of the time, there was no need for additional consultation with Jewish teachers or use of Jewish sources. Münster argued against this limited view in a variety of ways and asked, "How, I ask, does it come about that we have two Aramaic Targums which Jerome did not see since he does not mention them though they were written long before him?" Additionally, there was the old accusation that Jews corrupted the pure original Hebrew text so that it would not support Christian arguments. Münster, like Reuchlin, had much opportunity to examine a variety of Hebrew OT texts from various corners of the Jewish world, and his conclusion was that "they guarded their divine oracles, the whole body of Sacred Scripture so that no corruption could harm it." Then there was the opposite point of view, that Jews were so incredibly stupid and void of all learning that they could not possibly possess the correct Hebrew text. Tongue in cheek, Münster suggested, "If the Jews know nothing other than that which they acquire from Christians, then also the Christians must have provided them with their Hebrew Bible."

Yet another point Münster raised concerned the masoretic work done by Levita and himself. Münster noted that "Jerome's Hebrew text was without vowel points and there were no Hebrew [grammatical] commentaries in his time." Consequently, much as Jews maintained the authentic text, they were "also able to conserve the interpretation of their teachers, the traditions of their fathers." Far from being the ignorant and blind fools they were believed to be, Münster argued that "at the very least they must come to know the language and its idioms, and they did not *become* ignorant of the interpretation handed down to them from their elders." With a fair amount of sarcasm, Münster asked, "If the Jews were able to conserve the Holy Bible, its Aramaic translations, and even the Talmud, why not equally the [masoretic] expositions . . . ? Or did they have to obtain them by begging from Christians?"

Other critics conceded use of ancient sources but were disturbed by the use of medieval authorities, to which objection Münster noted, "Now if you say that from the time of Jerome to Rabbi Solomon the Jews had no learned men . . . [and were] destitute of all exegesis," as was the common charge, "read if you can, the book *Seder Olam* edited by Rabbi Abraham Levita ben David in which he writes about illustrious Jews and their works." Far from being destitute of scholarship and blind, "you will find in this book many worthy rabbis from Spain, Africa, Egypt, and other lands, who composed books . . . and I say these rabbis are famous and distinguished." Indeed, Münster noted, "I do not doubt that if the commentaries of Ibn Ezra, Moses Gerundis [Nachmanides], Ben Gerson or David Kimchi had been available to Jerome, he would not have needed living teachers."

Since Jews faithfully maintained the original texts, the accurate masorah, and the views of the ancients regarding proper interpretation and composed excellent exegetical guides during the Middle Ages, Münster's logical conclusion was that "we should be reminded therefore, not to listen to those who believe and despise the Hebrew writings as if they contained nothing good."

One additional statement by Münster may have alluded to what the author believed might have been a factor explaining some of the difficulty Christians experienced in finding Jewish teachers: overcoming their own sense of shame in turning to Jews for instruction. Münster reminded his reader that Jerome certainly felt no such shame: "This great and important man did not regard it beneath his dignity to have Hebrew teachers. Indeed, he admits that he would not have been able to interpret the sacred Scriptures without their help." Münster concluded his defense with the admonition, "Christian reader, if you have truly learned Christ, the lecture and interpretation of the rabbis will not harm you. Indeed, this information will be helpful to you whether they agree with us or not."

Münster's defense expressed little that would have troubled the overwhelming number of Christian-Hebraists in Europe. The appeal to the precedent set by Jerome was an effective argument with Catholic critics since it was his translation that the Church continued to use. Protestants may have had mixed feelings about much of Jerome's work, but certainly he was still considered a great cultural hero by all who had cause to work with the translation of Scripture. Moreover, even those most critical of the Vulgate would not have argued that its faults resulted from Jerome's learning Hebrew or his learning the contemporary mode of interpretation from those who knew it best. Even if one believed that Fagius's views too avidly aped rabbinic opinion, one would have to concede that it was far better to discover scriptural truth than to worry about agreement with Jews. Münster reminded his readers that Jerome, and perhaps even Fagius and Münster himself, "again became a student to those who were enemies of Christ" for Christian and not Jewish purposes.

A very different picture of Christian-Hebraica emerges from Lutheran centers, especially Wittenberg. We have had occasion to review some of Luther's basic premises regarding the supremacy of the spirit over the written word in translation. Similarly, we have had the opportunity to see how the views of the spirit were understood according to the *a priori* approach of the *loci* method which read NT concept into the OT text. We have also noted that Luther's notion of the dichotomy of Law and Gospel denied the same type of equal integrity to both halves of Scripture since one was essentially the good foil to the other's enslaving nature. Though the distinction between Law and Gospel was not a simple differentiation of OT and NT, concepts for the elucidation of both were primarily, if not entirely, drawn from the latter to apply to the former. Last, we have noted how Heinrich Bornkamm believed that the sum total of this method was, regrettably, the need "to carry the concepts of the NT revelation into the OT and put them into the mouths of the patriarchs."

The importance of Luther's views and his influence upon the nature and quality of Hebrew scholarship at Wittenberg cannot be overestimated. Without his persistent efforts to acquire a Hebrew teacher, his university might have gone without one for many years. And those who remained at that institution for any length of time found a need to accommodate their views to those of Luther. Consequently, nowhere was the subservience of linguistics to theology more clearly emphasized, possibly because no more leading scholar of the Reformation than Luther advanced this intellectual tendency more strongly. Additionally, no other Protestant intellectual center was so dominated by a single towering personality. Indeed, Luther himself gave clear testimony regarding his control over his Hebraists. Since he knew little Hebrew himself, Luther required the close cooperation of Wittenberg Hebraists to enable him to understand Scripture correctly. Of all of these none was closer to him than Johannes Forster (1495–1556), and Luther recorded a conversation they conducted concerning the translation of Scripture. According to Luther, the problem was to make the OT text rhyme with a portion of the NT: "It helped Dr. Forster and Zeigler very much that they talked with us . . . when he said: 'Ah, the rabbis interpret it this way.' I said: 'Could your grammar and your points allow you to render the sentence so that it rhymes with the NT?' Answer: 'Yes.' 'Then take it.' The result was that they themselves marvelled and said they never in their lives would have believed it."[3]

Johannes Forster originally learned Hebrew from Johannes Reuchlin but differed from his mentor in both enthusiasm for Hebrew and open-mindedness regarding Jewish authorities. Indeed, Forster's efforts in the area of Christian-Hebraica were quite unique and constituted a major effort to develop a concept of Hebrew studies that did not follow in the path of rabbinics and Reformed Christian-Hebraica. It is quite possible that Forster's greatest contribution was not in the area of Hebraica per se but in most clearly expressing the polemical character of Wittenberg Hebraica and in elucidating Luther's ideas on the subject.

Forster's approach to Christian-Hebraica and his polemical attitude were apparent in the very title of his only published work: *New Hebrew Dictionary, Not Arranged Out of the Comments of the Rabbis Nor Out of the Foolish Imitations of Our Native Doctors But Out of Our Own Treasures of Sacred Scripture and Developed by an Accurate Collation of Biblical Passages, Annotated with Passages and Phrases from the Old and New Testaments.*[4] The plain fact was, however, that aside from rabbinic guides, grammars, and commentaries, the only available sources were those composed by such "foolish imitators" as Sebastian Münster and Paul Fagius, who were in turn dependent upon rabbinic sources as well as the work of their contemporary Elias Levita about whom I have already written. Forster's program was more a goal than a true possibility, and he had the distinction of being the only Hebraist of his age who believed, quite incredibly and as his title indicated, that NT Greek might elucidate the meaning and construction of OT Hebrew. This polemical approach was further elucidated in the work's preface: "Many years after the restoration of the gospel I have seen that—as in the synagogues and schools of the Jews so too among Christians—the rabbinic commentaries control the work of translating and explanation, and that their commentaries are adored and worshipped by all with the highest reverence as sacrosanct mysteries of God."[5] Although it is possible that Forster was upset by the widespread use of Jewish sources or what he perceived as the judaizing tendencies of such orthodox scholars as Fagius and Münster or the works of a radical like Servetus, it is also possible that he alluded to a different problem altogether. Conceivably, Forster believed that Reformed Hebraists were more Law-oriented because of Jewish influence much as Sabbatarianism was allegedly caused by Jewish influence. Considering Lutheran opposition to Reformed covenantism, the accusation that this form of Protestantism was the result of Jewish sources and influence would make much sense. Expressing open contempt for such scholars, Forster continued, "Often I have wondered about the feeble-mindedness of my Christian colleagues who without discrimination have happily embraced the commentaries of the Jews."[6] The result of such Jewish influence was confusion within the Christian community where none should have existed, and "therefore we could not arrive at the true sense of Scripture."[7]

Considering the many faults he attributed to the work of other Hebraists, one should not be surprised that his *New Hebrew Dictionary* was organized along vastly different lines. Rather than provide dictionary-type explanations for OT Hebrew terms, his work was more of a lexicon and compendium of some 1,758 root verbs that had a bearing on Christ. The student using Forster's dictionary would learn no Hebrew and acquire no understanding of the OT idiom but would be able to locate references to many terms that demonstrated a specific understanding of Jesus. This understanding of Christ, in turn, was based upon NT sources that were then read back into the OT Hebrew, hence, the importance of using the Greek NT in determining the meaning of the original Hebrew. In short, this was a linguistic version of the loci method and purpose. Forster must have taken Luther quite literally about the need to find Christ in every Hebrew word because that is precisely what, in this work, he intended to do. Indeed, even Forster's treatment of points of grammar was so imbued with theological concept that he permitted himself many flights of fancy when discussing the elemental structure of Hebrew verbs: "The first rule of all is that all terms and roots of the Hebrew language consist of three original letters . . . just as the divine essence is divided into three distinct persons."[8] In similarly mystical (and mystifying) fashion Forster went on to discuss Hebrew verb classes, but rather than use standard Hebrew names for classes of conjugation, he made up his own system and pattern based partly on Latin and partly on German concepts of verb function. Had this innovation been of educational or linguistic value, it would have proved interesting if not significant. The pattern's only characteristic, however, was its nonreliance upon standard Hebrew or Jewish sources. Moreover, the remainder of the lexicon smacks more of ignorance than innovation, and Forster's list of verbs is filled with errors resulting primarily from a consistent lack of understanding of the most basic concepts of Hebrew syntax and grammatical structure. As examples, verb number 774, *lahag,* "to prattle or talk idly," is related by Forster to *lahat,* "to burn or blaze," and to *shalhevet,* "a flame." Verb number 681, *yashar,* "to straighten," is incorrectly related to *ēēshare,* "to become wealthy," and *nesher,* the noun for "eagle."

When discussing letters that might be interchanged under certain circumstances, Forster listed as equivalent such words as *beged* and *meged* as examples of interchangeable first letters. In fact, *beged* means "cloak" whereas *meged* means "excellence," and they constitute no such example of possible letter transference. Essentially, Forster built so much ignorance-born pliability into his grammatical system that the text might be made to support almost any translation at all.

Although Forster's approach to Hebrew was limited by his own native inabilities in linguistics, one must wonder to what extent the overall character of his work would have differed had he possessed a better grasp of basic Hebrew grammar. Forster was doing no more for linguistics than Melanchthon's loci method had done for theology; both created closed systems in which concomitant elements of the structure were carefully tuned to deliver desired results. Forster's pliability, like Melanchthon's selectivity, may well have been the result of a specific method and approach to Scripture which had already predetermined OT value and meaning.

Nowhere did Forster demonstrate his lack of ability in scriptural Hebrew studies in more convincing fashion, and nowhere is the difference between Protestant and Reformed Christian-Hebraist tendencies more in evidence, than in the area of Aramaic, the "chaldean" of the Reformed school. Many sixteenth-century Hebraists like Fagius and Münster considered knowledge of Aramaic fundamental to the pursuit of the rabbinic idiom from which Jesus and the apostles emerged. Forster was of another opinion. Much as he wished to present a Hebrew devoid of the influence of rabbinic gloss, and much as he did present a Hebrew devoid of traditional notions of grammar and syntax, so too did Forster attempt to strip Hebrew of its Aramaic legacy: "Moved by a holy zeal I have written this dictionary in which the true and certain significance of the Hebrew words is indicated from Moses and the Prophets lest the student of this language be confused by that Babylonian confusion and variety of meanings."[9]

Surely none would fault Forster his zeal to learn and teach classical Hebrew if in point of fact that is what he had attmepted to do. Yet, when one considers Forster's general incompetence in that language and his thorough ignorance of Aramaic, a rather clear picture emerges. Forster would have had his students study a Hebrew devoid of rabbinic opinion, devoid of Pharisee influence, devoid of the proper rules of grammar and syntax, and devoid of any sense of linguistic tradition at all since that tradition involved Jewish influence. Indeed, Forster attempted to defend this rather extreme position. If Jews knew no Hebrew and if the text had been tampered with continually—as Melanchthon claimed—and if the OT Law was the embodiment of all the NT Gospel came to rectify and if Jews remained steadfast in their error, then it was only logical that Jewish influences, glosses, and commentaries possessed "no light, no knowledge of God, no spirit, no real and solid knowledge of any discipline and art, no learning of any language not even Hebrew."[10] Since it was axiomatic that Jews could possess no beneficial knowledge of wisdom, "Their dictionaries and commentaries have brought more obscurity and error into the church of Christ than light and truth.''[11] Similarly, the Jewish-influenced works of Münster, Fagius, and all others were tainted and "the result is that not only they fall into error but they also mislead their readers.''[12]

The poor quality of Forster's work did not go unnoticed by other Hebraists within the German community. A year after Forster's work appeared, Johannes Isaac, professor of Hebrew at Cologne, published a very sharp attack on Forster's approach and his thorough incompetence in Hebrew studies entitled *Against the Confusion of Dr. Johannes Forster's Lexicon*.[13] Similarly, Professor William Schichard of the University of Tübingen accused Forster of gross incompetence and of impeding Hebrew studies.[14]

Unfortunately, Forster's overall approach to and concept of Hebrew studies was characteristic of the quality of work done in Wittenberg in general. These same attitudes, prejudices, and biases can be found in the studies composed by Avenarius toward the end of the century. His grammar (1586) and lexicon (1589) were essentially more complete versions of Forster's *New Hebrew Dictionary* and expressed the same ignorance of Hebrew grammar. Yet other Wittenberg Hebraists also demonstrated a very narrow conceptual base for Hebrew studies. Matthias Flacius Illyricus did not devote his efforts to Hebrew study to the same extent as Münster, Fagius, or even Forster, yet he still expressed many of the same hesitancies and fears regarding Jewish contamination of the text. Interestingly, Falcius's *Clavis Scripturae* of 1567, 1580 and 1581, like Forster's earlier study, was published in Basel and not in Wittenberg because of the latter's poor facilities. Considering that Wittenberg alone among Protestant centers produced a great number of anti-Semitic polemics, one is tempted to see Forster's work as the intellectual aspect of a more general problem plaguing this main Lutheran center.

The condition of poor-quality Hebrew work plagued other Lutheran institutions as well as Wittenberg.[15] Bernard Zeigler, Anton Margaritha, and Matthew Adrianus taught at Leipzig, but none produced a single notable linguistic work although Margaritha was quite adept at writing anti-Jewish polemics. The University of Marburg's efforts to locate talented teachers of Hebrew met with a similar lack of success. Sebastian Nucenus, a student of Ardianus, was the first teacher there in 1536 and was succeeded by Johannes Lincerus, who remained at that institution until his death in 1569. Neither produced a single grammar or other form of educational material, not to speak of scholarly output. The University of Konigsberg established Hebrew instruction in 1546, as did Rostock in 1553 and Jena in 1558. No instructor at any of these institutions produced scholarly, educational, or linguistic materials. In all these institutions Hebrew instruction never progressed past the stage of service to faculties of theology and, as such, provided only meager instruction in that language.

Luther was certainly pleased with the professors of Hebrew at the University of Wittenberg, a group he referred to as "a sanhedrin [i.e., a collection of rabbis] of the best people possible."[16] Understandably, he was upset by the type of work being produced in Reformed centers where scholars may have known more grammar but not the Holy Spirit. Had it been possible to create a Christian scholar of Hebrew incorporating all of Luther's hesitancies and fears concerning judaization, all of his biases against Jewish opinion on the OT, yet knowing enough Hebrew to facilitate NT study, Johannes Forster would have been that creation.

There can be no question that Forster's criticisms of contemporary Christian-Hebraica would have been more effective had he been a more qualified linguist. Yet, it would be a mistake to dismiss Wittenberg's fears concerning alleged Christian-Hebraica judaization as the mere expression of an overly narrow point of view. The same concern was expressed just a few years earlier in 1553 when Michael Servetus stood trial in Geneva. Both Calvin and others were horrified by Servetus's boldness and his ability to defend his views through the use of rabbinics. Calvin repeatedly referred to Servetus as "this excellent rabbi" and noted that "in truth you argue as the Jews and Mohammedans are accustomed to do."[17] The Company of Pastors expressed similar sentiments.[18] In many religious centers the line separating valid use of Jewish sources from judaization seemed increasingly vague if only because the new art of printing made both so much more apparent.

By midcentury, Hebraists increasingly found themselves under pressure to disavow the judaizing tendencies they allegedly fostered. This accusation was particularly troubling to Protestant Hebraists since their scripturalism, devotion to rabbinic sources, and even more open attitude toward the Jewish people provided Roman Catholic polemicists with a negative image with which to identify Protestantism as a reemergent Judaism. As incredible as it seems to identify Protestantism with Judaism, we shall see in the next part of this study that Hebraists and Luther himself were primarily responsible for this accusation and negative image.

Other factors, too, contributed to a more defensive Hebraica after midcentury. The onset of the religious wars, continuing strife with radicals and within the ranks of the magisterial reformation, and a new spirit of reform in the Catholic church were all important factors bringing an end to the intellectual openness characterizing the first half of the sixteenth century in favor of a spirit of factionalism, dogmatism, and a new scholasticism. In this atmosphere Hebraists defended themselves as best they could by attacking one another and, where possible, the very Jewish sources they found so important.

NOTES

1. Sebastian Münster, *Mikdash YHVH: Hebraica Biblia* (Basel, 1534, 1546).
2. *Ibid.* All the following Münster citations were taken from his reader's preface entitled "Hebraeorum Commentarij non Contemnendi," script b1b–b2b.
3. Luther, *LW*, 54:445–46, no. 5,533. See also 54:375–76, no. 5,002.
4. Johannes Forster, *Dictionarium Hebraicum Novum, non ex Rabbinorum Commentis nec ex Nostratum Doctorum Stulta Imitatione Descriptum, sed ex ipsis Thesauris Sacrorum Bibliorum et eorundem accurata locorum Collatione Depromptum, cum Phrasibus Scripturae veteris et Novi Testamenti Diligenter Annotatis* (Basel, 1557). Concerning Forster, see my article "Luther, Forster, and the Curious Nature of Wittenberg Hebraica," *Bibliotheque D'Humanisme et Renaissance*, 42 (1980): pp. 611, 619.
5. Forster, preface.
6. *Ibid.*
7. *Ibid.*
8. *Ibid.*, p. 2b.
9. *Ibid.*, preface.
10. *Ibid.*
11. *Ibid.*
12. *Ibid.*
13. It may seem strange to the reader that Cologne, a Catholic university, would employ a Protestant Hebraist. It seems the shortage of competent Hebrew scholars was so acute that religious irregularities were quite commonplace. Indeed, the greatest problem was not the specific denomination to which the Hebrew scholar in question belonged or identified, but the suspicion of Jewish origins. Johannes Isaac, whose *Contra Confussimum D. Joh. Fursteri Lexicon* was published in Cologne in 1558, was mentioned in the text and was clearly of Jewish origin but claimed he was a "genuine" Christian since his parents converted before his birth. Similarly, Leo Judd of Strasbourg also denied Jewish origins. Indeed, every Hebraist at one point or another had to defend his origins against the taint of Jewishness and compared with such charges, being normally Catholic, Protestant, or Reformed was a smaller matter. See Geiger, *Studium* . . . , pp. 136–38.
14. See Ch. F. Schnurer, *Biogr. und Literar. Nachrichten von den Hebr. Literatur in Tübingen* (Ulm, 1792), p. 112.

15.   See Geiger, *Studium* . . . , p. 106–18 ff.

16.   Hans Schmidt, *Luther und das Buch der Psalmen* (Tübingen, 1933), p. 60. Concerning this "sanhedrin," see Siegfried Raeder, *Das Hebraische bei Luther* (Tübingen, 1961); G. Bauch, "Die Einführung des Hebräischen in Wittenberg," *Monatschrift der Gesellschaft für Wissenschaft des Judentums*, vol. 48 (Breslau, 1904).

17.   Calvin, *C.O.*, 8:620, 695.

18.   See Kingdon and Berger, eds., *Registres de la Compagnie des Pasteurs.* . . .

PART IV

The Battle for Christian-Hebraica

Chapter Ten

Overview: Hebraica, Christians, and Jews

Despite the widespread appeal of Christian-Hebraica to devotees of the ancient theology and its popularity in scholarly exegetical circles, concern was also widespread regarding potential misuse of Jewish sources. Even so erudite a scholar as Erasmus, not to mention his more conservative co-religionists in the Dominican order and elsewhere, had misgivings about where this new study would lead. Three of Erasmus's statements summed up these fears and delineated the contours of this concern.

> The restoration of Hebrew learning may give occasion to the revival of Judaism. This would be a plague as much opposed to the doctrine of Christ as anything that can happen.
>
> The Christian Church should not put so much emphasis upon the Old Testament.
>
> Is there anyone among us who does not curse this species of mankind enough? If it is Christian to hate Jews, are we then not all Christian in over abundance?[1]

In short, Christian-Hebraica used too many Jewish sources too frequently, placed too much emphasis on the OT, and could in turn diminish the significance of that purely Christian social science, anti-Semitism. But were Erasmus's views anti-Judaic or anti-Semitic?

Some critics will point to the important difference between maintaining a point of view that encompasses anti-Judaism and one that encompasses anti-Semitism, usually a racial theory. One can quibble about whether anti-Semitism must necessarily express a racial distinction since a great many prejudiced people do not subscribe to these views but dislike Jews all the same on social, if not biological, grounds. However one defines anti-Semitism, it is understandable that Christianity, Judaism's daughter, would seek to define itself against its origin and in distinction to its source. Consequently, one can appreciate that a faith-oriented Protestantism would view Judaism's good-works approach to religious salvation with horror and repugnance. Similarly, Roman Catholicism would view Jewish literal interpretation of the OT Scripture with more than skepticism. Yet, without diminishing the importance of the distinction between anti-Judaism and anti-Semitism, we must also realize that often the former is only a mask for the latter. In Spain, for instance, anti-Judaic statutes forbade the practice of Judaism and brought about the large-scale conversion of tens of thousands of Jews. To ensure religious uniformity, the Spanish Inquisition maintained a rigorous standard of orthodoxy among these new converts. One can regret Spanish enthusiasm for religious regularity and the often cruel practices of the Inquisition yet still recognize that all sixteenth-century societies, Protestant and Catholic alike, attempted an institutional form of religious uniformity. Consequently, the anti-Judaic practices of the Inquisition were unfortunate and regrettable but were in keeping with the age.

Can the same theory of anti-Judaism be found in the "pure blood laws" that tormented and persecuted New Christian converts much as the anti-Judaic practices of a previous generation distinguished Jew from Christian? These laws stipulated that one was not a Christian for three full generations and then only if the New Christian convert married old Christians in each generation.[2] Clearly, anti-Judaism and anti-Semitism must be distinguished though they often traveled the same route and were but flip sides of the same coin of discrimination.

Luther, too, as we shall see, reflected a confusion of anti-Judaism and anti-Semitism common among the Spanish. He started out writing in favor of Judaism (and therefore of Jews) and became increasingly upset with the judaization of Christianity and expressed this through treatises directed against Jews. By the early 1540s Luther's clearly anti-Judaic stance had given way to the most extreme racial anti-Semitism.

In a society that predicated so much social policy on religious bases, it is difficult to differentiate anti-Judaic policies from anti-Semitic ones. Consequently, if indeed Jews were persecuted on religious grounds, that is, on grounds of anti-Judaism, and not out of anti-Semitic sentiment, we are only expressing the common Jewish view that Christian religious thought lay at the basis of modern anti-Semitism. Since the sixteenth-century Christian mind did not necessarily distinguish between Jews and Judaism, anti-Judaism and anti-Semitism, one can understand the acceptance of the assumption, however illogical, that those Christians knowing Hebrew were Jews. Those who openly advanced Jewish learning unwittingly encouraged this identification, and whether or not one wishes to view sixteenth-century sentiment as anti-Judaic rather than as anti-Semitic, one will still be forced to concede that Christian-Hebraists had a problem. Roman Catholic polemicists seized upon Protestant scripturalism as proof of its practioners' identification with Judaism and Jews. Protestants countered this accusation with charges of their own and noted the similarity between Catholic and Jewish ritual. As the conflict between the two Christianities increased and became more and more hostile in nature, Jews, necessarily bystanders, were increasingly drawn into the conflict as the polemicists' tool against the adversary. Consequently, the study of Hebrew among Christians in this tumultuous age must necessarily touch upon the issue of Christian attitudes toward Jews. Since these attitudes played so prominent a role in the increasingly important anti-Judaic position of those who expressed hesitancies about Hebrew study—and these attitudes soon found expression in anti-Semitic treatises—not treating this digression is to miss the vehemence of Hebraists and anti-Hebraists alike.

The Reuchlin-Dominican controversy of the previous generation heightened the tensions surrounding Christian use of Jewish sources but did not resolve any of the fundamental issues. The Dominicans argued on a purely anti-Semitic level, and the issue seemed to drag on without end, making any discussion of the true issues impossible. Those opposed to Reuchlin had not been won over, and although Christian-Hebraica made important strides during the subsequent two to three decades, the basic tensions remained.

The Protestant Reformation further complicated the question of language study in general and Hebrew learning in particular. Even though the linguistic skills themselves were neutral, many of Reuchlin's defenders were active Protestant leaders as were most of the foremost Hebraists of the day. Since, with the exception of Italy, western European Catholic countries were largely without Jewish population, the twin successes of the Reformation and Christian-Hebraica may have had the effect of consolidating anti-Reuchlin and anti-Protestant forces into one conservative anti-Hebrew block. Thus, many Roman Catholic leaders understood the Reformation movement as nothing more than the resurgence of Reuchlinist-judaized Christianity stressing Jewish sources, the OT, and a reevaluation of Jewish-Christian relations. Consequently, the charge of judaization came to have special meaning when used against the Protestant movement.

Protestant leaders such as Luther and Bucer attempted to clear their religion of the accusation of judaization by blaming eastern European Sabbatarianism and other manifestations of a pro-Law mentality on Christian-Hebraists and Jews. For their part, Christian-Hebraists attempted to avoid any guilt by association with Jews by writing anti-Jewish polemics under the guise of missionary works. At first these writings were just anti-Judaic, but as the antijudaization campaign raised its voice, they soon became shrill anti-Semitic blasts. Both Protestants and Hebraists essentially avoided the charge of judaization by pandering to popular anti-Semitism and by demonstrating that they too hated Jews.

Sensing Protestant discomfort regarding the "Jewish question," which was really only a Hebrew-studies question, Charles V altered his traditionally anti-Jewish policies in Germany and forbade Protestant states from expelling Jews. He granted German Jews liberal charters of tolerance, extended trading rights, and in general encouraged the Imperial Jewish community to remain in Germany as an irritant to Protestants. Along the way, an already beleaguered small Jewish community was caught between Catholic and Protestant charges that it was responsible for the ills of Christendom and became, despite its neutrality, an unwilling participant in a conflict not of its own making. Some Jewish teachers like Levita lived long enough to see former students like Münster and Fagius turn on Jews in barbarous fashion. The result was an intensification of Protestant anti-Semitism that finally culminated in feelings so intense that Christian-Hebraica itself was seriously threatened. Another result was the expulsion of Jews from most of Germany as soon as Charles V died.

In this part of this study, entitled "The Battle for Christian-Hebraica," we are turning our attention to the questions of judaization, Protestant-Jewish relations, and Christian-Hebraist missionary activity as part of the conflict regarding the use of Jewish sources within the Protestant community. In short, we shall attempt to determine how Christian-Hebraists understood the relationship between anti-Judaism and anti-Semitism in combating the judaization charges of their opponents.

NOTES

1. D. Erasmus, *Opus Epistolarum Des*, 2:508; Werner Welzig, *Erasmus' Werke* (Darmstadt, 1967), 4,46:138–43. See also M. A. Screech, *Ecstasy and the Praise of Folly* (Duckworth, 1980).
2. See chapter one, note 9.

Chapter Eleven

Judaization: Theory and Practice

Any discussion of Christian-Hebraica must consider the problems of judaization, the inappropriate use of, or influence by, Jewish religious sources. Unfortunately, what should be a fairly clear problem in religious systematics is, in truth, quite vague. This term was often used as a catchall epithet to describe the religious views of all opponents no matter how incongruous the charge. Thus the Lutheran author Hunnius described John Calvin as a judaizer much as Calvin believed Lutheran liturgy was highly judaistic.[1] On the other hand, Roman Catholic spokesmen thought Lutheran preoccupation with scriptural literalism was judaistic while both Reformed and Lutheran thinkers assumed Roman Catholic interest in ceremony and ritual reflected judaizing tendencies. Expressing a rare ecumenism, all agreed that Michael Servetus was a severe judaizer by any and all standards. For his part, Servetus lamented his being persecuted by judaizing Christians, Calvin in particular.

Judaization was not confined to the Reformation debate, for even before the posting of the Ninty-five Theses, an act provoked by "German judaizing tendencies," the Dominican order charged Johannes Reuchlin, who remained a Catholic, with judaizing when he defended the right of Jews to use the Talmud and other religious writings. Of course, the Dominicans felt they were authorities on the subject since their charges were built upon the writings of Johannes Pfefferkorn, who had been Jewish at one time and therefore ought to have recognized judaizing when he saw it. Some who defended Reuchlin (and were therefore judaizers) thought that Pfefferkorn was even worse than a judaizer, and they claimed that he was no Christian at all but was still actually a Jew. Indeed, some contemporary authors advanced the notion that the Reuchlin controversy was sparked by the Jews themselves. For their part, Jews, who were always regarded as judaizers by everyone, claimed Pfefferkorn was no Jew at all and in any event knew so little about Judaism that he could not possibly be a judaizer.

The same scintillating debate was conducted farther south in Spain.

The theologians of the Court of the Inquisition were concerned about Jewish converts to Christianity known as Marranos, who, the courts claimed, were judaizing the Christian religion by converting to it; there could be little doubt about the essential Jewishness of these New Christians (to be distinguished from old Christians) since they observed such obvious Jewish practices as changing linen on Fridays, cooking with olive oil rather than with lard, and facing the wall when hearing of a death. Of course, this simplistic narrative might become terribly convoluted *if* we attempt to discover whether the Dominicans in the north and the Franciscans in Spain and Italy ever agreed upon the nature of judaization and what they shared with other notable experts on the subject.

Considering the very small number of Jews residing in western Europe in the first half of the sixteenth century, the smaller number of Christian scholars able to read Hebrew, and the even smaller number of nongrammatical Jewish works of a religious nature available to these scholars, one can only be astounded at the incredible influence allegedly exerted by Jewish thought. If indeed such charges are to be taken seriously, one might consider an entirely new classification of Renaissance-Reformation intellectual life organized according to degrees of judaization. Such a system would enable us to dispense with all traditional concepts of classification which have only served to divide historians since the sixteenth century.

In point of fact—and in all seriousness—the term *judaization* was so variously used by different groups for different reasons that it is often difficult to discern the reasonable from the absurd. Indeed, it is unfortunate that Christians insisted upon obscuring this issue with interecclesiastical politics since there were serious fears regarding the use of Jewish sources. Moreover, Christian uneasiness regarding Jewish influence, like Jewish uneasiness regarding Christian influence, reflected the simple fact that while the two religions disagreed on a host of issues, there was also a large common ground shared by both. Christianity, however, had an additional problem in that it required a positive assessment of ancient Judaism at least whereas for Judaism Christianity was simply one more heresy deifying its founder in the traditional manner of Egyptian and Mesopotamian religions.

Since its earliest days Christianity has been required to define its peculiar relationship with Judaism, which definition demanded both proximity and distance. The notion of the *second* covenant, Jesus *fulfilling* messianic expectations, and the possible *continuity* of the Law required that Christianity understand itself as a logical extension of Judaism. Yet, the *new* good news of the Gospel, the *obsolescence* of the Law, a *different* concept of faith and works advanced by Paul all required that Christianity understand itself as a very different religion able to provide salvation precisely because Judaism could not. James and possibly Peter reflected the continuity of Judaism's transition into Christianity and accepted the continuing validity of the Law and many Jewish observances. Paul, on the other hand, stressed the inefficacy of these rituals and their replacement by a new form of worship and a new concept of faith. The Reformation conflict concerning the efficacy of works and faith was essentially an updated version of the Peter-Paul struggle between more-Jewish Christians and less-Jewish Christians. This was a central pivot of the Reformation debate and a point of strong discussion throughout the Middle Ages. It is not surprising that different churches and denominations have attempted to balance these two tendencies by stressing the importance of both in a variety of carefully worded formulations. Similarly, the importance of Scripture, the significance of its wording, and the question of whether the OT or the NT was more important were all related issues as was the question of use of Jewish sources.

The Roman Catholic position may have stressed the efficacy of works more than Protestant authorities believed best, but then Luther's suggestion that the Epistle of James should be eliminated from the corpus of NT Scripture no doubt left many Roman Catholics and other Protestants quite cold. The myriad of Christian sects, churches, denominations, and groupings is adequate evidence of the desire to reexamine many hitherto acceptable Christian positions. That many of the scholars carrying out this reexamiantion turned to the languages of the Bible to determine the inner meaning and thinking of the apostolic age is logical even though their conclusions differed quite significantly. It is thoroughly absurd to blame Jews for any of the formulations or positions taken by Christian theologians, much as it would be absurd to speak of James reflecting judaizing tendencies.

Similarly, the dogma of the Trinity—soteriologically necessary, yet conceptually awkward—had always proved a difficult concept to grasp, especially when compared with the pure monotheism of the OT Jewish tradition. If one considers that dissension regarding the Trinity is as old as the concept itself, blaming antitrinitarianism among Reformation Christians on Jewish influence was absurd. The conflicts at the councils of Nicaea, Chalcedon, and elsewhere, as well as the Germanic tribal proclivity toward Arianism, should have been sufficient to demonstrate the total unimportance of Jews to the entire conflict.

The issue of judaization has only one proper context, which is its importance and function in meeting the conceptual needs of a Christianity in search of its intellectual origins. One might argue that Jewish sources would be beneficial to this search or one might accept the opposite point of view, but the only position that would reflect a judaized tendency would be one that denied the Christian belief in favor of a Jewish one. Very simply, the rejection of a Christian position in favor of a clearly Jewish position did not occur. Even Sabbatarianism can hardly be considered a good example of judaization since the liturgy such Christians used was a Christian service and not a Jewish one. Indeed, it is doubtful that anyone would have objected had these same Sabbatarian Christians said these same prayers on Sunday morning rather than on Saturday. The only thing "Jewish" about Sabbatarianism was the day in question, and surely one does not cease being a Christian if Christian prayers are said on Saturday rather than on Sunday any more than a Moslem becomes a Christian if he says his Arabic prayers in a mosque on Sunday rather than on Friday. Similarly, no one would consider a person praying in Hebrew according to traditional Jewish liturgy any less Jewish if those prayers were said on Sunday rather than on Saturday morning. Certainly if the choice of Saturday as a day of prayer constitutes a judaization, Jesus Himself was guilty of this serious crime, for He not only prayed on Saturday but also even preached on the wrong day of the week—and in a Jewish temple, no less.

Despite the confusion surrounding the term *judaization*, it is possible to distinguish four basic tendencies that would be of legitimate concern within the Christian community.

OT Ceremony

Any religious position that advocated a return to specifically Jewish practices such as circumcision or the laws of kashruth or which recognized the continuing religious validity of these acts might conceivably detract from Jesus' efficacy in providing all that was needed for salvation. Then again, such behavior might be acceptable in addition to belief in Jesus as the messiah if these rituals were not presented as conveying grace but as mere ethnic practices.

Confusion of Ceremony

Similar to the above, this form of unacceptable judaization involved the maintenance of perfectly Christian rituals for Jewish reasons. As an example, baptism and circumcision might be confused, with the former understood only as an updated version of the latter. Many of the arguments concerning the proper time and method of baptism, that is, whether it is for children or adults and whether it is performed with full immersion or just sprinkling, often used Jewish circumcision as a foundation. Equating these two rituals can prove a problem unless both are accepted as legitimate forms of religious expression. If both practices are accepted, however, one must then discuss the relationship of Law and Gospel lest one accept the validity of OT ceremony discussed above.

Conceptual Justification

Some Christians wished to prove the truth of their views on the basis of Jewish religious sources even if the same dogmas could be satisfactorily validated with Christian sources. An entire generation of Christians was fascinated by the Cabbalah because they believed such concepts as the Trinity could be demonstrated through its methods. At the same time, others believed Jewish sources could be used to disprove the Trinity, as Servetus and others maintained. Since in either case Jewish sources were used, both tendencies should have been rejected; yet many of those defending Reuchlin argued against Servetus. Possibly defense of an accepted dogma with Jewish opinion was accepted as harmless whereas rejection of orthodoxy with use of Jewish opinion was perceived as far more dangerous. Then again, anyone accepting Plato and Pythagoras as Christian-in-spirit thinkers would have a hard time disclaiming Moses or the Cabbalah.

Interpretation of Scripture

Judaizing the text of the OT might serve the interest of those wishing to interpret Scripture in some alternate fashion in order to support an alternate view of Christian dogma. Those wishing to alter normative Christology would begin by describing messianic sections of Isaiah, Jeremiah, and others along lines that would not culminate in the person of Jesus as described in the NT. In turn, the NT might be interpreted according to certain concepts found in the OT which spoke of messianic expectations in a temporal rather than a spiritual sense. Thus, when Jesus "fulfilled" the Law, he did not so much complete its prophecies as order the fulfilling of the Law's ritual requirements. Scripture might be conceived of as a historical document rather than as a spiritual revelation, and use of Jewish sources might result in particularly Jewish interpretation of many key phrases and words. Essentially, judaization of Scripture came down to interpreting part or all of the Bible in any fashion that might deny Christian, or support Jewish, understanding of God's Word. Beyond this generalization there was great vagueness, for in one case citing a Jewish source might constitute judaization even if the interpretation was fully orthodox. In another case all historical interpretation was suspect despite the fact that the gloss was fully Christian and not at all Jewish. For some any use of a Hebrew text constituted judaization, and for Luther even adhering to Jerome of the NT reflected judaization.

Another point of view through which to understand all of the above concerns is to speak of degrees of christianization rather than judaization. As examples, let us look at some of the thinkers we have dealt with thus far, for all, though accused of judaization, attempted to make contributions to Christianity. Paul Fagius made extensive use of rabbinic glosses to interpret Scripture and expressed inordinate interest in those Jewish rituals that might help elucidate Christian practice. Surely none would have denied Fagius's orthodoxy, for his use of Jewish sources, however extensive, was for orthodox Christian purposes and not Jewish ones. It was the Lord's Supper Fagius hoped to illuminate, not the Jewish rituals he recognized as similar. Similarly, Fagius's interest in Jewish anthropology led to a distortion of rabbinic opinion in favor of, and in order to support, Christian concepts of man and sin. Judaization should have entailed the perversion of Christian belief and practice to support Jewish ends, not the reverse, which is what we found in Fagius's writings. Fagius might have been condemned for christianizing Jewish sources but certainly not for judaizing.

Reuchlin sought a variety of things from Cabbalah, including a magical wonder-working word and a numerological code through which the OT might be understood. The wonder-working word was to perform miracles described in the NT and to support a divine sense of Jesus' person as incorporating the power of God, hardly a Jewish position in any sense. Reuchlin's numerology is charming; but if deemed successful, it must still be considered fully Christian since this method was employed to prove the truth of the Trinity, not Jewish monotheism.

Luther, Bucer, Capito, Pellican, and others discussed might be considered judaizers only by the intellectually inept and emotionally peculiar. Even Münster, the great popularizer of Elias Levita, publisher of rabbinica, and pioneer in Aramaic did little more than provide the materials others, such as the editors of the Geneva Bible and the King James Version, found so necessary.

Servetus might be considered a judaizer, but he used no sources unused by Bucer, Capito, or Pellican. The antitrinitarian positions he advanced were no more acceptable to his Jewish sources than the position he sought to use them against. After all is said and done, Servetus did accept a modalistic concept of the Godhead and hardly needed rabbinic opinion when he could and did use a host of ancient Christian sources that also rejected Athanasian trinitarianism. Servetus's Christology did not reduce Jesus to a mere man, in Jewish fashion, but stripped Him of His humanity in order to create a fully divine Son of God. Surely, one cannot argue that this position, too, like its opposite, is a judaization.

Erasmus maintained that simple use of rabbinic materials constituted judaization, indicating that method and not goals might be important. On this basis Thomas's use of Maimonides would be judaization and his basic acceptance of Aristotle even worse. Jerome too would be a judaizer, as any translator of the OT Hebrew must be if more than the original Hebrew text is consulted.

Perhaps the clearest indication of the nature of judaization comes from Jewish authorities rather than from Christian sources. Two Jewish controversialists have indicated their own contact with judaizing Christians. Writing in Italy in 1512, Rabbi Abraham Farissol composed the anti-Christian polemic *Magen Avraham* ("Shield of Abraham"), in which he described the beliefs of the judaizing Christians with whom he was in touch:

> One of the sages described their faith in the following manner . . . one should take heed to keep all the practices enjoined . . . in the Mosaic Law . . . while remaining faithful to the mystery and prefiguration that is alluded to or ordained in the new teaching of Jesus. . . . And he believed and affirmed that it was necessary to be circumcised and baptised, to wear a prayer shawl and phylacteries and observe all the practical precepts [of the Law] and at the same time to remember the Christian concept of God.[2]

Understandably, Farissol did not list the names of such Christians. George Williams, too, has recently written about strong radical-Jewish ties in Italy, some of which at least might have been Farissol's associates.[3] It is likely that Marranos were important in these judaizing circles and may have even constituted the totality of judaizers in Italy.[4] Given the early date of Farissol's work, the large number of Spanish Jews and Marranos in Italy, and the description of Jewish-Christian practice, it is difficult to believe Farissol could have written about any group other than Marranos.

The situation was somewhat different in Poland and Lithuania where the intellectual and religious climate was more amenable to all forms of radical religious sentiment including judaization. The weakness of centralist political institutions and the inability of the Church to exert the sort of political clout it possessed in western Europe made these areas an attractive location of settlement for many Christian sects as well as many Jews expelled from Germany during the 1480s and 1490s. Isaac Troki, author of the best anti-Christian polemic of the sixteenth century, *Hizzuk Emunah* ("Faith Strengthened"), noted, "In our generation many of their scholars called Ebionites and Unitarians believe in the unity of God and oppose belief in the trinity. . . . Marcin Czechowic, in his Book of Dialogues, in Part 2, writes in Polish and repudiates the belief in the trinity with strong proofs based on Scripture and reason."[5] In another location Troki noted, "The Christian scholar Simon Budny wrote that the divine law given to Israel by Moses at Horeb is pure and eternal and there is no other divine law besides it . . . and he substantiated this position with prophetic and rational proofs."[6] In the most telling citation of all, Troki wrote, "We likewise meet with gentile authorities who state that the Law of God given to Israel is eternal and perfect [and] that no succeeding Law has ever been given [and] that they are mistaken who assert that Moses gave the first and Jesus the second Law [and] that Jesus gave no new law but merely confirmed the commandments given through Moses. Thus in all these doctrinal points they are found to agree with us."[7]

The antitrinitarian tendency mentioned by Troki is not surprising considering the popularity of Servetus's writings in the east and their influence through some important indigenous leaders. Jacob Paleologus, a former Dominican monk and leader of the Arian sect, defended Servetus's writings and views.[8] His considerable volume of 1572, *De Discrimine Veteris et Novi Testamenti*, argued that the NT did not abrogate the authority of the OT. Marcin Czechowic, mentioned by Troki, was called the "Rabbi of Lublin" because of the strong OT ritualistic tendencies in his thinking.[9]

Yet other names are known to us including Francis David, Christian Francken, Walenty Krawiec, Marciej Vehe-Glirius, Daniel Bielinski, Simon Budny, and John Kratiowicz, scholars whose works and opinions reflected an acceptance of OT ritual on the basis of NT argument and/or strong preference for OT monotheism over Christian trinitarianism.[10] It is possible that in Poland and Lithuania where Jewish-Christian relations were often quite cordial, Jewish influence was a significant factor in the development of pro-Law, antitrinitarian sentiment. Then again, Poland

and Lithuania were something of a dumping ground for all of Europe's most radical thinkers, and such sentiments may only have found freer expression in the east.

There is another dimension to the accusation of judaization which may have been less intellectually cogent but was far more effective socially and politically: the use of judaization as a guilt-by-association slur. This accusation was predicated upon the strong tradition of medieval anti-Semitism and the Christian proclivity to blame all change on Jews, not only because both change and Jews were considered disagreeable but also because the belief prevailed that Jews were in league with the devil.[11] Another feature of this specific accusation of judaization was the idea that Jews somehow possessed near-miraculous powers and were engaged in a continual effort to destroy Christ's true church. Many important Catholic authorities sincerely believed that the many problems plaguing the Church *must have been* the responsibility of Jews.

After four hundred years the absurdity of these sentiments is self-evident, but in the sixteenth century such accusations were taken quite seriously. Even before Luther challenged papal authority, John Huss was condemned as a judaizer, much as other so-called trouble-makers had been so accused before him. When Huss was condemned at the Council of Constance, the curse against him specifically listed the Jews as the responsible party: "Woe unto thee accursed Judas since thou hast forsaken the counsel of peace and hast adhered to the counsel of the Jews, therefore do we remove from thee this cap of salvation."[12]

Luther too, it would appear, was considered a judaizer, and Josel of Rosheim, representative of German Jewry to the court of Charles V, reported that "we were severely taken to task for having taught the Lutherans their faith."[13] Hans von der Planitz, Elector Frederick's spokesman at the Council of Regency, reported to him that at the 1522 meeting of the Diet of Nürnberg, many Catholic princes and Church spokesmen were spreading the rumor that Luther accepted such Jewish ideas as Jesus' being born of Joseph's seed, Mary's not being a virgin, and her giving birth to many children.[14]

Luther, it seems, had been hearing similar reports from other sources, and in 1523 he wrote his response in the curious treatise *That Jesus Christ was Born a Jew*, in which he hoped to set the record straight concerning his feelings about Judaism. Luther opened this treatise in forthright fashion: "A new lie is being circulated. I am supposed to have preached and written that Mary, the mother of God, was not a virgin either before or after the birth of Christ, but that she conceived Christ through Joseph and had more children after that. Above and beyond this I am supposed to have preached a new heresy, namely, that Christ was of the seed of Abraham."[15] To clear himself of these charges, the first part of the treatise was devoted to his defense of orthodox and traditional positions on these issues. Perhaps trying to kill two birds with one stone, Luther also wrote with one eye toward that other renegade community, the Jews, with the hope that some might find the Reform movement less objectionable than Catholicism. Early in the treatise Luther answered the charge that Jesus was of Abraham's seed or lineage: "We should remember that we are but gentiles while the Jews are of the lineage of Christ. We are aliens and in-laws; they are blood relatives, cousins, and brother of our Lord."[16] Far from disavowing Jews, Luther believed he might diffuse this claim by pulling its teeth: "Accordingly, I beg my dear papists, should they be growing weary of denouncing me as a heretic, to seize the opportunity of denouncing me as a Jew."[17] Compounding his insult to Catholicism, Luther went on to congratulate the Jews for not having converted to that religion: "If I had been a Jew and had seen such dolts and blockheads govern and teach the Christian faith, I would sooner have become a hog than a Christian."[18] Indeed, going to a new extreme, Luther wrote, "Anyone wishing to be a good Christian would almost have had to become a Jew."[19] Though he would change his opinions rather severely in just a few years, Luther was willing in 1523 to accord Judaism a respectable position in terms of Scripture. Indeed, considering his views of the dichotomy of the Law and Gospel, one is almost shocked to read, "When the Jews then see that Judaism has much strong support in Scripture, and that Christianity has become a mere babble without reliance on Scripture, how can they possibly compose themselves and become right good Christians?"[20]

Luther was also the first Christian authority to discuss the gruesome treatment accorded Jews in Christian lands, and he noted, "They have dealt with Jews as if they were dogs rather than human beings; they have done little else than deride them and seize their property."[21] Luther closed the opening section of this remarkable work with two important points. First: "I hope that if one deals with the Jews in a kindly way and instructs them carefully from Holy Scriptures, many of them will become genuine Christians."[22] The second point was a first recognition of ethnic Jewish ties and their importance: "They will only be frightened further away from [Christianity] if their Judaism is so utterly rejected that nothing is allowed to remain and they are treated with arrogance and scorn."[23]

Most of the treatise dealt with scriptural passages Luther believed important for Jews to understand. There was little that had not been written by previous Christian authors concerning the coming of the messiah, God's rejection of the Jews, and other traditional arguments. Given his polemical nature and the polemical tone of much of this treatise, Luther's moderation is surprising but evidently quite genuine: "Let them first be suckled with milk by recognizing this man Jesus as the true messiah; after that they may drink wine and also learn that He is the true God. They have been led astray so long and so far . . . that one must deal gently with them and instruct them from Scripture; then some of them may come along."[24]

Perhaps the most important part of the treatise was Luther's discussion of the violence and brutality usually constituting Christian love of the Jews. He noted, "We only try to drive them by force, slandering them, accusing them of having Christian blood if they do not stink,"[25] and he warned, "So long as we treat them like dogs, how can we expect to work any good among them? Again, when we forbid them to labor and do business and have any human fellowship with us thereby forcing them into usury, how is that supposed to do them any good?" Less than half a century after most German Jews had been expelled from their homeland, thirty-one years after one quarter of a million Jews had been expelled from their ancient homeland in Spain, seven years after the first ghetto was created in Venice for Jews living in Italy from before the time of Christ and long before the Barbarians conquered the peninsula, Luther wrote, "We must receive them cordially and permit them to trade and work with us that they may have occasion and opportunity to associate with us, hear our Christian teaching and witness our Christian life."[26]

However well-intentioned Luther's motives, his treatise of 1523 caused much trouble for both the Lutheran movement and the Jewish people. It confirmed Catholic suspicions that the rebellious monk was under the influence of Jews and damned the reform movement in the eyes of many whose aversion to Jews may have been greater than their dislike of Rome. For their part, Jews were cautiously hopeful. Some rabbis were so shocked that they believed the end of the world was at hand or the coming of the messiah imminent. Others were convinced that the Catholic reaction against Jews would be so strong that the gains of Luther's friendship would be offset by a new round of persecution. In one treatise Luther had fulfilled three precepts that placed his Christian integrity in question. He and Protestantism were very OT oriented; he and Protestantism were fundamentally important to the revival of Hebrew studies; he and Protestantism exhibited a profound and unusual interest in Jews and their fate.

NOTES

1. Aegidius Hunnius, *Calvinus judizans* (Wittembergae, 1593); see also O. Kluge, "Die Hebräische Sprachwissenschaft . . ." *Zeitschrift für Geschichte der Juden in Deutschland*, 3:180 f; 4:100 f; and Calvin's letter to Guilaume Farel, *C.O.*, vol. 10, part 2, col. 340.

2. S. D. Löwinger, "Selections from the Magen Abraham of Abraham Farissol" (in Hebrew), *Hazofe le-Hochmat Yisrael* (Budapest, 1928), SII, pp. 277–97; and by the same author, "Recherches sur l'oeuvre Apologistique d'Abraham Farissol," *Revue des Etudes Juives*, 105 (1939):24; David Ruderman, "The Polemic of Abraham Farissol with Christianity in its Historical Context," unpublished doctoral dissertation for Hebrew Union College-Jewish Institute of Religion, New York, 1971.

3. George H. Williams, "The Two Social Strands in Italian Anabaptism, ca. 1526–1565," *The Social History of the Reformation*. ed. L. P. Buck, J. W. Zophy (Columbus, 1972), p. 161 f.

4. The same may have been true of Spain as well. See John E. Longhurst, *Luther's Ghost in Spain* (Lawrence, Kansas, 1969), p. 86; "One of the noteworthy things about the Illuminist movement is that many of those involved in it were conversos, or persons of Jewish ancestry."

5. Isaac Troki, *Hizzuk Emunah*, in Hebrew (Breslau, 1873), ed. D. Deutsch, chap. 10, p. 86. Concerning Marcin Czechowic, see Ben-Sasson, "The Reformation in Contemporary Jewish Eyes," pp. 300 ff. Concerning Troki's arguments, see my article "The Reformation and Jewish Anti-Christian Polemics," pp. 85–97.

6. Troki, p. 129; Concerning Budny, see S. Kot, "Szymon Budny: Der grösste Haretiker Litauens in 16 Jahrhundert," *Studien zur Älteren Geschichte Osteuropas*, 1 (Graz, 1956):63–118; also, E. M. Wilbur, *A History of Unitarianism* (Boston, 1949), pp. 349, 368–71.

7. Troki, chap. 19.

8. Concerning Paleologus, see Karl Landsteiner, "Jacobus Paleologus," in *XXIII Jahres Bericht über das K. K. Josefstadter* . . . (Wien, 1873); Antal Pirnat, "Jacobus Palpaeologus," *Studja nad Arianizmem pod redakcja Ludwicka Chmaj* (Warsaw, 1959), pp. 73 ff.

9. See Ben-Sasson above and Judah M. Rosenthal, "Marcin Czechowic and Jacob of Belzyce: Arian-Jewish Encounters in 16th-Century Poland," pp. 77–95; also, Alexander Brückner, *Roznowiercy polscy* (Warsaw, 1905), p. 263.

10. See S. Kot, *Polski stownik biograficzny* (Krakow, 1938).

11.   See, for instance, the excellent work by Joshua Trachtenberg, *The Devil and the Jews* (New Haven, 1943). See also the anti-Semitic-satanic motif in A. Falb, *Luther und die Juden* (Munich, 1921).

12.   M. Spinka, *John Hus at the Council of Constance* (New York and London, 1969), p. 230.

13.   "Journal de Joselmann," ed. J. Kracauer, *Revue des Etudes Juives*, vol. 16 (1882), no. 22; L. Feilchenfeld, *Rabbi Josel von Rosheim* (Strasbourg, 1898), suppl. 16, p. 183.

14.   See Luther, *LW*, vol. 45, (Philadelphia, 1962), ed. and intro. Walter I. Brandt; see p. 197 of introduction.

15.   *Ibid.*, p. 199. Since many of Luther's polemical works, including this treatise of 1523 and other works of 1538, 1542, and 1543 are extremely controversial and subject to misinterpretation and may portray Luther in a very unfavorable light, I have chosen to use this authorized Lutheran translation of the reformer's treatises concerning Jews rather than make a personal translation of the standard Weimarer Ausgabe. Concerning Luther's attitudes toward Jews, see R. Lewin, *Luthers Stellung zu den Juden* (Berlin, 1911), and a volume with the same title by C. B. Sucher (Munich, 1977).

16.   *LW*, p. 201.

17.   *Ibid.*

18.   *Ibid.*, p. 200.

19.   *Ibid.*

20.   *Ibid.*

21.   *Ibid.*

22.   *Ibid.*

23.   *Ibid.*

24.   *Ibid.*, p. 229.

25.   *Ibid.*

26.   *Ibid.*

Chapter Twelve

The Year 1538:
A Turning Point

Luther's enthusiasm for persecution as a Jew was short lived. It was clear that he had bitten off more than he could chew and that Luther would now have to disavow his enterprise of 1523 and reiterate his position regarding Jews and judaization. Moreover, Luther's hopes that kindness would result in significant Jewish conversion did not meet with tangible results. However unreasonable it may have been to anticipate Jewish conversion after centuries of mutual hatred, Luther seems to have believed Jews would convert.

Compounding matters were the disturbing reports Luther received of judaization in eastern Europe. In one location he noted, "In Moravia many Christians are circumcised and they are called by the name Sabbatarians."[1] In yet another, he again lamented, "I hear that in Moravia and Austria some judaizers urge [the observance] of Sabbath and circumcision . . . which is certainly a great danger."[2] In some places the fear gave way to anger: "I hope I shall never be so stupid as to be circumcised. I would rather cut off the left breast of my Catherine and of all women."[3] Before 1523 Luther heard reports that he too was a judaizer, and now he was hearing about Protestant judaizers. Had Luther credited these rumors with the same degree of authenticity he credited those about himself earlier, he might have let the matter die of its lack of merit. Had Luther not embraced Jews in 1523, he could have done this, but the rumors of judaization in the east in addition to his own words of just a few years earlier meant Luther had to disavow any connection with Jews and judaizers. In 1538 Luther wrote the treatise *Against the Sabbatarians* in an attempt to set the record straight for both Protestantism and his own integrity.

Luther wrote that he received news from Graf Wolfgang Schlick zu Falkenau concerning Sabbatarian Christians. In his *Table-talk* of the previous year Luther had indicated that he believed Jews responsible for such developments: "In Moravia they [Jews] have circumcised many Christians and call them by the new name of Sabbatarians. This is what happens in those regions from which preachers of the Gospel are expelled; these people are compelled to tolerate the Jews."[4] In his treatise of 1538 Luther again confused Jews with Sabbatarian Christians: "You [Count Schlick] informed me that the Jews are making inroads at various places throughout the country with their venom and their doctrines and that they have already induced some Christians to let themselves be circumcised and to believe that the messiah or Christ has not yet appeared, that the Law of the Jews must prevail forever, that it must be adopted by all Gentiles."[5] The peculiar quality of this work was that it was directed against Sabbatarian Christians yet was in actuality a polemical exercise against Jews, Jewish interpretation of Scripture, and Jewish religious concepts.

Among the different themes covered by Luther in this treatise were such issues as the applicability of the Law outside Israel and the question of whether Jews truly observe the true Law and the Ten Commandments. Many of these arguments could have been effective against Sabbatarian Christians as well as against Jews were it not for the overall tone of the work, which was clearly directed against Jews while the whole avoided more central issues of importance to Law-observing Christians. Luther did not once refer to the works-faith controversy described in the NT, nor did he deal with the Epistle of James. Indeed, even Matthew's recording of Jesus' statement that not the jotting of an *i* nor the crossing of a *t* should be changed was shrugged off as somehow irrelevant: "We have neither time nor space to discuss what our Lord Christ says here about fulfilling the Law. Moreover, the Jews could not understand this and we would be diverted from our subject."[6] And should the reader forget who the real subject of the treatise was, Luther reminded him often enough. In place after place Luther began his discussion with "But if the Jews claim . . . " or "But when the Jews bandy about . . . " and raised such irrelevant issues as whether or not Jews understood Hebrew.[7]

In most of the treatise Luther abandoned reasonable argument for outright polemic. Arguing that Jews are treated poorly by Christians because they had killed Christ, "because of which they are suffering such misery and exile,"[8] would have little impact upon Sabbatarian Christians. The same Luther who just a few years earlier had found such strong scriptural support for Judaism now wrote that if Jews could make even one valid point, "then I, old fool and miserable *goy* [derogatory term for Christian] that I am, will immediately have a stone knife made and become a Jew. And

I will not only circumcise that one member but also my nose and ears."[9] The end of the treatise expressed the same confusion about whom Luther was writing against: "I hope my dear friend, that you will have at least been supplied with enough material to defend yourself against the Sabbatarians and to preserve the purity of your Christian faith."[10] And yet a page later Luther blurted out, "If you are unable to convert the Jew, then consider that you are no better than all the prophets who were always slain and persecuted by this base people."

The most striking feature of this work was how much it differed from Luther's earlier treatise. Most of Luther's points in this second work were traditional Christian anti-Jewish arguments seemingly written with little awareness of the first work. It is difficult to understand how both treatises could have been written by the same person.

The year 1538 also witnessed Martin Bucer's Cassel Advice, the first Protestant plan for the treatment of Jews. This document, like Luther's treatise, was of fundamental importance in reflecting the future course of Protestant-Jewish relations. Protestant states were in need of guidelines for Jewish policy to complement the many other changes and alterations in previous policy brought by the Reformation. Most Catholic countries had expelled their Jewish populations, with only Italy retaining a large number of Jews. Even in Italian cities, however, the traditional freedom accorded Jews was increasingly giving way to a new pattern of restrictive laws governing residence and trade, which restrictions were collectively known under the term *ghetto*. This institution—wall, gates, guards, and all—was quickly taken up by other cities after Venice founded the first such institution in 1516.[11]

The circumstances surrounding Bucer's Cassel Advice were as follows.[12] From 1526 to 1537 Philip of Hesse undertook the reform of the Hessian church along Protestant lines of thought. Hoping to consolidate these reforms into some coherent pattern, Philip requested that Bucer systematize the efforts of the previous years into a constitution of ecclesiastical organization. At the same time, Philip also requested that Bucer address the issue of Jewish rights and privileges in Protestant Hesse.

Bucer was no doubt aware of Luther's feelings since the Saxon Reformer had been somewhat instrumental in the expulsion of Jews from Saxony in 1536. Moreover, Capito had written to Luther in 1537 requesting that Josel of Rosheim be supplied with a safe-conduct pass through Saxony. Luther had requested such passes from the elector in the past, but this time he noted, "Why should these rascals who injure people in body and property and who withdraw many Christians to their superstitions be given permission? . . . I'll write this Jew not to return."[13]

In formulating his own policies, Bucer could also rely upon the traditional relationship that had existed in Hesse for many centuries. This relationship was summed up in the document entitled "A Proposal for the Toleration of Jews," which was submitted to the Landgrave in November of 1538. It is generally assumed that this document was composed by Philip's lawyers in consultation with representatives of Hessian Jewry. Such consultation had been past policy, and the stipulations of this program also expressed the continuation of traditional Hessian Jewish policy. The seven proposals were characterized by moderation and toleration and were not dissimilar to charters granted Jews by other rulers. Only the last two articles dealt with religious matters. These required that Jews attend special preachings several times a year and that Jews refrain from discussing religious matters with Christians. Both stipulations were fairly universal throughout Europe wherever Jews resided. Two of the articles dealt with the relationship of the Jewish community to the Hessian government. Here too the proposals expressed traditional policy. Each Jew was responsible for a special Jewish head tax. Though no specific sum was stipulated, the text called for the "traditional amount," a sum usually arrived at after much bargaining and bribery. The second stipulation recognized the existence of a corporate Jewish community within the framework of the Hessian state. An independent Jewish court system directed by special supervisors was to oversee civil and criminal matters within the Jewish community. The legal procedure and the nature of punishment followed traditional Jewish law (i.e., Talmud), but the document did not specify who would appoint the special supervisors or the scope of their legal authority. No doubt such decisions would be made between representatives of the Jewish community and the Hessian state, though it is also possible that the role of special supervisor was exercised only on those occasions when the state wished to overturn a decision of the Jewish court. The extensive autonomy granted Jews was traditional in Hesse and elsewhere and reflected the corporate nature of medieval law.

Three economic stipulations define Jewish trading rights and privileges; here again tradition seems to have been the main motivation. Jews would have full trading rights only in small nonguild cities with no provision made for trade in larger guild cities. Usury would not be tolerated, although the lending of money at a "just" rate and in small amounts was permitted. These economic articles, like the political ones, attempted to provide a pragmatic pattern that was loose enough not only to permit the state to intervene whenever it wished to do so but also to permit Jews to organize their own affairs under the authority of the state.

Granting Jews extensive autonomy was not necessarily a positive thing, for it permitted the institutionalization of ghettos upon the foundation of this autonomy. It is also true, however, that this format enabled Jews to live according to their traditional religious codes with little interference from the state, the Church, or nobility. If this arrangement did not provide adequate provision for legal cases involving Jews and Christians, the trade stipulations tended to diminish such contact insofar as that was possible. Whatever its limitations, this was a moderate document reflecting the desire of the Hessian state and the Jewish community to live at peace with each other despite their obvious differences.

Bucer's Cassel Advice was a far different sort of document, for it approached Jewish rights from a Christian religious vantage point rather than from the perspective of tradition, Christian-Jewish neighborliness, or any other pragmatic base. Bucer presented five axiomatic principles through which the specifics of Christian-Jewish relations were to be formulated.[14] The first axiom was that there was but one true religion, and it was the responsibility of the magistrate to protect this religion. The second axiom was no less obvious to Bucer than the first: Jews were dishonest and considered it a religious obligation to cheat Christians. Third, Jews had been condemned by God; consequently, Christians were under no moral obligation to treat them fairly. Fourth, all economic activity between Jews and Christians was to be avoided. And last, all specific stipulations had to be in accordance with God's law, presumably determined by Bucer.

Because Bucer understood this document as religious rather than as civil in nature, religious stipulations came first, followed by his economic and trade regulations. Among the former, Jews were to take an oath "not to harm Christ and His religion." This was translated into meaning that Jews could not build any new synagogues or discuss religious matters with Christians. Bucer also believed that Jewish use of the Talmud for the regulation of internal affairs could harm Christ, and consequently, Jews would be permitted use of the Pentatuech and the Prophets but not the Talmud, which was forbidden. Last of the religious stipulations, Jewish attendance at special preachings was required.

In themselves most of these religious articles were similar enough to the program proposed by Philip's lawyers. Inability to use the Talmud, however, meant an end to Jewish legal autonomy since that legal code provided for the regulation of religious as well as economic and civil affairs. In this regard Bucer's proposals marked a stern departure from traditional Hessian policy.

Bucer's rejection of acceptable trade and economic ties between Jewish and non-Jewish residents represented a far more radical departure from traditional policy. Jews were to be excluded from all money lending, commerce, and industry. By statute, Jews were to be forced to fill positions defined as subordinate, wearisome, and ungainful, in which they were to be protected from competition. Among areas of employment open to Jews Bucer listed ditch digging, wood cutting, lime burning, chimney sweeping, sewer cleaning, and the carting of ash, waste, and other garbage. Other economic provisions called for an increased head tax, and Bucer ended the document with the statement that Jews should be expelled from Hesse but that the above regulations were acceptable since they were in accord with the Christian religion and morality.

The difference between Bucer's proposals and those submitted by Philip's lawyers is clear and needs no elaboration. It would appear that Philip thought more of the work done by his own staff, for he wrote to the Cassel Town Council strongly urging the rejection of Bucer's draft and predicated future Hessian Jewish policy upon the more moderate document. In arguing on behalf of his Jewish constituents, Philip pointed out that Jesus Christ was born a Jew and that Jews possessed many virtues. Moreover, he noted how the NT called for tolerance toward Jews. Bucer attempted to defend his rejected advice in both a letter to Philip and in a treatise of the following year, *Von den Juden*, essentially a more complete version of the Cassel Advice. While complimenting Philip on his generosity and good intentions, Bucer argued that government was responsible for fostering proper religion and subduing false religion. Moreover, Bucer argued, NT admonitions for tolerance applied to Jewish-Christians and not to Jews, certainly a curious argument considering the ethnic composition of the early church, apostles, disciples, and founder.[15]

Bucer did not explain how harsh economic regulations favored the proper religion, but in *Von den Juden* he elaborated upon a new justification for his Jewish policy. First, God always ordained that unbelievers should serve believers, but most important, the Jews were really Catholics in all but religious affiliation: "Nor should it surprise you that they [Jews] are more inclined towards the atrocities of the papists than towards our own pure doctrines and the pure ritual of our churches. For, except that the papists venerate icons and idols and set them up for worship while giving lip-service to Christ . . . the faith and religious practices of papists and Jews are really identical."[16]

The identification of Jews with Roman Catholicism by Bucer was as intellectually cogent as Catholic identification of Jews with Huss and Luther. In both cases Jews proved to be the only losers while providing an easy explanation for the difficulties of both religions. Of course, it was particularly important that Bucer clear the good name of the new Reformed church from the taint of Jewishness since he was one of that church's leading spokesmen. Also, a significant campaign had long advanced the idea that Bucer was born of Jewish parents.[17]

NOTES

1. Luther, *WA*, 50, 309.
2. *Ibid.*, 42, 306.
3. Leon Poliakov, *A History of Anti-Semitism* (New York, 1974), p. 223.
4. Luther, *LW*, 54:239, no. 3,597.
5. *Ibid.*, *Against the Sabbatarians*, 47:65.
6. *Ibid.*, p. 89.
7. *Ibid.*, pp. 83–84, 80–81.
8. *Ibid.*, p. 69.
9. *Ibid.*
10. *Ibid.*, p. 95.
11. For further discussion, see Roth, *History of the Jews in Venice.*
12. Concerning the Cassel Advice, the reader might consult the following: Hastings Eells, "Bucer's Plan for the Jews," *Church History*, 6 (1937):127–36; W. Koehler, *Hessische Kirchenverfassung im Zeitalter der Reformation* (Geissen, 1894), pp. 4–34; A. Glaser, *Geschichte der Juden in Strasbourg* (1894); M. Lenz, *Briefwechsel Landsgraf Philipp's des Grossmüthigen von Hesse mit Bucer* (Leipzig, 1880).
13. *LW* 54:239, no. 3,597.
14. The Advice was published the following year in Strasbourg under the title *Von den Juden*. Pages Ai-B deal with religious policy and pages B-Biii are concerned with social and economic regulation.
15. *Ibid.*, p. Ci–Ciii, and Lenz, pp. 59–60.
16. *Ibid.*, p. cii.
17. Nicolas Wurmser, dean of the chapter of St. Thomas in Strasbourg, wrote in his *Protocol*, "Audi aliud novum de Buzerio iudeo" and "Vicesima prima Buzerius

iudeus ex patre et matre christiana natus, conductus a crutariis et parochianis eccle-
siae S. Aureliae iniuta capitulo fecit primum sermonem." Citation taken from
Hobbs, "Introduction . . . Bucer." Hobbs cited the *Libellus Conclusionem Capi-
tuli Sancti Thomae* in J. Ficker and O. Winchelmann, *Handschriften proben des
sechzehnten Jahrhunderts* . . . (Strasbourg, 1905), II, f.47a.

Chapter Thirteen

Luther, Charles V, Jews, and Hebraists

Catholic and Protestant identification of Jews as one of the main culprits disturbing sixteenth-century Christendom conveniently served the interests of both in their conflict with each other. The greater Luther's fears of Jewish responsibility for Protestant judaization and dissension and the greater his paranoia about Jewish residency in Germany, the more Charles V attempted to ameliorate Jewish conditions in Germany and prevent expulsion of Jews from Protestant areas. It is clear that Charles V understood Protestant fears of Jews since he expressed many of the same sentiments, yet Jews might fit into his plan of irritating Protestants. Before dealing with Charles's political machinations, however, let us look at Luther's anti-Jewish views as they continued to develop during the 1540s.

Luther's thought shifted in two ways after writing against the Sabbatarians in 1538. His anti-Semitism deepened considerably, and he came to believe that Jews not only perverted Christianity and the world order but also his own health.[1] Luther increasingly allied the image of the Jew with that of the devil, and his works expressed an inability to distinguish among Jews, sectarians, Turks, and the devil. The second shift concerned the handmaidens of the Jews, the Christian-Hebraists. Since Jews were the essence of foul corruption, Christian-Hebraists were no less dangerous than Jews since both attempted to spread the same perverted approach to Scripture and religion. Luther's anti-Semitism consumed him so completely that by the time he died he believed that everything touching Jews became equally evil, including the beneficial Christian study of Hebrew. In an earlier chapter we have already had the opportunity to analyze the very strange form of Christian-Hebraica that developed in Wittenberg during Luther's declining years, an Hebraica devoid of any Jewish contact.

During the 1540s Luther wrote three anti-Semitic treatises and delivered numerous sermons against Jews, including the very last before his death.[2] *Concerning the Jews and Their Lies* was the longest of these trea-tises and will be dealt with in this chapter. The other two works, *The Last Words of David* and *Concerning the Ineffable Name*, are so vicious, so hate-filled, and so completely devoid of any concept of human decency that they are best left untreated, especially since they ramble and are also incoherent. Had these works confined themselves to attacking Jews, their study would be of marginal interest to us in this work and might best be dealt with in a volume concerned with anti-Semitism. Luther's opinions seriously af-fected Christian-Hebraica circles, however, for he dealt with the role of Jewish sources in these works. Moreover, if the separate issues of Christian-Hebraica, judaization, and anti-Semitism need be treated as interrelated themes, Luther himself must bear much of the responsibility for this confusion.

Even before composing these works of the 1540s, Luther expressed in-creasing displeasure with Christian use of Jewish sources. Consequently, when describing these treatises he added, "Oh the Hebraists, and I say this also of our own, judaize greatly. Hence in this book which I have written against the Jews, I have also had them in mind."[3] In yet another place Luther wrote in frustration, "Some Christian-Hebraists are more rabbini-cal than Christian."[4]

Axiomatic to all three works of this decade was Luther's belief in the evil desire of the Jews to convert Christians: "For the Jews would like to entice us Christians to their faith and they do this whenever they can."[5] Jews were able to accomplish this, according to Luther, by abusing the OT text and interpreting it to their liking: "The Jews tear apart the text wher-ever they can, solely for the purpose of spoiling the words of Scripture for us Christians."[6] In many places Luther subscribed to the idea that many a Jew secretly believed in the Christian religion, though "outwardly he may pre-tend he does not believe it."[7] Proper exegetical method, therefore, could not possibly include use of Jewish sources since those sources were composed only to fool Christians: "We do not give a fig for their crazy glosses which have spun out of their own heads. We have the clear text."[8] What followed, however, was a series of paradoxes that are difficult to understand. On the one hand we are told that Jewish grammarians "conjure up the Hebrew words before our eyes as though we were not conversant with the Chaldee text."[9] And we are similarly informed that Jewish use of Aramaic was used only to subvert the text, which ploy did not fool Luther since "Chaldee and Hebrew are closely related, indeed, they are almost identical."[10] Yet, in another location Luther informed us that Jews were able to confuse Christians "since we are not conversant with the Hebrew, they can vent their wrath on us secretly."[11]

Luther was able to cite several instances in which Jews perverted the text. In so doing he demonstrated his total inability to distinguish between Jewish exegetes and Christian-Hebraists. "They invent many lies about the name of God, the Tetragrammaton, saying that our Lord was able to define this name . . . and whoever is able to do that, they say, is also able to perform all sorts of miracles."[12] Clearly, Reuchlin was being included in the group of Jews against whom Luther inveighed. Indeed, only Christian-Hebraists argued about the magical powers in Christ's name since Jews did not accept that Christ or His name had any magical or religious significance. Continuing to confuse Reuchlin with his Jewish sources, Luther noted, "In addition they rob Jesus of the significance of His name which in Hebrew means savior or helper. . . . But the Jews, in their malice, call Him Jesu, which in Hebrew is neither a name or a word but three letters, like ciphers or numerical letters."[13] Not only was Luther incorrect concerning the meaning of Jesus' name—in itself not surprising considering the state of his Hebrew knowledge—but he also continued to confuse Jews and Christians: "It is as if, for example, I were to take the three numerical letters C, L, V, as ciphers for the word CLU. That is 155. In this manner they use the name Jesu signifying 316."[14] The result was, "Here we poor *goyim* [derogatory term for gentiles] are really despised and are mere ciphers compared to the holy, chosen, noble, and highly exalted people which is in possession of God's word."[15]

Luther's confusion of Jews and Christians, Jewish sources and their use by Christian-Hebraists, runs throughout these later works. In turn, these were but part of a larger group of troublemakers, and we are informed that "Jews, Turks, Papists and radicals abound everywhere."[16] It was also difficult for Luther to differentiate between Jews and Turks: "He [Mohammed] is a genuine Jew and the Jews are genuine saracens."[17] Similarly, Jews were confused with the devil: "Whenever you see a genuine Jew [i.e., not a Turk] you may with good conscience cross yourself and bluntly say: 'There goes the devil incarnate.' "[18] The result of obvious Jewish evil was that Jews controlled the entire universe and persecuted Christians: "They cannot treat us too harshly or commit enough sins against us for they are lords of the world and we are their servants, yes, their cattle."[19]

Luther was able to chart how Jewish persecution of Christians was carried out. First, "they steal and murder where they can and even teach their children to do likewise."[20] Second, "their Talmud and their rabbis record that it is no sin for a Jew to kill a Christian."[21] The result of all of this was as clear as the logic that conceived it: "The accursed *goyim* must be servants . . . to the Jews and let themselves be slaughtered like wretched cattle."[22] Throughout these treatises Luther reiterated how "they are our masters and we are their servants."[23]

Despite his disavowing such claims in 1523, Luther devoted considerable space to all the traditional lies concerning Jews: "The history books often accuse them of contaminating wells, of kidnapping and knifing children, as for example at Trent, Weissensee, etc. They of course, deny this."[24] And again contradicting his earlier statements of 1523 where he conceded Christian abuse of Jews, Luther now wrote, "We show them every kindness. They live among us, enjoy our shield and protection, they use our country and our highways, our markets and our streets."[25] And how did evil Jewry repay these kindnesses? "They remain our daily murderers and bloodthirsty foes in their hearts. Their prayers and curses furnish evidence of that, as do many stories which relate their torturing children and all sorts of crimes for which they have often been burned at the stake or banished."[26]

The last part of the treatise concentrated upon the actions Germans might take to protect themselves from being overwhelmed by Jews. In one location he wrote, "In my opinion the problem must be resolved thus: If we wish to wash our hands of the Jews' blasphemy and not share their guilt, we have to part company with them. They must be driven from our country."[27] And expressing a rare ecumenism, Luther wrote in another place, "Let us emulate the common sense of other nations such as France, Spain, Bohemia etc. [and] eject them forever from this country."[28]

In yet another location Luther devised a different seven-step proposal concerning possible treatment of Jews which did not include exiling Jews from their natural homeland. The proposals are as follows:

> First, to set fire to their synagogues or schools, and to bury and cover with dirt whatever will not burn. . . .
>
> Second, I advise that their houses be razed and destroyed. . . .
>
> Third, I advise that all their prayer books and Talmudic writings in which such idolatry, lies, cursing and blasphemy are taught, be taken from them.
>
> Fourth, I advise that their rabbis be forbidden to teach henceforth, on pain of loss of life and limb.
>
> Fifth, I advise that safe conduct for Jews on the highways be completely abolished.

Sixth, I advise that usury be prohibited to them . . . [for] they have no other means of earning a livelihood than usury.

Seventh, I recommend putting a flail, ax, hoe, spade, distaff or spindle into the hands of young strong Jews and Jewesses.[29]

Though these stipulations were very harsh, Luther presented what he believed was the best rationale possible: "This is to be done in honor of our Lord and of Christendom, so that God might see that we are Christians."[30] Luther also made another proposal for clearer Christian-Jewish relations, though he did not explain its relationship to the above: "So we are even at fault in not avenging all this innocent blood of our Lord and of all the Christians which they shed . . . and the blood of the children they have shed (which still shines forth from their eyes and their skin) we are at fault in not slaying them."[31] Clarifying even further why and how Jews and Christians were so very different and, conceivably, why the above measures were necessary, Luther again appealed to the Bible: "Scripture tells us of two seeds, the serpent's and the woman's. It says that these are enemies and that God and the devil are at variance with each other."[32]

Historians have cited many different factors to account for these extreme writings, though most biographers of Luther usually avoid mentioning them altogether. Certainly such factors as ill health in his declining years, dissension with sectarians and the German-Swiss, and a growing realization that Europe might soon be at war help explain some of the tensions contributing to these works. Mitigating factors of authorship do little, however, to lessen the impact of these treatises on Jews and Christian-Hebraists—in Luther's time or in the Germany of the twentieth century.[33]

During the years that German Protestants were becoming increasingly hostile to Jews, Charles V became increasingly receptive to Jewish needs. Curiously, Charles V's views changed in inverse ratio to those of Protestantism. At the age of fifteen Charles campaigned against Reuchlin, and through the 1520s his German policies were consistent with his policies in Spain.[34] Much as Luther's views changed, by 1530 Charles's attitudes made an abrupt aboutface.

At the Diet of Augsburg in 1530, Josel of Rosheim was requested to debate Luther's protégé, the Jewish convert Anton Margaritha, concerning the merits of both religions. The ostensible purpose of the debate was the determination of true religion so that blasphemy might be eliminated from the empire.[35] It is difficult to understand how and why Josel was declared the winner of the debate with Margaritha personally banished from Augsburg by Charles V. Whether Josel actually merited victory or whether Charles was making German Jewry a personal political concern at the expense of Protestantism, declaring Josel the winner of this confrontation was daring, controversial, and very anti-Protestant. Significantly, two years later Josel had an audience with Charles concerning the state of German Jewry, and at that time Charles accepted as binding in all Germany Frederick II's list of Jewish privileges of 1216 and Frederick I's list of 1182.[36] It is quite possible that Philip of Hesse called upon Bucer in 1538 to create an equivalent Protestant plan for the Jews because of Charles's actions of 1532. We have already noted that Philip rejected Bucer's advice and instead promulgated laws more in keeping with Imperial policy.

Even more indicative of Charles's changing attitude was his apparent response to Luther's alarmingly hostile anti-Semitic blasts of 1542–43, where that reformer called for the most severe measures against Jews. A year later, in 1544, Charles issued a new statement of Jewish privileges which surpassed his actions of 1532 and did much to ameliorate Jewish conditions throughout Imperial Germany.[37] Jews were granted full freedom of trade, and Charles even granted Jewish bankers the right to charge higher interest rates than those permitted Christian bankers. Closing of synagogues was forbidden as was interference with Jewish ritual and religious practice and observance. It was forbidden to spread false rumors regarding ritual murder, the desecration of the host, or other alleged Jewish practices. The expulsion of Jews was forbidden except with the direct approval of Charles himself. It is perhaps just coincidence, but Protestant expulsion of Jews during the late 1550s and 1560s occurred after Charles resigned as emperor in 1556 and even more so after his death three years later.

It is curious that Charles's German policies should differ so greatly from Imperial policies in Spain, but perhaps this single factor more than any other illustrates the poverty of anti-Semitism as the sole explanation for the treatment of Jews. It is likely that Charles's personal feelings about Jews were similar to Luther's and those of the overwhelming number of people in the sixteenth century. Given his early support of the Dominicans against Reuchlin and his approval of the Spanish Inquisition, Charles would not have become pro-Jewish in Germany were it not to his advantage. It is also reasonable to assume that Charles would have done little to hurt German Catholicism and to permit Jewish religious influence to exist if Catholic political leaders had indeed been concerned about judaizing, whether from Jews or Christian-Hebraists. It is reasonable to assume that Charles's pro-Jewish policies were a direct response to Protestant anti-

Semitism and represented an attempt to keep the "Jewish problem" alive in his enemies' lands. By extending the traditional view that Jews were *servi camerae*, Charles protected Jews in Germany at the same time that he aggravated his Protestant enemies and provided a pretext to interfere in the internal affairs of Protestant states.

Charles could use "Jewish policy" against his Protestant enemies *because* the latter came to see Jews and Hebraists as a fifth column bent upon subverting the new religion. This general fear of all religious irregularity was mirrored in Protestant fears of judaization, in its treatment of radicals (and the enormous fears associated with such persons), and in Protestant attitudes toward even minor dissension within its own ranks. Surely the Germans were not unique in this regard; both Calvin's anxiety over Jerome Bolsec and his grave concern regarding Michael Servetus are well known. But when we consider the Luther-Zwingli tangle at the Colloquy of Marburg and the continuing eucharistic battle dividing Swiss and German Protestants for the remainder of the century, it is apparent that even normal intellectual and dogmatic differences constituted a dangerous and serious threat to all concerned. Similarly, the Philipist and Osiandrian controversies in the Lutheran camp and the events surrounding the Council of Dort in the Calvinist camp amply illustrate that total religious conformity was a basic demand even after Protestantism had sunk deep roots and was no longer in danger of internal subversion.

The possibility that earlier in the sixteenth-century Jews were the scapegoats needed by Christian-Hebraists to defend their own orthodoxy from charges of judaization becomes all the more apparent when so important a humanist and scholar as Johannes Agricola stooped to attack another Hebraist, Osiander, in self-serving fashion. Agricola attempted to clear his own name of the accusation being "too Jewish" when he wrote, with neither proof nor justification, that "a cat never ceases to be a mouser. He [Osiander] was a Jew, is a Jew, and will remain a Jew" and concluded by stating that Osiander was obviously under satanic influence.[38]

The pressure on other Hebraists was equally great, and we have already noted Münster's defense of Jewish sources as well as Forster's attack upon them. But even before Münster finally wrote a forthright justification of Jewish scholarship, both he and Fagius attempted to placate potential critics by authoring some very unusual missionary treatises that were allegedly directed toward the Jewish community but which in fact were written for Christian readership.

NOTES

1. See Luther, *LW*, 50:290, letter dated 2 Jan. 1546 from Luther to his wife.
2. See *LW*, 50:303, note 19.
3. Martin Luther, *Tischreden in der Matheischen Sammlung*, ed. E. Kroker (Leipzig, 1903), p. 588; See also R. Lewin, *Luther's Stellung zu den Juden*, p. 60.
4. Martin Luther, *Briefwechsel*, ed. E. L. Enders (Leipzig, 1884), 15:274, no. 3,342.
5. *LW, On the Jews and Their Lies*, 47:149.
6. *Ibid.*, p. 244.
7. *Ibid.*, p. 205.
8. *Ibid.*, p. 196.
9. *Ibid.*, p. 186.
10. *Ibid.*, p. 180.
11. *Ibid.*, p. 257.
12. *Ibid.*, p. 256.
13. *Ibid.*, pp. 256–57.
14. *Ibid.*, p. 257.
15. *Ibid.*, pp. 164–65.
16. *Ibid.*, p. 175.
17. *Ibid.*, p. 212.
18. *Ibid.*, p. 214.
19. *Ibid.*, p. 227.
20. *Ibid.*, p. 227.
21. *Ibid.*, p. 226.
22. *Ibid.*, pp. 215–16.
23. *Ibid.*, p. 266.
24. *Ibid.*, pp. 217 and 264–65.
25. *Ibid.*, p. 217.
26. *Ibid.*, p. 288.
27. *Ibid.*, pp. 287–88.
28. *Ibid.*, p. 272.
29. *Ibid.*, pp. 268–70
30. *Ibid.*
31. *Ibid.*, p. 267.
32. *Ibid.*, p. 217.
33. It is noteworthy that these several treatises by Luther were reprinted by the German government on the occasion of Kristalnacht on 9 Nov. of 1938 when Jewish homes, shops, and synagogues all over Germany were destroyed. Much of Luther's program had been codified earlier in the Nuremberg Laws of 1935. Indeed, the Kristalnacht pogram of 1938 was carried out in commemoration of Luther's birthday. See Malcolm Hay, *Thy Brother's Blood* (New York, 1975), p. 169. Other works dealing with the relationship between Luther and twentieth-century anti-Semitic

thought include G. van Norden, *Kirche in den Krise* (Dusseldorf, 1963); W. Jannach, *Deutsche Kirchendocumente* (Zürich, 1946); F. Zipfel, *Kirchenkampf in Deutschland, 1933–1945* (Berlin, 1965); O. Diehn, *Bibliographie zur Geschichte des Kirchenkampfes 1933–1945* (Göttingen, 1958); W. Niemoller, *Kampf und zeugnis der Bekennenden Kirche* (Bielefeld, 1948); *idem, Die Evangelische Kirche in Dritten Riech* (Bielefeld, 1956).

34.   See Charles's letters to the papacy of 16 May 1515 and 24 Sept. 1519 in Geiger, *Johannes Reuchlin*, p. 311; F. Fita, "Los Judaizantes españioles . . . " *Boletin de la Real Academia de la Historia* (Madrid), 33:330 f.

35.   See Selma Stern, *Josel of Rosheim* (Stuttgart, 1959), Eng. trans. Gertrude Hirschler (Philadelphia, 1965); S. Baron, 13:426–27, note 21.

36.   Stern, *Josel*, p. 107 f (German), p. 129 f (English); S. Baron, 13:276 and 453–54, note 80.

37.   The *Privilegiorum Universorum Teutoniae nationis Hebraeorum Confirmatio*, dated Spire, 3 April 1544, has been reprinted in A. Engel, "Die Ausweisung der Juden," *Jahrbuch der Gesselschaft für Geschichte der Juden in der Cecheslovakischen Republic*, 2:69; See also, S. Baron, 13:454, note 82.

38.   See J. Agricola's *Grüntlich anzergung was die theologen des chufürstenthums der Mark zur Brandenburgk von den christlichen Evangelischen lehre halten, lehren und bekunen* (Frankfort om Oder, 1552).

Chapter Fourteen

The Jewish Mission

Missionary activity is far more complex than is usually assumed.[1] On its face, missionary activity simply attempts to spread the good news of the Gospel much in the manner of the apostles and Jesus Himself. More complex factors include the psychological need of some to defend their possibly insecurely held beliefs from imagined enemies of truth. Even more removed from Jesus' good news are the economic and political factors motivating centralist governments and industrial cliques that profess to be carrying the white man's burden of spreading civilization and Christian truth. Such multiple layers of motivation are common knowledge and require no elucidation here.

The Jewish mission was peculiar on many levels. At once the oldest, since it dated from the time of Jesus' preaching and the activity of the apostles, it was also the most meager. Traditional medieval missionary policy toward Jews consisted of preachings several times a year, financial reward to voluntary converts, the forced baptism of Jewish children, and outright persecution of those rejecting conversion. In all instances more was lost than accomplished through such measures. The sermons were more often harangues against Jews than presentations of Christian belief, and forced baptism created deep distrust of such Christian love that would take children from parents.[2] Conversion to avoid persecution was often short lived, and the quality of belief of those converting for financial gain was predictable. One need only note that Johannes Pfefferkorn converted for the financial reward offered by the Dominicans in Cologne.

In retrospect it may seem odd how often Christians hoped and prayed for the successful conversion of Jews yet did almost nothing positive to bring about this goal. Indeed, much Christian activity had the effect of alienating potential Jewish converts from the Church. Until Münster translated the Gospel of Matthew and the Epistle to the Hebrews into Hebrew, not a single page of NT Scripture existed in that language. Despite the great number of anti-Jewish polemics written from the earliest of Christian times, I have yet to find a single work written to explain Christian belief to Jews which did not devote far more space to anti-Semitic themes. The most prevalent argument of all, however, was that Jews' inability to understand the NT and their ignorance of church teaching was the result of Jewish failure rather than the result of Christian failure.

Blaming Jews for not converting to Christianity is truly to put the cart before the horse, and it is safe to assume that had Jesus felt similarly, His sermons to the people of Judea and Samaria would have been filled with hate-filled frustration rather than with patient love. Similarly, Paul would have written many fewer letters had he believed it was the prior responsibility of the Ephesians, Thessalonians, and Galatians to understand the Gospel. Yet the reverse approach was taken in missionary writings to Jews. These works began and ended by blaming Jews for Jesus' execution at Roman hands, for their ignorance of the NT, for provoking Christian persecution, for plagues, poor harvests, the Turkish menace, and a myriad of other vexing problems.

If haranguing Jews for their ignorance of Christianity was not conducive to Jewish conversion, neither was the unwillingness of Christianity to accept those Jews who had converted. The Spanish Inquisition was horrified by the intensity of Jewish religious belief but even more horrified by Jewish conversion to Christianity. Luther, Erasmus, Capito, Bucer, and so many others speak only of "Jewish-converts," never of "Christians of Jewish origin." Indeed, Luther most often thought of such converts as Jews and not as Christians. To this day the stigma of Jewish origins is often so great that many converts create their own churches rather than join existing institutions. Indeed, the existence of such organizations as Jews for Jesus is adequate testimony to Christian unwillingness to accept Jewish converts. The large number of Jews returning to the Jewish fold after conversion to Christianity is even greater testimony to this historic problem.

The rise of Christian-Hebraica in the fifteenth and sixteenth centuries and the Reformation provided a rare opportunity to create the sort of climate that might accommodate Jewish conversion. The unprecedented split in Christian ranks made possible an appreciation of many points of traditional Jewish resistance to Catholicism. Indeed, we have noted how Luther complimented Jews for their not converting to the Church of Rome. The significant number of Christians increasingly familiar with Jewish thought and scholarship enabled the creation of special works directed at Jews. If conceptual advice was needed, the large number of Christian-Hebraists of Jewish origin we have encountered could certainly have provided insight and advice. Moreover, Christian-Hebraists could write in Hebrew, using the Jewish religious idiom for emphasis and clarity. In short, just as Reformation Christian-Hebraica expressed the greatest borrowing *from* Judaism, it also represented the greatest possibility for Christian expression *to* Jews. In actuality, the results of the Reformation Jewish mission were most peculiar, and the reality did not meet the potential. Some of the missionary writings were innovative and interesting, but most give strong indications that they were written for Christian audiences or at least with an eye toward potentially critical Christian readers.

The Christian-Hebraist was in the paradoxical position of being both the best and the worst spokesman for the Jewish mission. Compounding such objective problems that Jews were not pagans and were not ignorant of God or His written word was the peculiar position of the Christian devotees of Judaica. For these scholars, Judaism provided Christianity with tools, resources, and even wisdom for the elucidation of Christian concepts, thereby making the Hebraist mission both obvious and complicated; obvious because they understood Judaism better than anyone else, but more complicated because the Hebraists found themselves in the position of attempting to convert the very people upon whose tools, resources, and wisdom they had come to rely. Moreover, this reliance, as we have seen, did not elicit respect so often as it invited the accusation of judaizing. Consequently, the Hebraist was often forced to justify his studies by disavowing Judaism and disclaiming any respect for Jewish scholarship. Such disclaimers took the form of missionary works and polemical treatises, and although such writings might pacify potentially critical Christians, they could only confuse Jewish readers and nullify possible missionary effectiveness.

The result of these many demands and difficulties was a missionary movement at once effective and ineffective, at once open toward Jews yet hostile toward them. Much as Luther was friendly toward Jews in 1523 only to become vehemently hostile and vicious just a few years later, Münster and Fagius reflected the same ambivalence and inconsistency.

There was yet an additional function to these missionary treatises and polemics. Such writings enabled Hebraists to publish much information they might otherwise have been unable to present without encouraging scalding criticism. As we shall see, both Münster and Fagius were able to publish some of their most controversial works by including in the same publication and binding a missionary work or polemic that had a potential to make the entire endeavor more acceptable. Let us now turn to these writings to understand better the many different uses and functions of the Jewish mission and the complicated profile of this literary form.

In 1537 Sebastian Münster produced the most significant missionary treatise written to Jews ever produced by a Christian scholar. It was entitled *Torat ha-Mashiach: The Gospel According to Matthew in Hebrew with a Latin Version and Notes by Sebastian Münster.*[3] First published in 1537, it was reprinted again in 1557 and in 1582 with the latter editions also presenting a Hebrew and Latin translation of the Epistle to the Hebrews. Additionally, the first 120 pages consisted of a missionary treatise entitled "This is the Holy Christian Faith," which attempted to express Christian belief in an idiom accommodated to Jewish readers since this work too was written in Hebrew and Latin. Despite many centuries of attempts to convert Jews to Christianity, it is a curious fact that before Münster's work of 1537 not even a single page of NT Scripture had ever been translated into Hebrew. Similarly, no author before Münster ever produced a missionary treatise written in Hebrew using a Jewish religious idiom to explain Christianity. Moreover, Münster's gloss on the Gospel of Matthew was filled with rabbinic commentary and other materials from Jewish literature to demonstrate a point Paul Fagius would champion in the next decade: the continuity of Pharisaic and apostolic thought. On the face of it, this work would appear to be the complete missionary treatise consisting of explanation, text, and gloss. For purposes of clarity, the two sections of this volume will be analyzed separately.

"This is the Holy Christian Faith" was actually only the first of a four-part, 120-page work attempting to explain Christian belief. The second part was an explanation of Judaism with the two remaining sections devoted to rebuttal of Jewish and Christian charges, rejections, and erroneous claims. Taken together, all four sections attempted to demonstrate the continuity from Judaism to Christianity.

The first part, "This is the Holy Christian Faith," presented a very rudimentary understanding of Christianity. Considering the limited space allocated to this section, some thirty-five pages, Münster's primary efforts centered on explaining such central doctrines as the Trinity, the nature of the messiah, the virgin birth, and the new covenant. Other fundamental issues such as scriptural method, Christian tradition, and the relationship of the OT and the NT were left untreated or were dealt with in later sections. If Münster did not succeed in presenting the totality of Christian concept, those issues treated were explained intelligently with many arguments specifically worded and explained with Jewish readership in mind.

Münster opened this section with a statement affirming the unity of Scripture and its complete expression of the divine will. Although such explanations may seem rather obvious, Münster may have understood that the "unity of Scripture" was often used by Jewish polemicists as a starting point for their attack upon Christianity. From the Jewish viewpoint, this concept excluded NT writings from the corpus of canonized writings on the premise that the quality of its language, apocalyptic concept, emphasis upon a negative anthropology, as well as Paul's concept of the Law, were incompatible with OT ritual, concept, and observance. Consequently, much as Christians might understand this term to express the compatibility of the OT and NT spirit, Jesus' fulfilling of the Law, or the single messianic thread running through both sets of writings, Jews used this same concept of the unity of Scripture to separate and exclude the Christian set of works. Another reason why it was important for Münster to have begun with this point was that it enabled him to lay a basis for a continuing theme of the smooth transition of the Pharisaic into the apostolic religious concept. Despite his inclusion of Paul's Epistle to the Hebrews in later editions of this work, Münster did not accept the notion of the dichotomy of Law and Gospel.

Next, Münster directed the reader to that other concept of unity dividing Jews and Christians, the unity of the Godhead. Rather than build upon the premise that Cabbalistic emanationism was essentially similar to trinitarian personification, a route taken by Pico, Reuchlin, and others, Münster accommodated his Jewish reader in a different manner and wrote, "And we completely believe that God, blessed be His name, is one and that there is no second to compare to Him, to place beside Him. He is my God, my living redeemer, my stronghold in times of distress, my bliss the day I call. To Him I entrust my spirit, always and at all hours and in every moment. He was, is, and will be, in glorious eternity and He is a living, awesome, and holy God."[4] Perhaps the most striking feature of this almost personal description of the Christian Godhead was its Jewish origin. Translating a part of a Jewish prayer from the daily morning liturgy, Münster used this stridently monotheistic prayer to describe the Trinity even though it was originally composed to preclude Christian pluralism from acceptable Jewish monotheism. As in the case of the "unity of Scripture," Münster purposely used a Jewish idiom to express a Christian truth. Considering his missionary objective, one can speculate that Münster no doubt felt it wise to demonstrate his familiarity with Jewish prayer and ritual and its applicability to Christian purpose. Utilizing the same logic and perhaps anticipating Jewish objections, Münster additionally cited Maimonides to the effect that only when the soul is still with God before birth can the mystery of the Godhead be understood.

Moving from the realm of Jewish prayer to Christian definition of the individual persons of the Godhead and their relationship, Münster wrote, "And similarly, we believe there are three names [*nomina*] and attributes [*middoth*] in God and that nothing differentiates [*divisio*] between them for He is one reality [*essentia*], one power [*potentia*] and one substance [*substantia*]."[5] Using an almost Servetan formula stressing names and attributes rather than divine persons, Münster attempted to demonstrate why the Trinity was not polytheistic. He explained that the Trinity was not like the three sons Reuben, Simon, and Levi who shared a common father (i.e., origin) but were separate expressions with individual personalities. Similarly, Münster explained that the persons of the Trinity were not analogous to the relationship of the sun and moon in which the latter reflected the light of the former and in which each was created separately. On the other hand, the Trinity might be compared to the unity of ice, water, and steam, each of which manifested one characteristic or nature of a greater totality. Using his knowledge of Hebrew, Münster took another approach and argued that such synonyms as *enosh, adam,* and *eesh* for "man," or *adamah, eretz,* and *tayvail* for "earth" were essentially the same as the different expressions of Father, Son, and Holy Spirit for God. Despite the different names, "all are one God, of one essence, and of one substance."[6] Bolstering this linguistic-synonymic approach to the Godhead, Münster noted that Scripture "spoke in the singular as 'the Lord' and yet at times in the plural, as in '*Elohim*' " with other names also used as "Adonai," "Eloha," "Shaddai," and others. The one drawback of this argument was the possibility that Münster's description was more in keeping with economic trinitarianism or some form of Servetan modalism than with orthodox trinitarianism. Still, this was an intelligent and successful approach to a difficult Christian concept for readers who were predisposed to reject the argument in its entirety. In using such concepts as divine names or attributes, Münster did no more than use traditional Jewish terminology, even though the rabbis used these ideas somewhat differently.

Münster's difficulties increased when he attempted to discuss the person of Jesus Christ. No less troubling to the Jewish mind than the hypothetical plurality within the Godhead was the notion of a plurality of natures in the second person of the Godhead. Even Jews accepting diverse divine personae would be hard pressed to accept the idea that each synonym could possess a different physical nature. Moreover, Münster could not utilize the same method used earlier. No Jewish prayers advanced the view that the second person could incorporate a physical nature, and the OT tended toward the total removal of God from matter. Arguments from the NT would be dismissed by Jews, and traditional theological formulations would leave them cold. Still other difficulties would entail explaining how God could/would be born of a virgin. No less difficult would be an acceptable explanation for Jesus' vicarious atonement for mankind since the very essence of rabbinic anthropology moved in the very opposite direction.

Münster began this discussion in a traditional fashion: "Isaiah said about the birth of the messiah, 'Behold the *almah* is pregnant and has conceived and His name is called Emanuel.'"[7] Realizing the long controversy surrounding the term *almah*, which Christians claimed meant "virgin" and Jewish scholars, "young woman," Münster cited other OT examples of this expression used in relation to the matriarch Rebecca and Moses' sister Miriam. This was not an effective argument, however, since "young woman" was the Jewish translation in these instances, too. Moreover, if *almah* always meant "virgin," as Christian authorities claimed, the result was that both Miriam and Rebecca shared in Mary's miracle, without having given birth to God, however. Seeking firmer support, Münster argued that both the Targum of Jonathan and many Cabbalistic writings assumed the messiah would be born of a virgin, but he did not pursue the point.

Moving to the relationship Jesus enjoyed with God though he was corporeal, Münster observed, "It is within the scope of God's ability to be born as a body within a body and to give it a soul and spirit . . . without annihilating His own substance because of it since He has no need for a special form."[8] Yet, despite Jesus' apparent removal from God He "was like a candle from which several other candles are lit and from which no detraction is apparent."[9] If Münster did not attempt to argue through a Jewish idiom in defense of this concept, it may have been recognition on his part that none existed. He faced a similar difficulty when explaining Jesus' relationship with the Law and His vicarious atonement for mankind's sins. Münster wrote that after "revealing to Israel how He was the messiah through miracles that were not performed by any prophet, He demonstrated to the whole world how He came to redeem man from sin as it

was written in Isaiah."[10] He was able to redeem man because "Christ fulfilled the old Law with His own circumcision and He gave a new covenant
sealed with a new rite of baptism applicable for males and females and all
people."[11] In this manner, Jesus did not do away with the Law, but converted its essence into a new form that expressed its truth while also expressing the new truth of the new covenant. Countering the Jewish argument
that the rituals of the Law were not observed by Christians, though God
commanded their continued observance as the Epistle of James indicated,
Münster argued on several levels to advance his Christian argument. On
the one hand, "in His life He taught man and lifted from them the severity
of the Law . . . from which men could not liberate themselves."[12] On the
other hand, Jesus did not do away with all aspects of the Law for "all commandments that are natural and consonant with reason, He placed upon us
. . . such as [laws regarding] theft, murder, etc."[13] Consequently, Christianity was less a negation of Judaism than a widening and spreading of its
message to those previously excluded. Again citing baptism as an example,
Münster wrote, "Just as the messiah eased the unnatural severity of the
Law, He eased circumcision and created equality between males and
females."[14]

The last point Münster made regarding the rituals of the Law centered
upon the word *l'olam*, the term used by the OT to describe the duration of
these observances. Along with Luther and most traditional exegesis, Münster claimed that *l'olam* did not mean, as Jews claimed, "forever" or, literally, "for the duration of the world," since *olam* meant nothing more than
"world." Rather, he argued that this expression meant only "until the fifty-
year jubilee" or "for the duration of the Temple."[15] These were unfortunate arguments, as Münster himself realized, since the Christian meaning
was not consonant with Hebrew linguistics, and although in other places
he indicated his displeasure with this view, he may have presented it here
since it was a traditional argument against Judaism. Perhaps in attempting
to bolster this view, Münster also noted that "in the wilderness of Sinai the
Hebrews practiced none of these rituals,"[16] though it is also true that they
were not yet demanded of Israel by God.

The last remaining issue raised by Münster was Jewish abdication of
the status of "true Israel" in Jews' rejection of Jesus as messiah. The section
was concluded with a translation of the Nicaean creed.[17]

Despite apparent gaps, lacks, weaknesses, and an error or two, Münster's brief description of Christian belief was written in Hebrew with many

arguments accommodated to Jewish readers. Many of his points were intelligently argued and made use of applicable Jewish views toward a Christian end. In all these senses, this was a good missionary effort.

The second section of Münster's book of faith was devoted to a description of the Jewish religion. To an extent this section was the acid test of missionary Christian-Hebraica, for it would demonstrate whether an understanding of Judaism would enable Christians to make greater numbers of Jewish converts more easily as Christian-Hebraists had indicated for several decades. The Jewish reader would be able to gauge the extent of Münster's comprehension of Judaism from this section, an often overlooked, but essential, aspect of successful missionary writing. There was important Christian significance in this section, too, since Münster's covenantal views were predicated upon the notion that the old Law gave way to the new and that consequently many Christian arguments might conceivably receive their best definition from a Jewish base. In terms of intellectual systematics then, from both a missionary and a Christian perspective, this section would demonstrate the proper reading of Judaism which would lead directly from the old religion into the new.

Much as Münster used Jewish prayers to begin his description of Christianity to win the confidence of his reader, many aspects of Jewish belief were presented through the wording of Jewish liturgy. The prayer descriptions used by Münster in this section covered a wide range of issues and points of belief. The first concept advanced was that of Jewish monotheism: "We Jews believe in the living God of the universe who ruled before any being was created. Indeed, His existence transcends time. He is one and there is no singularity like His. He is unknowable, His singularity is unique and endless. He has no semblance and He is bodiless. He preceded all that was and He is the first though He Himself had no beginning."[18] Though many descriptions of Jewish monotheism might have served Münster's purposes, this citation demonstrated why Jews viewed Christianity as a blasphemy. The notion that Jesus as God could be corporeal represented the essence of idol worship for Jews since it implied that God could be finite, whether as a man or as a statue. The essence of Christian heresy was not so much that it taught that a man was God but that God could be a man.

The next theme described by Münster was the place of the Law in Jewish thought. First, because God was its author, the Law was perfect, for "He gave a true Law to His nation through Moses, His faithful prophet, and He will never amend or change His eternal Law." Second, because He is perfect and His perfect Law eternal, the people of Israel, too, acquired a special status in receiving the Law: "He chose us and selected us with His commandments and ordered us to study His Law. He chose us of all the peoples and we are *His* people, the descendants of *His* covenant . . . whom *He* called Israel." Far from accepting Christian notions of negative anthropology because of Original Sin, Judaism saw in the Law the perfect expression of human potential: "Blessed is he that adheres to His commandments and Law and follows His word in his heart." Indeed, human capability toward both good and evil was the basis of true righteousness, and "He accounts to mankind righteousness according to their activities [deeds] and will repay the wicked with equal evil." Although sin and temptation were true factors in human behavior, God remained a loving father to all those that sought him because He is a merciful and clement God, He is our father, king, creator, redeemer . . . giving free grace to each and every generation . . . opening His hand in repentance to receive transgressors and sinners." Most important, since He is perfect, loving, and the Law a code of behavior expressing these qualities, man needs no intermediaries between himself and God: "For He is first and last, and aside from Him we have no king, no redeemer, and no savior."

The remaining two-thirds of this section of some twenty-two pages dealt with two other issues: the nature of the messiah and the world in the messianic age. Münster's opening statement represented the overwhelming consensus of Jewish thought: "When the messiah comes he will return us to our land."[19] In another location Münster added, "[The messiah] will be a man and not God and it is not within his power to give life."[20] And a few pages later: "The messiah has not yet come but will come. He will be a complete man from a mother and a father and from their union, from the seed of King David, and filled with the spirit of God."[21] One striking feature characterizes these and other statements by Münster concerning the messiah. Rather than present Jewish views about the role the messiah would play in the universe at large and his relationship to God, topics constituting the full Jewish understanding of messianism, Münster primarily presented opinions that demonstrated how the Jewish messiah would differ from Christian understanding of Jesus. Essentially, Münster was less concerned with how the messiah fit into the rest of Jewish thought than in the fact that many Jewish scholars believed "that his son would rule after him and his son thereafter, each father granting his title to his son."

Münster was also curious about differences of opinion concerning the location of the messiah before he appears on earth as God's messenger.

Münster noted that some rabbis postulated that "the messiah will remain in Rome until it is destroyed as we find with Moses our rabbi, may he rest in peace, who was found in the Pharaoh's house until he left there. . . . He did not redeem Israel immediately after being born but waited several years according to God's will."[22] Other rabbis claimed, "He was born long ago on the day the second temple was destroyed and remains in the Garden of Eden," whereas "others maintain the messiah will not be born until close to the time of his appearance at the end of the world, when he comes to redeem us from exile."

All authorities were in agreement that in the messianic age there would be an in-gathering of exiles from all parts of the world "even though we have been exiled to every corner."[23] Moreover, there will be an end to all war between nations, and even nature itself will undergo transformation in that neither plants nor animals will harm man or each other. More significant still, the messianic age will mark a worldwide turning to the true God whose proper worship will again be instituted in Jerusalem "because the land of Israel is in the center of the world and Jerusalem is in the center of Israel and the temple is in the center of Jerusalem and the Holy Chamber is in the center of the temple and the Ark [of the Covenant] is in the center of the Chamber and this is called the Seat of Glory."[24]

Though one cannot fault Münster for misrepresenting the Jewish religion, there is a certain sense of balance and proportion missing in these pages. Briefly stated, Münster devoted two-thirds of the space allocated to Judaism to a discussion of messianic and apocalyptic concerns whereas only a third of the space described normative Jewish thought. Moreover, normative Jewish thought was described in terms of its ancient legacy rather than through its medieval rabbinic understanding. Despite the fact that the sixteenth century was a high-water point in Jewish messianic thought, such speculation never approached the importance of talmudic concerns or other aspects of the medieval Jewish legacy.[25] Although it is possible that Münster felt the constraint of limited space, there are other explanations as well.

It is conceivable that Münster's presentation of Judaism was a Christian reordering of Jewish priorities. Rather than place Judaism within its own conceptual framework and development, Münster highlighted those aspects and areas of greatest interest to Christians, the messianic, and glossed over those issues of least interest, including the rabbinic and talmudic. This understanding of Judaism may or may not have been intentional, but it certainly followed Münster's own interest in Jewish literature which concentrated upon ancient scriptural matters to the detriment of medieval and talmudic concerns. In turn, this approach to Judaism, consisting largely of an ancient rather than a medieval legacy, represented a very traditional bias that conceived of Judaism as an ancient religion with little change in the period after Christ's coming. In essence, from the point of this orientation, Münster viewed Judaism as a Christless Christianity. Thus the importance of the Law is emphasized but not the mature flower of the Law, the Pharisaic revolution that produced the Talmud. For much as Christianity did away with the Temple and its sacrificial worship, Pharisaic Judaism did away with the same ancient basis in favor of a modified rabbinic-talmudic religion of ethics and community-based religious practices.

Another explanation that does not preclude the above is that it hardly made sense for Münster to describe a Judaism that was post-Jesus Talmud-oriented since that religion could not possibly find its culmination and expression in Christianity. Moreover, stressing the rabbinic aspects of talmudic Judaism would make the conversion of Jews to Christianity that much more difficult, for in this light Christianity stands as an alternate religion to Judaism and not its fulfillment.

Yet a third reason to account for Münster's reading of Judaism might have been the desire to present that religion as somehow "incomplete" since its messianic basis had not been fulfilled. In stressing the messianic aspect of Jewish thought, Münster was also necessarily emphasizing the inability of the Pharisaic Jewish religion to complete itself. Recognition of the rabbinic-talmudic orientation of contemporary Judaism would have vitiated this understanding of Judaism as a failed religion.

A fourth factor that must be considered was Münster's own orientation that understood the second covenant as built upon the shoulders of the first covenant. In this light, the Jewish premise was extremely important for a proper understanding of the Christian development. Thus, Münster's presentation of Judaism, no less than his presentation of Christianity, was an intelligent and carefully guided orientation to religious history and development important to both Jews seeking to convert as well as sixteenth-century Christians searching for the roots of their faith in a nostalgic and past-oriented age.

The second half of Münster's treatise dealt with his perceptions of traditional Jewish objections to Christianity and an attempt to answer them. At the very outset of this section entitled "Some Answers to the Vanities and Errors of the Jews," Münster wrote, "And here is the difference between the

Christians and the Jews concerning the issue of the trinity and the messiah in the trinity. The lying Jews state that we believe in three Gods because we accept a plurality in authority."[26] The next few pages consisted of answering traditional Jewish arguments, including the inequality of the Father and the Son, according to a sequential basis, their distinction at the time of Christ's assumption of flesh when the Father had none, and yet other arguments. Most of these objections appear to have been taken from David Kimchi's commentary on the Psalms—parts of which were collected into his *Answers to Christians*—which so influenced Michael Servetus. After stating, "That which the Father does, thinks, understands, and desires, the Son and Spirit similarly do, think, understand, and desire,"[27] Münster shifted to more comfortable and possibly more effective linguistic arguments: "Elohim is one but not singular . . . and if He is not singular but one, we correctly say that He is triune but not three."

Concerning the division of Father and Son during Christ's tenure on earth, Münster wrote, "And if you say 'Who ruled the world when God died and was buried?' I answer . . . He did not die in His divine aspect because He is God . . . but only the singular aspect of His humanity died." And to explain further how one element could die when the other did not, he continued, "Much as when a person dies, the body dies but the soul does not. Similarly, the Son of God died; that human aspect united with the divine, but not God."[28]

Münster also attempted to answer objections regarding the two natures constituting Christ's being. Essentially, Jewish objections surrounded what they saw as an opportunistic approach to Christ's strengths and weaknesses. He could perform miracles but cursed the fig tree when it bore no fruit. He could raise the dead but could not avoid death. He defied death in His Resurrection but required food and nourishment while alive. He was God in power and yet man in His wrestling with the devil. He could walk on the water but could not carry the cross without great exertion. Münster's answers surrounded conventional formulae of Christ's two natures, at once stressing that "in this one aspect each nature itself was separate" to account for Christ's human behavior, yet also emphasizing that "body and soul came together in on personality much as a soul gives life to the body" to explain Jesus' divine powers. Münster also attempted to differentiate between the divine power possessed by Moses and Elijah and that expressed by Jesus: "If you say that divinity was with Moses and the other holy prophets since His spirit filled them and they did great miracles and signs and knew the future through God, I respond that this is in error because this divinity was not joined in one person as in the messiah . . . because He was man and God in one person." Considering the complicated nature of these views and perhaps Münster's own recognition that his answers merely raised the same Jewish objections yet again, one notes his frustration: "If you Jews would understand this secret you would not have such contempt for us and our teachings as if we held a wrong faith." In yet other places in this third section Münster again appealed to faith and the Holy Spirit as the only true sources of understanding: "We have shown you many sentences demonstrating the secret of the divine triune but he who does not believe cannot understand."[29] In another location Münster wrote, "If you say 'I do not understand,' the answer is that you do not believe and therefore you do not understand."

Münster was far more effective using arguments tailored for his Jewish audience than utilizing Christian formulae more likely to be rejected if only because their wording reflected an alien religious development. In such an effort, Münster wrote, "According to our faith the messiah already came where you say He will yet come. I will prove our position—that He came—on the basis of your Talmud."[30] He noted, "It is written in the treatise *Olam Zootah* that there are 3558 years from the creation of the world to the destruction of the second Temple. And 2442 years from that destruction until the end of the world, altogether 6000 years [and] since it is written in the treatise on Idolatry that the Law was given for only 2000 years and before the Law was given 2000 years had already passed, the world will exist for 2000 under the authority of the messiah." Münster also tried to support his position on the basis of other Jewish sources. He cited Rabbi Joshua ben Levi's view that the messiah would come in the age of the second Temple, and Maimonides' position "that it should not occur to you that in the days of the messiah anything from the normal workings of the world from the time of the six days of creation will change or become different."[31] Consequently, if all the prophecies have not yet been fulfilled, Jewish sources, too, conceded that the first coming of the messiah would not initiate a messianic age.

Going on the offensive, Münster also tried to discredit traditional rabbinic positions regarding the messiah and rabbinic authority in general: "One says the messiah will not come until there is one completely just generation [while another says] only in a time of total impiety. One says redemption will come with Israel's repentance. One says the messiah was born during the second temple and another says he won't be born until he is due to come. One says that in the days of the messiah sacrifices of atonement will be made while another says only sacrifices of thanksgiving."[32] Münster's conclusion was, "Do not listen to your rabbis and their limited teachings."[33] or "It is important to know that your rabbis do not interpret in truth."[34] Münster mentioned the advent of the false messiah, Asher Lammlein, who in 1502 claimed he would lead all Jews back to the Holy Land: "For how did that repentance of 1502 help you, when all Jews in their habitations and places in exile . . . young and old, infants and women, repented as never before and nothing was revealed to you."[35] The result was that "you Jews [too] see and understand that your rabbis are confused and wrong."[36]

It is difficult to assess the actual impact of Münster's argument though it is reasonable that Jewish readers would be more easily influenced by his Jewish sources than by his NT citations. Indeed, use of such sources in this context as well as creating special arguments was the unique ability of Christian-Hebraists, and Münster certainly exploited his abilities to the full. It is true that use of an adversary's sources sometimes caused anger, too. In his treatise against the Sabbatarians in 1538, Luther wrote that Jews could not make use of NT arguments in their anti-Christian polemics because they did not otherwise accept the validity of these writings.[37] Luther referred to Jewish controversialists who exploited the tension between Paul and James regarding good works, certainly a sensitive point for a Protestant reformer debating the merits of Catholic rite and ritual. Nonetheless, Münster did make use of Kimchi and other sources in an exegetical setting, and this may account for both his familiarity with some of their polemical views and the absence of contempt on his part as well. Münster did not abuse his Jewish sources, and if he pointed to what he believed was their error in thinking, he demonstrated no ill will or scorn. All together, Münster did his job well, demonstrating more tact and inventiveness than is usual in this sort of literature. Indeed, perhaps because this treatise was so well written thus far, the fourth section stands out in bold relief.

The last section of this treatise is puzzling and confusing. Entitled "Errors, Fabrications, and Vain Opinions Against Christians," this section was to deal with Jewish claims against the Christian society in which European Jewry found itself. In actuality Münster ended this missionary endeavor with a six-page section outlining those factors keeping Jews from converting to Christianity. Among others, Münster listed the following as primary factors.

> 1. Jews refer to converts as "destroyed ones," indicating that such Jews
>   have no place in the world to come and are considered deceased.

2. Jews consider converts sectarians and heretics and refuse to marry them.
3. Jews will not eat or drink with Christians or consume any food prepared for them by Christians.
4. Jews do not wear Christian clothing.
5. Jews take usury because they love money more than God.[38]

It is very difficult indeed to understand why Münster would end a treatise written to Jews with such nonsense. Surely if Jews wore different clothes, perhaps a yellow star, such was required by civic statute in most locations. Jews were forbidden to eat with Christians for the same reason that Christians were forbidden to make use of Jewish physicians: There was widespread fear of Jewish poisoning. And condemning Jews for involvement in usury without an equal condemnation of a society that permitted Jews no other economic participation in society was more than absurd. Of course, Münster did not endorse the Spanish Inquisition or charge Jews with the blood-libel or the poisoning of wells, yet the effect was much the same for the Jews whom Münster would have liked to convert.

It is not difficult to clarify why Münster wrote the last section of this missionary work since the author himself clearly noted that the last two sections of the work were directed toward Christians and not toward Jews at all. Each of the rebuttal sections possessed its own one-page Latin introduction without Hebrew translation. The first such introduction was entitled "A Censure of the Faith and Errors of the Jews," in which Münster hoped "to describe the monstrous opinions and most crass errors of the Jews which conflict with true Scripture interpretation and authority regarding the messiah and His age."[39] This motivation is easily enough understood, but then the author continued, "I wanted here briefly in both the Latin and Hebrew languages to respond to these blind and obstinate people so that Christians can frankly elude their false arguments and opinions." In short, Münster joined the battle against judaization. The introduction to the fourth section was even more clearly directed toward the Christian reader. Entitled "Sebastian Münster to the Pious Reader," the author argued that since the earliest days of the Church, Jews had persecuted true Christians.[40] Moreover, this persecution continued in the form of erroneous opinions regarding religion and Scripture. Münster spoke of Jewish false interpretation as "depraved and corrupted," the usual epithets, and maintained that such views were held in order to hurt Christian truth.

In themselves, such charges and accusations were fairly routine and usual and as such they need not be taken seriously. But their inclusion in a missionary work, at least an alleged missionary work, must raise the possibility that the entire treatise, like these short introductions, was actually written for Christians and not for a Jewish readership. At the very least, these Latin introductions must demonstrate that Münster wrote this work with at least one eye carefully trained on a potentially critical Christian readership. If there is a small indication that he was concerned with potential judaization in this work written in 1537, Münster did not act on these fears during the next decade or more when he published huge quantities of rabbinica and Jewish exegesis. Moreover, we have already read his defense of Christian-Hebraica written in 1546 wherein he defended not only his Christian colleagues but also the sources and the Jewish tradition itself. Similarly, during these very years Münster's collaboration with Elias Levita reached the point where the former gave up writing his own grammars and simply collated material written by Levita. Then again, perhaps his very defense of Levita and his strident use of Jewish materials necessitated the disclaimers found in this missionary work. Perhaps this confusion can be cleared up somewhat by looking into the remainder of the work, Münster's annotations to his translation of the Gospel of Matthew.

The annotations placed at the end of each chapter of the Hebrew and Latin translation are both polemical and informative. Most of the arguments against Jewish objections were fairly traditional and covered many of those points of NT Scripture Jews found impossible to understand or accept. Consequently, the first issues raised by Münster have to do with Christ's lineage and Mary's virginity. Jews have traditionally argued that it is impossible to trace Jesus' relationship to the tribe of Judah and David's family through Joseph since he was not His father. Scripture, however, says nothing about Mary's family.[41] Similarly, the term *almah*, the female version of the expression *elem*, which means simply a "young man," does not mean a "virgin."[42] Münster's answers were fairly routine. Joseph's lineage was presented because that was the scriptural idiom even though Mary, too, was of Judah, and *almah* meant "virgin." Neither argument was terribly effective since their acceptability depended upon a prior orientation and acceptance of the Christian message. Other traditional arguments were equally ineffective. The verse "The scepter shall not pass from Judah until Shiloh" received attention, with Münster taking the traditional position that Shiloh was Jesus and that Jewish sovereignty came to an end with the Jews' rejection of Jesus as messiah. Thus when Matthew mentioned Herod, Münster wished to comment upon this point. Countering Christian claims, Jews pointed out that sovereignty had been lost several centuries before Jesus and that in any event, Herod was not Jewish and he possessed no sovereignty. Unlike Luther, who ignorantly maintained that Herod was Jewish, Münster conceded, "This Herod was a foreigner . . . therefore the Jews before Christ did not have a king from the tribe of Judah . . . but they had *m'chochakim* [i.e., "lawmakers"] that is officers or intermediaries who governed the tribe of Judah."[43] One could debate whether local mayors and other similarly local positions constituted sovereignty, but here again a prior commitment and understanding of Christianity would determine the position accepted.

Other points discussed by Münster related to Christ's person, His mission, and His unique relationship with the Father. Since Jews rejected all three positions, a variety of arguments were presented by Münster along with an equal number of answers. He noted that some Jewish authorities asked what miracles Christ performed that had not been previously discharged by Elijah, Hanoch, or other OT miracle makers. Münster noted that "Christ did all things according to His own authority and according to His own command,"[44] whereas Elijah and others acted only on God's power. This in turn raised other problems. Why did Jesus take on flesh and not appear in some more divine fashion if he was unlike other men, especially since his followers would exhibit difficulty in understanding his human divinity. Münster answered, "He covered Himself [with flesh] in order to give us an example of modesty and not demand honor from mankind other than for His works and miracles which He performed and which give evidence of His nature. He covered Himself because His actions demonstrated His divinity."[45] This answer was thoroughly consistent with Christian teaching and thoroughly incomprehensible from a Jewish standpoint that saw little divine modesty or human divinity in the OT. Moreover, Jewish systematics had little need for a divine intermediary between man and God and consequently were not receptive to the basic idea itself. For Jews, Christian apologists shifted from Jesus' humanity to His divinity and back again too easily for the entire framework to be acceptable. Münster presented many of the questions asked by Jewish polemicists, such as why Jesus did not know that Judas would betray Him and, if His mission was to die for mankind, why did He ask of the Father, "Why have you betrayed me?" at the time of His death. Similarly, why did Jesus not know the time of His return at the end of the world? Why was Jesus both man and God in some senses but fully human in others? On what basis did Jesus determine whether to react as a man or as a God?

Münster presented traditional answers to all these questions. "It is not written that the Son did not know the time of the last days but only that the Father knew."[46] Similarly, Jesus' prediction that He would be betrayed indicated that he knew who would betray Him and He did not feel betrayed at His death but that "He prayed at His crucifixion for His enemies, to show that He came for the salvation of all and that He was not bereft of divinity."[47] Such arguments can prove effective only with those already accepting the truth of the Gospel while for Jews all these traditional responses were evasions for the actual wording of the text.

Jewish polemicists read the NT with the same literal method utilized in interpreting the OT text. Consequently, when Jesus was referred to as the Prince of Peace, Jews questioned the accuracy of this designation. Two points in particular troubled Jews: Jesus' own words and the condition of the world during his lifetime. On the one hand, Jesus Himself said that He came with the sword; on the other, His sword notwithstanding, there was no peace during His lifetime or thereafter. Münster wrote as follows regarding these issues: "The messiah did not come to give peace to the world, that is, external peace, but spiritual peace. And as for bringing the sword . . . this refers to non-believers who hate Christians and their peaceful ways."[48] It is possible that Jewish critics would have had less difficulty with the bringing of spiritual peace had the sword not been quite so literal. In any event, the Jewish query and Münster's answer indicate that much of the disagreement characterizing Jewish-Christian interpretation of the OT was similarly reflected in their reading of the NT. It is reasonable to assume that were Jews to accept the validity of the NT, their method of reading that work would still distinguish them from traditional Christians.

The Jewish criticism that Christians interpreted the NT too loosely, using different methods at different times to deliver different types of interpretations, found expression throughout Münster's Matthew. When Jesus claimed that He came to fulfill the Law and not to destroy it, Jews have interpreted this statement as an affirmation of the "Jewish Jesus" who still accepted the continuing importance of good works, sacrifices, and other prescribed rituals. In defense of this position, Jewish controversialists often pointed to the large number of times when Jesus sent the person cured of some malady or disease to the Temple in Jerusalem to issue thanks to God with a sacrifice. Aware of these positions, Münster gave very traditional and straightforward responses. Jesus fulfilled the prophecies of the Law if not the letter-perfect ritual requirements of that code.[49] Consequently, the question of whether or not Jesus did fulfill the Law depended upon how the expression "fulfill"' was understood. "Ritualistic" Jews would have seen this as compliance with observance and practice whereas more "spiritual" Christians would have explained this term in light of a tradition of prophecy of the messiah. Yet, Münster also argued that Jesus could prepare food on the sabbath because sacrifices were made to God on that day in the Temple.[50] Since Jesus was "the true temple of God," He was justified in his activity on the sabbath day despite the fact that on the very same page Münster argued against Temple practice and demonstrated its lack of religious validity. This argument concerning the fulfilling of the Law was essentially plagued by the same problem that affected the interpretation of Jesus as the Prince of Peace. In both instances Münster departed from what Jews would have understood as the literal, plain, and objective rendering of the text in favor of an allegorical or typological argument whose truth was axiomatic rather than demonstrated. Consequently, however fine Münster's explanations of the Christian position and however accurately he presented Jewish objections to Christian arguments, the differences between the two positions were in no way bridged by this treatise.

The problems involved with assessing the value of a religious polemic or missionary treatise are largely subjective in nature. The most convincing of arguments from the author's point of view may seem incoherent to the reader of a different religion. Consequently, it is extremely difficult to determine whether Münster's efforts can be called successful. He demonstrated great honesty and openness in grappling with Jewish objections and rejections, and much as he presented the Jewish position with admirable accuracy, Münster responded to these with a consistently traditional Christian approach. If Münster expressed some occasional exasperation, this is understandable; he was rarely defensive or quarrelsome. Münster accepted the honesty, if not the validity, of the Jewish position, and he responded with the best consensus-held Christian answer available to him.

It is apparent that only a Christian-Hebraist could have composed a work of this sort. The translation into Hebrew itself was both conceptually and technically difficult. Reading, understanding, and appreciating Jewish criticism of the NT and traditional Christian concepts were also demanding and difficult but no more so than attempting to respond to these positions with serious argument.

There is one difference between the arguments presented in the Matthew gloss and those advanced earlier in the missionary treatise bound along with it. Many of the arguments advanced by Münster in "This is the Holy Christian Faith" were carefully constructed for Jewish readers whereas virtually none of the arguments made in the gloss leave the same, albeit subjective, impression. All of Münster's responses in his gloss were so conventional and so very traditional that they were bound to have greater meaning for Christian than for Jewish readers. Indeed, it is impossible to escape the very definite impression that Münster wrote with at least one eye, and perhaps both eyes, on Christian readers and not on Jewish ones. Not only were all Jewish objections presented in Latin as well as in Hebrew but quite often the Latin version presented information not contained in the Hebrew equivalent. This is even more true of Münster's responses where again it was the Latin version that was favored with greater elucidation. Moreover, many of Münster's textual annotations make no sense at all unless they were prepared for a Christian audience.

In point of fact, most of Münster's gloss did not deal with Jewish objections but was filled with a variety of information valuable to the general reader. His notes are filled with such geographic information as the location of the Sea of Galilee and other areas mentioned in the text.[51] Similarly, the value of the drachma and other monies received extraordinary discussion.[52] If such information would be of little value to Jews or for missionary purposes, it might be of great interest to Münster's Christian students or other scholars.

Were this work primarily directed at Jews, it would not have been necessary for Münster to explain to them the ritual observance of such holidays as Purim and Chanukah or to describe at great length other feasts and fasts.[53] Many of these observances, perhaps the majority, were of rabbinic origin and had no textual basis in either the NT or the OT. When elaborating upon the ritual observance of the autumnal OT holiday of Succoth, to whom was Münster explaining the use of such ritual objects used by all Jews as the palm branch and the citron?[54] It was similarly unnecessary for Münster to explain to Jews how on the fourteenth day of the month of Nisan Jews searched their homes for unleavened bread before commencing the Passover celebration.[55] Even more unnecessary in a missionary treatise for Jews were Münster's explicit elaborations and descriptions of the ritual use of phylacteries and prayer shawls by the Jewish people since such objects were used by all Jewish males six days a week from the age of thirteen years.[56] Indeed, throughout the Latin presentation of Jewish views, Münster's annotations continually mention "our opinion" and "us" when referring to Christians and Christianity, and "they" and "their opinion" when referring to Jews.[57] In one location, when noting Jewish criticism of Roman Catholic laws of celibacy, Münster stated, "See how the Jews confuse us and use our own sword to pierce us through."[58] Yet other long presentations dealt with such issues as Josephus's description of the Temple and a very long piece covering several pages elaborating upon the process of conversion to Judaism.[59] More than anything else it is difficult to understand why long discussions of Jewish practice would lead to Jewish conversion to Christianity. Indeed, it is possible that such descriptions might have had a retarding effect rather than a beneficial one. On the other hand, much of this information might have been of interest to Christian students of Scripture seeking to discover apostolic roots in the NT and to learn what the first Christians saw about themselves, and possibly accepted, as normal religious observance.

In an earlier analysis of the fourth section of the missionary treatise attached to the Matthew text, we noted Münster's accusations against Jews and his explanations of why they did not convert to Christianity. At that time it was difficult to understand why Münster would use such arguments in an attempt to convert Jews to Christianity. The gloss on the Matthew text does not help explain those earlier charges and accusations, but it does complement them with accusations of indulgence in lewdness, hitherto unknown in Münster's work, as well as veiled threats alluding to possible Christian punishment of Jews.[60]

This is a very peculiar work, and it is impossible to account for its creation simply as a missionary treatise. Were it possible to write for both Jews and Christians, it would be far easier to understand the conflicting elements constituting this volume. Unfortunately, the separate demands of each religious community cannot find a single format of expression, and consequently it may be necessary to understand this not as one work but as two separate entities. The first part, "This is the Holy Christian Faith," was clearly written for a Jewish audience, but the second part may well have been written for Christian students of Scripture rather than for Jews. Whomever it was written for, however, there can be little doubt that its popularity lay in the Christian rather than the Jewish community since it went through three large printings—there simply were not enough Jews in Europe to account for such sales figures. It is possible that Münster's Matthew was actually an ethnographic study of the NT with the inclusion of Jewish objections to Christian claims as part of the overall information Münster wished to convey to the Christian reader. Although all scholars sought to explain the "Hebraisms" of the NT and many did appeal to Jewish sources to elucidate upon the Jewish background to the apostolic age, a cultural discussion of the Gospel of Matthew was both daring and possibly unacceptable in conservative circles. Perhaps the best way to present such a radical work to a Christian audience was in conjunction with a missionary treatise and as part of a missionary endeavor. Lest he be criticized, Münster might have pointed out that the primary intention of the work was to cultivate a Jewish audience and that he could not be responsible for Christian use of this volume. Moreover, there could be no accusing Sebastian Münster of judaization, for clearly he was able to counter Jewish polemicists and did in fact do so. Indeed, few could claim to have done so much to counter judaization, for who else had taken the bull by the horns and grappled with the Jew so convincingly? If indeed this work was written to counter judaization, surely it was written for a Christian audience and not a Jewish one. We must also bear in mind that Sebastian Münster gave up the study of Hebraica in his later years to devote himself to what soon would become his most significant contribution, his cosmologies and geographical studies.[61] The most outstanding feature of these later works was their interest in the mores and folkways of the many different peoples of the different locations he described. Quite possibly, Münster's Matthew was a first indication of his anthropological interests, here focused on the Jewish people. Of course it would be enormously helpful if some additional work existed which also demonstrated an intense interest in Jewish thought, folkways, mores, and even superstitions. Fortunately such a volume exists and that too was described by its author as a missionary endeavor.

Münster's alleged missionary treatise of 1539 entitled *Mashiach* ("Messiah") expressed a very different attitude toward Jews than the previous work of 1537.[62] Whereas the earlier work was written to answer wise Jews like Kimchi, Ibn Ezra, and Rashi, the later treatise encouraged the view that Jews were not quite human and were terribly strange, as anyone rejecting Christ must have appeared in the sixteenth century. Unlike the Matthew or its missionary preface, the 1539 volume was published in separate Hebrew and Latin editions, and with very good reason as we shall see. Equally noteworthy and curious was the total lack of hard Christian content. The one-page introduction stated that salvation came through Christ, but no other attempt was made to present even rudimentary points of Christian belief. Indeed throughout this dialogue between a Christian and a Jew the former was primarily passive, content to inquire about Jewish messianic expectation and apocalyptic speculation. The Jew described the human nature of the anticipated messiah, the coming battle of Gog and Magog, and the future condition of the world after the coming of the messiah.

When the Jew presented differing and often conflicting rabbinic opinions concerning the messiah's imminence, Münster highlighted these conflicts but without conveying viciousness or nastiness. When the Christian participant asked how long Jews would wait for the messiah and the Jew answered that they would wait forever, there was neither constructive nor critical response. Indeed, little the Jew said ruffled the Christian participant or elicited any response at all. Münster had the Jew poke holes in many Christian arguments without any attempt to rework or redefine orthodox positions. Considering that Münster wrote both sections of this dialogue, one finds the lack of hard Christian content and the flow of conversation often difficult to understand. Inconsistency is expressed in yet other ways, for the first half the treatise is rather inane whereas the conversation in the second half is far more cogent and intelligent. For all these reasons and others that will be soon apparent, it is likely that Münster was both uncomfortable and unskilled in the role of missionary/polemicist.

Münster's confusion was evident from the very first pages. Before any conversation began, when the Christian first saw his adversary walking along the street but was not sure whether he was Jewish or not, the Christian addressed the Jew in Hebrew, assuming that only a Jew would have been able to respond. The Christian wondered, "Is that man who comes to meet me a Jew? Truly his face and form show him to be a man."[63] Yet a moment later the Christian noted, "For you Jews have a peculiar color of face, different from the form and figure of other men . . . for you are black and ugly and not white as are other men." Having stipulated that Jews were racially different, Münster's protagonist then explained that Jews were also biologically different, for they did not menstruate, but this was only the beginning. The Jew responded to such comments by asking why Christian men lusted so after Jewish women if indeed Jews were so ugly. The Christian responded that this was unfortunately so, that "your women are indeed more beautiful than your men" and then added "but you seduce them most corruptly."[64] In less-than-convincing fashion, Münster had the Jew elaborate upon just how much Jews abused their women and why: "We adorn them with excellent apparel that they may find favor in your eyes and through them we obtain what we want that it may be well with us by reason of them and that we may live among you gentiles for their sakes."

Within the first three pages Münster made clear that Jews were black, not quite human, and whoremongers. Lest one assume that only some Jews were this immoral, Münster had the Jew volunteer that Jews had always been this way even to the time of Abraham the patriarch: "As it is written

[Genesis 12:16] 'And they treated Abraham well for Sarah's sake because she was a woman of comely countenance.' " Not content with the conversation thus far, the Christian respondent noted that Abraham and his progeny acted so disgracefully "because you are no longer God's inheritance and beloved people but rather you are an abomination in His eyes and a stink in His nostrils."[65] Münster's chronology may have been a bit imaginative, but the point expressed Christian sentiment. Considering how very foul the Jew was and how much his people were outside the pale of decency, Münster's protagonist responded to all this with the obvious: "I am ashamed to talk to you in public in the sight of those who pass." He then added, "Go and I will follow you," but was quick to add, "I have not entered the house of any Jew for a long time."[66]

Although it is altogether possible that Münster actually believed that Jews were of a separate, biologically and morally inferior species of humanity, it is reasonable that these opening pages were written for the edification of critical Christian readers who held suspect anyone with a knowledge of Hebrew and detested those who would use that language for legitimate Christian ends. Yet presenting the Jew as so deficient a being also helped explain the greatest anomaly of all: Jewish rejection of Jesus. Surely only the strangest of beings could have denied so obvious a truth, Münster may have reasoned, for following this racial description he turned to a discussion of the peculiarities of Jewish belief.

Again aping common views of the Jew, Münster's discussion of the Jewish religion began with the alleged Jewish belief in ghosts. Münster had the Jew explain that by drawing a white circle on a doorpost, "we . . . drive away the devil lest he enter and hurt the newly born."[67] Intrigued, the Christian responded, "You tell me strange things but go on and tell me what else your masters write." The Jew proceeded to describe how different ghosts affect mankind and how they might be warded off, but rather than present such views as a common legacy of all Europeans, Münster wished to demonstrate how this belief, like Jewish immorality, was grounded in religious precept. Thus the sabbath day was not described as a day of rest and prayer but as respite from devilry for "on the sabbath day no devil or other evil spirit['s] assault need be feared for they flee to the dark mountains and neither do they appear all the sabbath day . . . but when the sabbath is ended they return to fall upon men and hurt them."[68] To counter these evil spirits, the Jew volunteered, "They [rabbis] have taught us to make seven circles to drive away the seven troops of hurtful angels."[69] No longer interested in this issue, the Christian responded, "This is great folly in you Jews, yes, a madness of heart."

Since discussion of ghosts and evil spirits can yield only so many pages of copy, Münster shifted the discussion to other areas of alleged Jewish belief no less curious. The Jew began a long discussion telling about how the sun and moon were originally of equal size but that later God made the moon smaller as a punishment for its envy of the brightness of the sun. To this, the Christian responded, "It is not written that the moon envied the sun and desired to rule the world. Why therefore do you believe such things that even the philosophers never thought of?"[70] In reasonable fashion the Christian went on to explain how the moon reflects the sun's light and also discussed eclipses and other points of astronomy. Clearly demonstrated, however was that the Jew, so strange and immoral, was also rather superstitious and apparently ignorant as well.

Certainly the Christian community sensed that Jewish rejection of Jesus reflected a very peculiar frame of mind. Münster's treatise demonstrated just how very strange these Jews were who were willing to believe in ghosts, signs against the devil, and psychological tensions among the heavenly bodies. All of this, of course, might be expected from those who abused their women and who were not quite human. If one considers that this work was directed at Jewish readership, it is difficult to appreciate Münster's reasoning that this treatise would win Jewish souls to Christ. Far from breaking new ground, the first forty pages of this work thus described only affirmed conventional stereotypes.

Finally, on page forty, Münster asked the first central question, "Why do you Jews not believe in our Messiah, seeing that all the prophecies are fulfilled by Him, written in the law and the prophets concerning Him?" In what seems like a serious turn in the conversation, Münster's Jew responded, "You ask why we do not believe in the messiah, nor receive Him as you do to which I answer you thus: The words of the prophets are not fulfilled by your Christ which they foretold concerning the messiah, and neither are the mysteries of the law fulfilled." One objection raised by the Jewish participant was that "the prophets say that all the Jews shall live in quiet and peace, safe from all annoyance of foreign kings . . . but hitherto we have been in bondage under many peoples."[71] Yet other objections raised by the Jew included the continuing prevalence of war: "The prophets write that war shall be no more in the world and it is written thus: 'I will break the bow and sword from the earth' and again: 'Nation shall not lift up sword against nation, neither shall they learn war any more' [Isaiah 2:4]. But to this time they make wars . . . and all the earth is full of robbery and plundering as in ancient days."[72] The last objection to Jesus' fulfilling the prophecies which Münster had his Jewish antagonist mention dealt with the continuing problem of idol worship: "In that day the Lord alone shall be exalted, who shall cast our idols universally. And although idol worship has ceased among some peoples yet some are still found in the east," and referring to Christians, the Jew continued, "Likewise they are truly counted among worshippers of idols who bend their knees and make images. But in the days of the messiah idols shall be wholly rooted out."[73]

Münster answered these objections, but considering that it was he who posed the questions, one might anticipate somewhat better answers. He denied that any Christians were idol worshippers and similarly rejected the idea that icons and other likenesses were the images forbidden by the Ten Commandments. He argued that these statues were purely symbolic in nature and added that in any event did not the Hebrews worship the ark of the covenant in the desert? Münster was on weaker ground when he noted, "At this time and for many years there are not nor have [there] been idols in the world, as I said above, but all nations worship the one God."[74]

Jewish objections concerning the continuing existence of war in all corners of the world elicited several responses. In some locations Münster's Christian advocate argued that war would end with Jesus' Second Coming, but in one instance a different idea was advanced. Since the Jew had earlier pointed out that no OT prophecy of the messiah mentioned a second coming and Isaiah specifically wrote of a period of peace, Münster adjusted his argument accordingly, "Peace was also throughout the entire world in those days when Christ was born. For then one man, namely Octavian, did reign over the whole world in peace."[75] To consider the *pax Romana* the expression of biblical prophecy and the culmination of Isaiah's hopes would in itself be somewhat obscene were it not for the additional fact that Jesus' homeland and people were in a state of semiwar with Rome at the time of His birth. In any event, the bringer of this messianic peace, Octavian Caesar, could hardly qualify as God's messenger as defined by Isaiah.

The argument most important to Jews has always been the return to their homeland, which return the messiah would bring about. The continuing state of exile experienced by Jews was proof-positive that their messiah could not have come and that Jesus, eloquent moral teacher that He was, was not the messiah. Münster answered this objection according to traditional Christian interpretation: "All those evils which you Jews suffer from came . . . because your fathers slew Him and crucified Him."[76] Jews have always had much difficulty with this explanation since it would seem to imply a collective responsibility and a collective guilt while Christianity addressed the concerns of the individual soul. Moreover, Jewish critics have continually pointed out that only Roman authorities were authorized to carry out a death sentence. But even if Jewish culpability was assumed, controversialists often wondered how so small a number of Jews could have damned an entire people when Jesus, His mother, His apostles, an overwhelming percentage of the disciples (numbering 120 according to the Book of Acts), and a clear majority of Christians for at least a few generations were all Jewish. Münster addressed none of these related considerations though they must have been found in the same Jewish sources from which he took those issues he did address. We have already noted, however, that Münster was willing to predate Jewish immorality back to the time of Abraham and Sarah because of Jewish culpability and responsibility for Jesus' death. In this light, integrity of argument might not be anticipated.

In order to demonstrate the continuing responsibility of contemporary Jews for the actions of their God-murdering ancestors, Münster had his Jewish spokesman mouth violently anti-Jesus sentiments. In one location Münster wrote, "We cannot believe in your Christ because He was a magician and all His miracles were wrought by magical arts and therefore He was judged to death."[77] In yet other places the sentiments expressed were far more violent: "Jesus ought to have been hanged upon the cross so that all who should come into the world might see that He was not God."[78] Münster must have been charmed with this line of logic, for it was repeated over and over. In yet another location, the Jew gleefully recounted how his ancestors did the correct thing in killing Jesus: " . . . because Jesus, your messiah, was an evil man and His speeches were spurious and the glorious God saw that He would seduce the whole world and would set Himself forth as God and for that reason God said that that man should die."[79] To demonstrate continuing Jewish responsibility, the Jew continues, "We suffer from all these tribulations and this very long captivity because that wicked man, who made Himself God and seduced the whole world, was born of us and in our land."

It is undoubtedly true that, if for different reasons, many Jews and Christians alike would have preferred that Jesus had been born of a different people in a different land; yet the arguments Münster put into the mouth of his Jewish antagonist were far removed from actual Jewish sentiment and thought.[80] Moreover, these many arguments could have had but one goal—the continuing indictment of the Jewish people not for what they believed or did not believe, but for what they were. That Münster had the Jew willingly accept such responsibility rather than have the Christian participant make these charges must raise the question of who this treatise hoped to please and edify. If it was unfortunate that Münster could not deal with real Jewish objections to Christ and Christianity, it was even more unfortunate that all this information was presented in place of any hard Christian concept and teaching. Much as Münster might have presented a more credible portrayal of those factors involved with Jewish rejection of Jesus, he certainly could have made a better case for Christian acceptance of Jesus as the messiah.

There are yet other conceptual problems with Münster's treatise. The issue of proper exegetical method was not central in this work and was only touched upon in those instances in which Christian and Jewish participants differed regarding the interpretation of specific verses. In one instance the Christian observed, "You make me laugh when you bring Scriptural authorities and interpret them according to your folly."[81] Surely this sort of disagreement is understandable considering that differing interpretations of Scripture were one area of traditional conflict between the two religions. As we noted earlier in this work when dealing with scriptural exegesis, Jewish scriptural studies tended toward more literal-historical interpretation of the text whereas Christianity often understood the same texts along more spiritual and allegorical lines of thought. We also noted that Protestant Hebraists saw value in Jewish sources precisely because of the latter's literal-historical tendencies, and all claimed to follow the non-mystical, literal, or "simple" interpretation even though some fell short of this mark. It is therefore somewhat surprising to find Münster defending the older rejected allegorical approach in this treatise written against Jews when his scriptural works defended the literal approach against the Catholic fourfold method of interpretation and allegory. In one location the Christian disputant chided his Jewish antagonist for "understanding them [the prophets] according to the letter when in actuality they are metaphors."[82] In another location much the same sentiment was expressed when the Christian said, "The words of the prophets are not always to be understood according to the run of the words [i.e., simple interpretation] but in spirit, according to an allegory."[83]

The defense of allegory was not a small point since it was Münster himself who chose the texts in question and the arguments each side would present in defense of their interpretation. As an example, at one point the Christian asked that the Jew discuss the future third temple to be built when the messiah appears. Münster then had the Jew respond to this request with a long citation from Isaiah 54:11 in which this new temple was described: "Behold, I will lay thy stones with fair colors and lay thy foundations with sapphires and I will make thy windows of agates and thy gates of carbuncles and all thy borders of pleasant stones and all thy children shall be taught of the Lord."[84] Münster did not merely refer to this text or even cite a few words but put the entire verse into the body of the work. The Jew understood this magnificent description as nothing less than a blueprint of this future temple, but the Christian saw a far different thing: "By these words heavenly Jerusalem is figured out, or surely these words indicate the congregation and church of the faithful which is the spiritual Jerusalem."[85] Expressing amazement that a blueprint might be subject to such spiritual interpretation, the Jew continued to press his simple interpretation, but the Christian responded, "Neither Scripture nor the prophets make mention [of a third temple] but you have invented this opinion out of your own brain to seduce the simple."

Were this not a serious work, one would almost suspect that Münster chose this passage precisely because it made allegory look poor. Surely this competent student of Scripture and highly qualified translator of God's Word could have chosen a better citation to dispute.

Another area of conceptual failure on Münster's part involved his presentation of the Second Coming of Christ. Surely this was a central linchpin in the Christian-Jewish difference regarding Jesus as messiah. Since many of Isaiah's prophecies of a more cosmic nature, such as those regarding world peace, universal acceptance of God, and an end to Israel's exile, were not fulfilled by Jesus, Jews rejected Him as messiah. Christians have argued that these prophecies would be fulfilled at His Second Coming and that Jesus fulfilled other OT prophecies regarding His lineage, His mother's virginity, and His being the suffering servant sent to redeem mankind from sin. Jews countered that no OT prophecy alluded to a second coming and that this idea was a contrivance of the NT to explain Jesus' failure. Any successful resolution of the Jewish-Christian difference of opinion would necessarily build upon reaching some measure of consensus regarding which prophecies were central and which might be fulfilled either in the course of time or through a reappearance of the messiah. In the two locations where Münster dealt with this central issue, he studiously avoided making any concise statement that might convince Jews of the

Christian position. In one location Münster wrote, "You and your rabbis do err very much for all those wonderful things concerning which you have spoken to me are already fulfilled with some few exceptions which shall be brought about in the second coming of Christ."[86] In another location Münster again described this difference of opinion concerning comings, but again failed to bridge the gap or even attempt to do so: "These things shall be in the second and last coming of the messiah, that is, in the end of the world and not in His first coming as you think."[87] But if the Christian disputant could not argue away the Jewish position or adequately defend the Christian argument, he did succeed in muddying the water altogether with an enormous flight of fancy unwarranted by either the OT or the NT: "The world [will] come to joy which shall never be taken away . . . men shall live not only 500 or 1000 years but forever and ever."[88] Once again one must wonder why Münster chose to express so important a Christian concept in so unfortunate a manner.

It is possible that this treatise was not written with only Jews in mind or even primarily for Jewish readers. Münster's other missionary works were written for his students and possibly for critical Christian readers, and perhaps this readership was the intended one in this instance as well. There are many places where Münster expressed just the right amount of righteous indignation about the words he put into the Jew's mouth. When the Jewish antagonist expressed the view that the messiah would be a great king like David or one of the Hasmoneans, the Christian responded with shock and horror: "Oh thou blind Jew. Are you not ashamed to speak such things of the most holy messiah?"[89] Had this Jewish description come at the beginning of the treatise, Christian shock might have been more understandable, but it appeared almost two hundred pages into the text, approximately two-thirds of the way to the end of the treatise. Surely this dramatic reaction would be more effective with Christian rather than Jewish readers. Similarly, the lack of hard Christian content, the unsatisfactory presentation of the few Christian ideas mentioned, and the truly poor use of Jewish argument when Münster's other works demonstrate far greater sophistication all seem to indicate that there is less here than meets the eye. Additionally, the first half of the treatise where Münster presented the Jew in a very unfavorable light and Jewish thought in an equally poor light could not have been seriously written by a scholar familiar with the most sophisticated Jewish exegetical work. Indeed, it is doubtful that any Jewish reader able to read through the first fifty pages would be converted or have any desire to read farther. This treatise could only prove edifying to very ignorant anti-Semites, which many of Münster critics were.

Quite predictably, the end of the treatise did not find the Jew converted or even interested in conversion. The Jew said, "You shall never persuade me to receive your faith and believe in your Christ for no one can comprehend that which you believe."[90] Undaunted, the Christian said at the end, "I must depart from you now but I will return to you again and speak more with you about these matters." For his part, the Jew was at least civil by the treatise's conclusion, though still filled with hatred and evil: "Go in peace and see that you return to me again for I also have many things I would yet discuss with you concerning your Christ and your evil tidings."[91]

Before determining why Münster wrote this curious treatise, we might consider the companion Latin edition that appeared in the same year. Though the text was essentially the same with minor wording differences attributable to translation, the title was changed to *A Jewish-Christian Debate* from *The Messiahs of the Jews and Christians Compared*. The Latin introduction appearing only in this version explained that the work was published to express the foolishness of Jewish thought when compared with Christian enlightenment. The reader of this version did not have to progress very far into this introduction to detect Münster's new attitudes. Surpassing Luther, Bucer, and other Christian-Hebraists whose opinions of Jews had changed radically during the middle years of the third decade, Münster was the first Hebraist to call for the mass expulsion of European Jewry when he wrote, "These perfidious people should have been eliminated from all Christian boundaries long ago,"[92] a position adopted by Luther only in 1543. It is doubtful that this Latin version would have proven a very successful missionary treatise, but then again, even without this introduction the Hebrew version was a rather strange missionary work, too.

Attempting to place this treatise within the framework of Münster's publications is truly difficult. The admiration and respect he expressed for Jewish authorities is not present here; yet one cannot postulate that Münster's feelings about Jews underwent some alteration since that same congenial and open attitude was again expressed in the introduction to his great OT Bible translation of 1546 where he defended not only Christian-Hebraica and Hebraists but Jews too. Considering Münster's earlier efforts at missionary literature, this later work added nothing but confusion and ill will. If only the Latin version existed, one would be forced to conclude that this work of 1539 was an attempt to demonstrate that Sebastian Münster was no friend of the Jews. The Hebrew edition complicates matters, for it seems like a missionary work, and Münster had written one such treatise just two years earlier. Yet, there was a peculiar quality to Münster's 1539 Hebrew debate as well as the Matthew of 1537. Unlike the overwhelming number of Münster's other publications in Hebrew, these two presented the Hebrew text with vowel points. The overwhelming majority of Jewish publications dispensed with this reading aid as an unnecessary and very expensive printing addition. Münster's publications followed the Jewish practice, and as we have seen, Münster accepted Levita's view that these and masoretic markings were not part of the original ancient texts. The two contexts in which vowel points continued to be used were in grammars and OT texts where absolute accuracy was necessary, especially for elementary students of Hebrew. Any work written specifically for Jews could have easily dispensed with vowel points if only because their addition was costly. However, any work Münster prepared for his own students presented both vowel points and masoretic markings. It is possible that the 1539 Hebrew text and, no doubt, the 1537 Matthew were both prepared for his own students and not for Jewish readers.

One cannot help but note the strange coincidence of a missionary treatise accompanying a radical ethnographic approach to a NT writing. The coincidences continue, for when Münster published his incomprehensible works of 1539, it was but one year after the publication of the Cassel Advice and Luther's first attack on judaization and Jews in his tract against the Sabbatarians. Both Luther and Bucer had expressed admiration for Jewish exegetes earlier; yet the sentiments of both changed. Münster, it would seem, was in good company.

The coincidences will continue, however, for Paul Fagius did the very same thing. Certainly no Christian-Hebraist was more vulnerable to the accusation of judaization than Fagius, and by the logic of the 1530s, this meant that Fagius should have written the most anti-Jewish polemic of all. Not only was that the case but it was also published right in the middle of his most serious judaizing treatise. Let us turn to Fagius, however, to appreciate the logic forming this coincidence.

In 1542 Paul Fagius published two allegedly missionary treatises that clearly demonstrated the need felt by Christian-Hebraists to put distance between themselves and the possibility of judaization. In what was becoming a standard format, both works appeared in both Hebrew and Latin.

The more complete work was entitled *Sefer Emunah* in Hebrew and *Liber Fidei* in Latin with the title page noting, "Book of Faith, a good and pleasant entreaty written by a wise and proper Jew several years ago, to demonstrate and prove in complete, simple and clear fashion the Christian faith's belief in God, in a Father, Son, and Holy Spirit and other things . . . and called therefore the Book of Faith to illuminate the eyes of the blind and to lead the erroneous along the path of righteousness. Translated from Hebrew to Latin by Paul Fagius and printed in Isny."[93] Despite the apparent missionary intent of the original author's purpose and Fagius's missionary description of the work, it was clearly intended for a Christian audience. The Latin half of the volume presented several introductions not found in the Hebrew section with the first taking the form of a long dedicatory letter to the Roman Catholic Hebraist Andreas Massius, to whom the volume as a whole was dedicated. It was in the second Preface to the Reader that Fagius's true intentions were made clear, for he explained that this missionary work required translation from Hebrew to Latin "to communicate the holy tongue for the benefit of students." The missionary intent of the Latin translation was further diminished when Fagius noted how "they [Jews] hate anything not presented in their language."

Despite the pleasant words used on the cover page to introduce the work—no doubt for the benefit of the casual bookstand browser—this introduction noted, "If these arguments in this book against the blindness of the Jews are a little feeble . . . remember good reader, it was written by a Jew." Evidently, somewhere between the cover page and the reader's introduction the value of the work declined considerably with the author diminished from a Jewish convert to Christianity to a Jew. Fagius ended this preface with the very clear statement that the Latin translation was initiated "to advance and cultivate the study of the Holy tongue." Essentially, Fagius hoped to provide his students with a Latin translation of a rather well-written Hebrew text.

Lest the reader accidentally associate Fagius with the original author, our scrupulous translator included an end-piece after the conclusion of the volume entitled "To the Christian Reader."[94] In stronger terms than used previously, Fagius again emphasized that the Latin translation was made "for students of the Hebrew language who desire to read intensely in the Hebrew language." And yet once again Fagius noted, "If perhaps not all the arguments of this author in this book against the Jews glitter, and do not appear well founded, solid, and firm, remember—as I admonished in the preface—it was a Jew who wrote it." Adding contempt for Jewish converts to a condescending tone regarding Jews, Fagius continued, "It is therefore not surprising that he dragged in much Jewish foolishness for these people, [even] if they do accept Christ, never fully abandon their Judaism always adhering to some Jewishness as if it contained some truth."

More than any other publication by any other Christian-Hebraist, this volume reflected the age-old wisdom that one cannot tell a book by its cover. Presented as a missionary work by a wise Jew making a clear demonstration of the Godhead, Fagius then argued that the demonstration was weak, that the author was less than wise and not really a Christian but a Jew, and that Jews never convert anyway.

Without analyzing this treatise written by an anonymous source, it is important to note that the original work was indeed a very well-organized and thoughtful treatise. It consisted of nine chapters covering such issues as the Trinity, the Incarnation, OT proofs that Jesus was the messiah, and the resurrection of the dead. The original Hebrew was clear and concise with most arguments drawn from the Talmud, the Cabbalah, and scriptural exegesis. Two chapters in particular were of importance. Chapter seven dealt with "15 Answers to Jews" described by the author as "15 answers the Jews use to vanquish the Christians in their attempt to prove He did not come." The value of this chapter lay in the author's ability to argue against many Jewish claims from within the Jewish idiom. Chapter nine too was of interest, and it was entitled "Those Factors Preventing Jews from Accepting the Christian Faith."

If the overall judaizing quality of Fagius's publications required a disavowal of Jewishness in the form of the *Book of Faith*, certainly the most judaizing of his works—which equated the Lord's Supper with Jewish table blessings—required an especially strong disclaimer to such charges.[95] Unfortunately, Fagius was unable to find a short missionary work to translate and contented himself with publishing a chapter of the *Book of Faith* in the same volume as he published his *Hebrew Benedictions*. If only one chapter of the *Book of Faith* was to be published along with a thoroughly Christian work, the most likely missionary choice would have been chapter seven dealing with responses to Jewish claims and arguments. Publishing this chapter would have clearly demonstrated to any Christian reader that Fagius could not only differentiate between Judaism and Christianity but was also aware of the subtleties of Jewish argument and the correctness of Christian responses. Moreover, the volume's title page presented this excerpt from the *Book of Faith* as a wise Jew's contribution to the Christian mission, and certainly chapter seven was the most valuable single part of the book. Instead, Fagius selected a part of chapter nine entitled "Those Factors Preventing Jews from Accepting the Christian Faith." The intellectual content of this chapter was almost nonexistent, but the reader has already had opportunity to become familiar with it since in fact Sebastian Münster used it in the preface of his 1537 Matthew.

We have already noted that the fourth section of Münster's missionary treatise, "This is the Holy Christian Faith," was incongruous with earlier sections and was devoted to describing those factors that inhibited Jewish conversion to Christianity. In fact, the fourth section of Münster's work consisted of chapters seven and nine of the *Book of Faith*. Although the Hebrew text published by Münster in 1537 was somewhat different from that published by Fagius in 1542, the Latin translations appearing in both works was identical. Since this excerpt is but a few pages in length and was viewed by both Münster and Fagius as the epitome of Christian-Hebraist missionary intent, the English translations is provided below.

That Which Prohibits the Jews from Believing in the Messiah that was Sent

And this is what prohibits Jews from believing in the messiah that was sent. Because the Jews call them that believe in the messiah and take upon themselves His covenant and law "destroyed one" which is to say that person has no share in the world to come and that his soul will receive no forgiveness forever. And they spit in his face, call his children bastards and his wife impure. And they do not eat with him nor drink with him but ostracize and excommunicate him. And they curse him daily, three times evening and morning as [in the prayer] "The destroyed ones have no hope." And they abuse him and his family and they do not marry him or members of his family unless he and his family have much money. They seek out his life and permit his execution, that is to say, whoever kills him has neither responsibility nor the need for repentance but is considered as one who has brought a sacrifice. And they praise him [he who murders a convert] and say of him "Blessed is the memory of the righteous."

But he who believes in the messiah, they say of him after his death, "may the name of the wicked decay and rot." And when some bad occurrence befalls him they rejoice and say of him "In such a manner are the enemies of God lost." They rejoice in the bad circumstances that befall him. They confiscate his money and property and greatly disgrace and dishonor him.

When they remember him later [after his death] they say "may his name and memory be eradicated and may this destroyed one be our expiation. Woe unto him, unto his soul. Woe unto his father and mother who raised such a thing. Woe unto his mother that conceived him and woe unto his teacher who taught him Law," and all their thoughts concerning him are for evil and not for good.

And this too greatly contributes to their not believing in the messiah sent to redeem them. Their wise men determined that they should not eat or drink with Christians and everyone who eats with Christians does so as if he consumes corpses and cadavers from the open field. And they make this prohibition even more stringent that one should not eat butter or cheese cooked by Christians. And the Jews will not touch anything cooked by Christians, not even Christian milk. The Jews will not even eat those things permitted them [by laws of kashruth] unless they watched during the cooking period that it was cooked according to their wills. If they did not observe the period of cooking, it is forbidden to eat of any part of it. The Jews do not use the utensils used by Christians, such as metal pitchers or platters unless they place them in boiling water two or three times. They destroy Christian ceramic utensils and it is forbidden for the Jew to wear Christian clothes. It is forbidden for a Jew to marry them and they consider Christians gentiles regarding usury and they depend upon the Scriptural assertion that it is permissible to take usury from gentiles but not from brothers.

Because they believe differently, that the messiah did not come, they believe the Christians gentiles. But this is in error because they do not follow the true meaning of Scripture and they alter the text according to their desire and opinion in order to take interest and profit from their money without having to work and labor. They are so dedicated to usury that they cannot leave it and they seek profit from their money so that they can easily become rich without working. Because money is so dear to them and they worship money more than God, they lose their souls as if they worshipped idols. And this money causes them to be downtrodden in this world and they have no place in the world to come because they do not follow the text "By the sweat of thy brow . . . " which is to say that everyone who profits from his own labors is blessed in this world and fortunate in the world to come. But they who profit without labor and toil, who take interest, have no hope at all. And it is written about him that the crooked shall not be made straight, and he is also called a thief and transgresses against the commandment, "Do not steal."

And because they depend upon the above-cited text, they are lost in this world and this causes them to be exiled, vexed, and repelled among the nations and they have no share in the world to come. That is, because they do not believe in the messiah sent to redeem them, they have no share in the world to come. Additionally, they transgress against the words of the Law because the text is not as they interpret it regarding their treatment of Christians as gentiles because of their belief in the messiah. Indeed, it is incumbent upon them to see them as brothers since they believe in a living, universal God, much as they do, and do not worship idols as I described above. Those who worship idols should be considered gentiles.

Therefore, all who take interest from Christians transgress against the Law and against all the precepts against usury. But in any event, as they understand things, this generation is not bound in this matter, and claim the Scripture's meaning was altered by wise men after the appearance of the messiah. Thus they [Jews] blind the eyes of the masses with their various interpretations and from this they poison the heart of the masses and consider their own opinions correct and just. But as Scripture states, "the sons will not perish from the sins of the fathers" and who knows, perhaps when they know the truth they will not stiffen their necks.

Therefore it is necessary to speak to them with soothing and kind words in order to persuade them towards the path of righteousness and faith. One should speak to the Jews with wisdom and gentleness so that they will be inclined towards the correct path. Even though he does not want to hear about the messiah at first, do not leave him but continue until he is persuaded to listen. And whoever redeems them has participated in the salvation of the multitudes. Consequently, everyone is required to attempt to redeem his neighbor with selected good arguments from the works of the Cabbalah and from books of faith or from other arguments and responses [i.e., debates] until he convinces him and he ceases to sin and he leads him from hell to merit a life in the world to come.

Therefore, may it be God's will to justify us for life in the world to come and redeem us from our tribulations and listen to our prayers and save us from all trouble and affliction, from all plague and sickness, and justify our lives until the second coming of the messiah. Amen.[96]

Münster's familiarity with the *Book of Faith* went beyond the excerpts he included in his own treatise of 1537, for every single one of the arguments taken from the Cabbalah and from the Talmud which appeared in his treatises of 1537 and 1539 also coincidentally appeared in the *Book of Faith*. In turn, Fagius's familiarity with Münster's earlier works must be assumed since his Latin translation of the one excerpt translated above was identical to that published by Münster five years earlier despite some minor discrepancies in the Hebrew texts they used.

The picture that emerges is not a happy one and does not present either scholar as possessing vast quantities of personal or scholarly integrity. Both authors were severely criticized for judaization, and both were close personal and professional associates of Elias Levita. Both wrote bogus missionary treatises to demonstrate the Christian value of Hebrew study, and both in fact were dependent upon the *Book of Faith* for much of their material—in Fagius's case, for all of his material. Both included the same excerpt in their writings because of its anti-Jewish tone at the same time that both could have found better, more convincing missionary sections in the same work. It would appear that this anti-Jewish section served another purpose as well. In both cases it accompanied a very radical use of Hebraica for Christian purposes. In one case it was included in a treatise dealing with the Lord's Supper and in the other case in a translation of the Gospel of Matthew into Hebrew which, in turn, formed the basis of an ethnographic study of the NT. In short, both authors used prevalent anti-Semitic feeling, and their ability to pander to this sentiment, as a guise behind which to carry out their own scholarly pursuits. That Fagius might employ such tactics must surely merit condemnation and a charge of cowardice when one considers that he not only used the *Book of Faith* for his own purposes but also criticized its author as nothing but a Jew and its arguments as typical of the work produced by Jewish converts. Münster, at least, possessed the grace to refrain from criticizing the *Book of Faith*, which provided so many pages of copy and so many of his arguments.

According to the prevalent logic, Christian-Hebraists could write missionary treatises but only such that were not friendly to Jews. The hostility these works demonstrated might clear the author of the charge of judaization but would do little to advance the Jewish mission. According to this logic, only an ex-Jew could write a sincere missionary treatise since he was already tainted by his origins and might require some sort of proof demonstrating the validity of his conversion. If this logic seems overly perverse, one must consider that only one missionary treatise from the entire sixteenth century was open, friendly, and sincere in its desire to convert Jews to Christianity. This same treatise was the only such Christian-authored work absolutely avoiding any and all anti-Semitic denigration. This work, *Catechism of the Elect of God*, was published in 1554 by John Emmanuel Tremelius (1510–1580) of Ferrara, a Jewish convert to Reformed Christianity.[97] Tremelius had the distinction of suffering persecution as an ex-Jew and as an active Calvinist, but he contributed nonetheless to his new religion's growing interest in Hebrew studies. Among his accomplishments were various translations of OT books of Scripture, and numerous students studied Hebrew with him. He served as Fagius's successor at Cambridge in 1549 and translated Calvin's Catechism into Hebrew five years later in hopes of Jewish conversion. Unlike previous works, the Catechism was published only in Hebrew with a special Hebrew introduction. The friendly tone of the reader's introduction was undisguised: "Bountiful and ever increasing greetings to all descendants of Jacob from Immanuel Tremelius. Dear Brothers; I have seen the books among our people, [especially] the prayer books used to teach children to pray to the Lord and to thank Him for His blessings. A great many good and thankful prayers are included in these volumes and they are worthy of use by all descendants of Abraham."[98] Explaining why he took a pen to hand, Tremelius noted, "I wanted to write a single short book including the order of the prayers and other aspects of devotion practiced by our ancestors Abraham, Isaac, and Jacob, and which were commanded by God."[99] Rather than express anger, frustration, or hatred, Tremelius wrote, "I await the salvation [of Israel] and all my desires are for the redemption of Israel and therefore I have written this small book."

Despite the promising introduction and Tremelius's fine qualifications for missionary work, the body of the work itself was a straightforward presentation of Christian belief more geared to Christian than to Jewish readers. But if he did not attempt to accommodate Jews with special arguments, neither did Tremelius demonstrate the opportunism and nastiness found in works by Hebraists of Christian origin.

One must wonder to what extent Christian-Hebraists helped or hindered their cause of safeguarding Christian study of Jewish sources from accusations of judaization. If the rabbis were dull, foolish, and incapable of true scholarship and if Jewish converts were even worse, there was little to fear from those quarters but even less reason to read rabbinic literature in the first place. Yet Fagius did succeed in justifying his studies, for he was offered Capito's position when the latter died and was invited by Bucer to accompany him to England when both rejected the imposed Interim. In the long run, however, Christian-Hebraists would be forced to defend their studies from a Christian perspective on the grounds of those benefits gained from Jewish sources. Perhaps this explains why Münster reversed his position just a few years later in 1546 when he wrote his strong defense of Christian-Hebraica in his preface to his Bible translation. To an extent, the problem resolved itself, for by the end of the next decade all the Christian-Hebraists dealt with in this volume had died, leaving many students, if few great Habraists, to carry on after them.

NOTES

1. Surprisingly little has been written about the Protestant mission to the Jews during the Reformation period. Indeed, the only work dealing with this subject is Armas K. Holmio, *The Lutheran Reformation and the Jews: The Birth of the Prot-*

estant Jewish Missions (Hancock, Michigan, 1949). Unfortunately, Holmio knew no Hebrew and consequently could not study most of the missionary treatises of the period. See my "Sebastian Münster, the Jewish Mission, and Protestant Anti-Semitism," *Archiv für Reformations-geschichte,* vol. 70 (1970).

2.   See Steven W. Rowan's article "Ulrich Zasius and the Baptism of Jewish Children," *Sixteenth Century Journal,* vol. 4 (Oct. 1975). This article presents a good summary of medieval law and practice regarding the forced baptism of Jewish children and discusses one important case during the early sixteenth century.

3.   *Torat ha-Mashiach: Evangelium Secundum Matthaeum in Lingua Hebraica cum versione Latina atque succinctis annotationibus Sebastiani Münsteri* (Basel, 1537).

4.   *Ibid.,* pp. 2–3. The Jewish prayer from which this citation was taken is known as *Adon Olam,* "Lord of the Universe," found at the conclusion of the daily morning liturgy.

5.   *Ibid.,* p. 5.

6.   *Ibid.,* p. 8.

7.   *Ibid.,* p. 12.

8.   *Ibid.,* p. 20.

9.   *Ibid.,* p. 19.

10.   *Ibid.,* p. 23.

11.   *Ibid.,* p. 28.

12.   *Ibid.,* pp. 23–24.

13.   *Ibid.,* p. 24.

14.   *Ibid.,* p. 28.

15.   *Ibid.,* pp. 24, 25.

16.   *Ibid.*

17.   *Ibid.,* pp. 33–34.

18.   This and the next six citations appear on pp. 34–38.

19.   *Ibid.,* p. 43.

20.   *Ibid.,* p. 48.

21.   *Ibid.,* p. 55, and the next citation as well.

22.   *Ibid.,* p. 43, and the next two citations as well.

23.   *Ibid.,* p. 45.

24.   *Ibid.,* p. 51.

25.   Concerning sixteenth-century Jewish messianism, see A. H. Silver, *A History of Messianic Speculation in Israel* (New York, 1927; Boston, 1959); and my article "Sixteenth Century European Jewry: Theologies of Crisis in Crisis," *Social Groups and Religious Ideas in the Sixteenth Century,* ed. M. U. Chrisman, O. Gründler (Kalamazoo, Mich., 1978).

26.   Münster, *Matthew,* p. 57.

27.   *Ibid.,* pp. 59–60, along with the next citation.

28.   *Ibid.,* p. 63 and through p. 65 for the next four citations.

29. *Ibid.*, p. 61, and the following citation.
30. *Ibid.*, p. 66, and the following citation.
31. *Ibid.*, p. 82.
32. *Ibid.*, p. 84.
33. *Ibid.*, p. 75.
34. *Ibid.*, p. 89.
35. *Ibid.*, p. 61.
36. *Ibid.*, p. 83.
37. Luther, *LW*, 47:88.
38. *Ibid.*, pp. 108–13.
39. Münster, *Matthew*, p. 56.
40. *Ibid.*, p. 92.
41. *Ibid.*, p. 121.
42. *Ibid.*, p. 128.
43. *Ibid.*, p. 132.
44. *Ibid.*, p. 188–90.
45. *Ibid.*, p. 217.
46. *Ibid.*, p. 343.
47. *Ibid.*, p. 386.
48. *Ibid.*, p. 198.
49. *Ibid.*, pp. 215–16.
50. *Ibid.*, p. 187.
51. *Ibid.*, p. 148, 238.
52. *Ibid.*, p. 270, 353.
53. *Ibid.*, pp 247, 248, 249.
54. *Ibid.*, p. 402.
55. *Ibid.*, pp. 366–67.
56. *Ibid.*, pp. 325, 326, 327.
57. *Ibid.*, pp. 285, 301, 316.
58. *Ibid.*, p. 285.
59. *Ibid.*, pp. 329, 338.
60. *Ibid.*, pp. 214, 204, 260, 342.
61. For a complete listing of these works and editions, see Burmeister, *Bibliographie.*
62. Hebrew version: *Mashiach: Messias Christianorum et Iudaeorum* . . . (Basel, 1539). Latin version: *Havikuach: Christiani Hominis cum Judeo pertinaciter prodigiosis suis opinionibus* . . . (Basel, 1539).
63. All citations and references are taken from the Hebrew version with pagination following the letters of the Hebrew alphabet. Also listed are page numbers from the English translation by Paul Isaiah published in London, 1655, for those unfamiliar with Hebrew. Hebrew, aleph 2 a–b; English, pp. 1–2.
64. *Ibid.*, Hebrew, p. aleph 2b; English, p. 5.

65. *Ibid.*, Hebrew, p. aleph 3b; English, pp. 6–7.
66. *Ibid.*, Hebrew, p. aleph 4b; English, p. 9.
67. *Ibid.*, Hebrew, p. aleph 4b; English, p. 10.
68. *Ibid.*, Hebrew, p. aleph 6a, unpaginated; English, p. 16.
69. *Ibid.*, Hebrew, p. aleph 7a, unpaginated; English, p. 19.
70. *Ibid.*, Hebrew, p. bet 5a; English, p. 25.
71. *Ibid.*, Hebrew, p. zayin 4a; English, p. 173.
72. *Ibid.*
73. *Ibid.*, Hebrew, p. zayin 6a; English, pp. 180–81.
74. *Ibid.*, Hebrew, p. zayin 6b; English, pp. 180–81.
75. *Ibid.*, Hebrew, p. daled 8a; English, p. 104.
76. *Ibid.*, Hebrew, p. chet 8a; English, p. 215.
77. *Ibid.*, Hebrew, p. chet 7a; English, p. 211.
78. *Ibid.*, Hebrew, p. chet 7b; English, p. 214.
79. *Ibid.*, Hebrew, p. chet 8a; English, p. 214.
80. See my article "The Reformation and Jewish Anti-Christian Polemics," *Bibliotheque D'Humanisme et Renaissance.*
81. Münster, *Jewish and Christian Debate*, Hebrew, p. bet 2b; English, p. 31.
82. *Ibid.*
83. *Ibid.*, Hebrew, p. zayin 3b; English, p. 171.
84. *Ibid.*, Hebrew, p. hey 6a; English, p. 126–27.
85. *Ibid.*, Hebrew, p. hey 6b; English, p. 128.
86. *Ibid.*, Hebrew, p. chet 4a; English, p. 201.
87. *Ibid.*, Hebrew, p. daled 6a; English, p. 98.
88. *Ibid.*, Hebrew, p. chet 3b; English, p. 203.
89. *Ibid.*, Hebrew, p. chet 1b; English, p. 193.
90. *Ibid.*, Hebrew, p. tet 1a; English, p. 217.
91. *Ibid.*, Hebrew, p. p. tet 8a; English, p. 240.
92. Latin version, p. A3a.
93. Paul Fagius, *Liber Fidei* (Isny, 1542). Unfortunately, Fagius did not mention the name of this treatise's author, and I have not been able to locate this work or its author in any listings of missionary treatises.
94. *Ibid.*, p. 129.
95. Published along with *Precationes Hebraicae* . . . (Isny, 1542) was an excerpt of the *Book of Faith* with the cover page of the volume as a whole mentioning both works.
96. *Ibid.*, p. A–A4b.
97. Hebrew Title page: Immanuel Tremelius, *Sefer Chinuch B' Chirei Yah* (London, 1554). Concerning Tremelius, see the *Dictionary of National Biography*, ed. L. Stephen, S. Lee (Oxford, 1917), 19:1112–114.
98. Tremelius, p. 10.
99. *Ibid.*, p. 12, along with next citation.

PART V

CONCLUSION

Chapter Fifteen

A New Interpretation of Christian-Hebraica

Despite other differences, most historians agree that at bottom Renaissance humanism entailed an appreciation of the value of classical sources for contemporary purposes. This appreciation might be literary, political, legal, or aesthetic, but such individual expressions were secondary, for surely no one of these areas was more fundamental than the others in demonstrating the Renaissance yearning for the past. The ancient theology provided yet another dimension to this nostalgia if in a more religious or spiritual sphere. Whereas some humanists undoubtedly frowned at Zoroaster or simply preferred Cicero, an equal number found significant and refreshing meaning in Hermes Tresmegistus. Certainly the Christian-Cabbalah must be understood as a branch of this more spiritual humanism. Some critics will no doubt note a qualitative difference between the visceral appreciation of human potential implicit in much Italian humanism and Reuchlin's more spiritual quest for the wonder-working word typifying the ancient theology and Cabbalah. Such distinctions, however, are surely after the fact, for few sixteenth-century humanists differentiated between earthly pagan sources and more spiritual religious ones. Thus Cardinal Bembo inserted the names "Zeus" and "Apollo" into conventional Christian prayers while other scholars happily used Plato for Christian religious ends, as did Ficino in his *Theologica Platonica* by noting that such infidel sources had the imprimatur of the spermatic logos. Lefèvre d'Etaples combined an approach to Scripture not unlike Luther's with an ardent faith in Hermes and Cabbalah and a love of classical literature. Symphorien Champier was a greater juggler yet. Not only did he attempt to amalgamate Plato and Aristotle but he also tried to do so within a framework decidedly Hermetic and Cabbalistic and all toward a Christian end. And yet these all pale by comparison with Pico who managed to forage world culture for nine hundred axioms of truth, all of which supported Christianity despite their far-flung origins. Even great religious leaders of the age had more than passing interest in the pagans, and one too easily forgets that Calvin's first work dealt with Seneca and not Scripture. Melanchthon's love of the classical languages was surpassed only by Zwingli who earned Luther's wrath and perhaps jealousy when he preached in Greek, Latin, and Hebrew with as much ease as in the vernacular.

Had followers of the ancient theology pursued wisdom from scriptural sources, there would be little to differentiate them from Protestant scripturalists. Moreover, had Protestants sought religious insight from Homer, Plato, Herodotus, and Livy, they might properly be called classical humanists. Had followers of either group of scholars read Hebrew translations of any of this literature, they would be known as Christian-Hebraists; and had Italians pursued Mark, Luke, John, Matthew, and Paul with the same energy spent upon Cicero, Plato, and Pythagoras, no nineteenth-century scholars would have considered them pagans but "proto-Protestants." Essentially, "Italian humanism," and "ancient theology," "Reformation scripturalism," and "Christian-Hebraica" all constitute variations on a single nostalgic theme. Moreover, all these terms are the products of subsequent historiography and might be unrecognized by the subjects themselves. Categorical distinctions between these various pursuits of the past may result more from the value judgments of later ages and historians than from the sixteenth century itself. Hence, though historians have been presented with a solid wall of nostalgia running through much sixteenth-century culture, some have chosen the Christian religious pursuit of the apostolic age for separate study. Under the rubric "Reformation studies," as if the Protestant return to Scripture was somehow removed from similar efforts by other humanists such as Petrarch, Machiavelli, Reuchlin, or Bruno, this specific form of nostalgia acquired a degree of legitimacy imparted by Protestant historians. Surely there is no reason Protestant scripturalism cannot be studied apart from other forms of contemporary nostalgia though there is danger that such exclusive study will stress peculiarities of this one area to the exclusion of what it shared with other forms of humanism. In other words, there is the danger of missing the forest for the trees and creating artificial categories of thought within Reformation studies along doctrinal lines that make little sense in terms of the age as a whole. This indeed has often been the case, and one need only be reminded that Reformation studies have traditionally excluded the Catholic reformation, radicalism, Christian-Hebraica, and other tendencies often found confessionally unpleasant. The Catholic church hardly needed study since it was the bed of corruption from which the Protestant religion originated; the radicals were all *Schwärmer* and Christian-Hebraists were either more rabbinical than Christian or nothing more than a bunch of Jews. In fact, all these groups shared a great deal and differed primarily in terms of religious dogma, not intellectual tendencies or method. Artificial categories of thought have been suggested, such as justification by faith alone as if Catholic practice was nothing more than superstitious ritualism with no foundation in Scripture at all. In turn Protestant scripturalism was lauded to the exclusion of realizing that many Catholics never left Scripture and the Council of Dort may never have approached it. Many of these confessional developments and approaches find their explanation in the simple observation that many, if not most, students of the sixteenth century have traditionaly been Protestant ministers expressing a specific orientation to all the developments of that age. It is to be hoped that such strong confessionalism has weakened over the last several decades, and much new and good work has been conducted concerning Roman Catholicism, radicalism, the ancient theology, and even the contributions of Jewish literature to this age of ferment.

In approaching the sixteenth century as an age of multiple and variable nostalgia, we can appreciate the continuity of Renaissance into Reformation without indulging in that useless debate of Renaissance versus Reformation which makes sense only through a confessional perception of the age. Moreover, we can appreciate the various types and sorts of Christian-Hebraica which were so persistent during the sixteenth century and so worrisome to ecclesiastical leaders. Some Hebraists like Reuchlin were followers of the ancient theology. Others, like Servetus, were radical apocalyptic restitutionalists whereas Fagius's evaluation of Pharisaic morality was not unlike those many Renaissance writings lauding the virtues of Rome and Greece. Münster, the grammarian and teacher, was for Hebraica what Pletho and Chrysoloras were for Greek studies and Valla for the critical study of Latin philological development. Yet others like Bucer or Pellican were essentially traditional scholars utilizing any and all skills and sources necessary for the completion of their studies. In short, there were Hebraists to match every form and expression of nostalgia and scholarly pursuit found in the age in general. Christian-Hebraica, then, was not so much a branch of classical humanism or even a Hebrew version of it. It was a total reflection of the age as a whole through uniquely Hebrew eyes including such diverse tendencies as the Christian-Cabbalah, scripturalism, linguistics and philology, moral philosophy, and history. Yet even these categories are poor and insufficient in expressing the genius of the sixteenth century. How can we explain Servetus, who as a sideline to disturbing Europe's peace of mind as an antitrinitarian radical and servere judaizer, also made the revolutionary discovery of the pulmonary circulation of the blood a century before William Harvey? Sebastian Münster may have been the greatest Christian-Hebraist of his age, but he is remembered by posterity as the greatest geographer of the day.

The preoccupation with the past, whether secular or religious, literary or legal, scientific or mystical, yielded few fruits. It is incontestable that humanism widened cultural awareness, brought about by linguistic skills hitherto unknown or rare, and created a core of studies known as the humanities. But before Italy quite succeeded in restablishing the glory that was Rome, it was invaded by France, not once, but three times. Indeed, the sack of Rome in 1527 by the emperor of the Germans was less reminiscent of Republican or Imperial Rome than of that city's conquest by Alaric, an earlier German, in 410. Certainly this was not the ancient virtue lauded by Machiavelli, Petrarch, or Bruno. Of course, humanism did reform educational curricula and expressed the need for well-rounded gentlemen.

Other branches of nostalgia fared equally poorly. Reuchlin never found the miraculous wonder-working word, and by the middle of the seventeenth century Hermes was getting long in the tooth. Druids were out. Servetus's restitutionism did not fare well either. The age of the apostles surely retains its glow even today though the wars of religion dampened the human spirit's concern with such illusive goals. Whether or not Fagius was correct regarding the similarity between Jewish blessings and the Lord's Supper was soon a moot point. By the end of the century Lutheran, Calvinist, and Catholic eucharistic formulations were set in concrete hardly to change over the next centuries or to demand ethnographic elucidation for their justification.

Protestant scripturalism enjoyed a greater measure of success than other branches of the pursuit of the past, for this intellectual tendency alone created new institutions, altered older ones, and did away with yet others. Such structural and institutional changes are more easily quantified than substantive transformation of Europe's religiosity. But along with new translations of Scripture and a simplified form of worship came the wars of religion also apparently understood in every vernacular. By the time the wars and conflicts ended, Europe's condition reflected less the age of the apostles than Armageddon, or so Montaigne and Charron reported from France and the bloodied Grimmelhausen from Germany. The Roman

Catholic church too underwent reform with most pre-Reformation abuses slowly eliminated. Yet, these reformers—no less successful than their Protestant counterparts—were not nostalgic dreamers of yesterday but Spanish Jesuits deeply rooted in medieval Thomism as well as in Renaissance classicism.

The purveyors of nostalgia expressed a diminished faith in traditional Christian belief and practice. Indeed, the desire to return to yesteryear's simplicity was born of an age of crisis characterized by overpopulation, peasant rebellion, the plagues, the Hundred Years' War, institutional and class conflict so rampant that even knights were in active rebellion, and the Turks. In turn the church, that mirror of society's discontents, was crumbling. Multiple and rival papacies, papal-conciliar conflict, outrageous moral and fiscal abuse, and an inability to deal effectively with Hussites and many others all indicated that Europe was in a state of unparalleled crisis. The desire to return to the past was reasonable to the extent that programs of nostalgia were based upon what were conceived of as successful attempts by the ancients to deal with reality. Some, like Machiavelli, attempted to emulate those positions that seemed to bring about political stability in earlier ages of crisis. Others, like Reuchlin, attempted to renew man's ability to feel close to God; he forwarded a form of knowledge based upon the proposition that Hebrew was God's language. If the state of crisis so much in evidence seemed depressing, one had only to remember that the world must be perceived through mathematics, and underlying all reality was that great safety net of the wonder-working word. Despite appearances to the contrary, Reuchlin soothed his readers, Jesus was still with us. Europe's problems were far too serious and endemic to wish away through the use of magic. It was simply impossible to transmute lead into gold through the proper verbal formula and no less difficult to convert Europe into its own classical past. Those truly desperate returned, not to the age of the apostles, but to Sinai and the wisdom of Cabbalah, which would unify Hellenistic, Jewish, and Christian ideas into one synthesis. Poor Reuchlin was more desperate still and pushed the date of Cabbalah from Sinai to Eden in his attempt to return to the womb.

No one typified a greater lack of faith in traditional Christian ideas than Servetus. Not only did this radical thinker reject a great many standard and normative Christian views such as the Trinity, infant baptism, and a host of other ideas but he also dismissed Christian tradition as nothing more than the fruit of the antiChrist. Servetus would accept as comrades Jews, Arabs, Hermes, Zoroaster, and anyone else who disagreed with Christianity, although his reliance upon early Jewish concepts was predominant.

Even Paul Fagius, secure in his orthodox belief, found need to justify Christian belief and practice upon a Jewish foundation in much the same manner as Servetus. Luther understood the dangers in this religious insecurity and feared for the judaization of Christianity, but he also rejected Greek sources and wished to reduce Aristotle's dominance in higher education. Calvin too understood the problems involved with alien sources and, while he wrote on Seneca, he correctly perceived the danger Servetus posed in using Jewish sources and even such ancient Christian sources as the Clementine Recognitions and Pseudo-Dionysius. The problem was not Hebrew per se but a nostalgic Hebraica that translated into the Reuchlin, Servetus, and Fagius types of doubts about Christian belief.

Orthodox Protestantism was in little position to stem the tide of such unconventional source use since it had returned to Scripture as a reaction to the same medieval past troubling more radical thinkers. If one was justified in cutting away centuries of church tradition and practice to return to Scripture, the same process might entail a return to yet other sources of value to Christians. We have noted that many sixteenth-century figures did not distinguish between pagan and Christian sources and combined the use of both as did Lefèvre and others mentioned above. The fact is that, many Reformation historians notwithstanding, the sixteenth century was not so source oriented (i.e., Christian *vs.* pagan) as it was time conscious (i.e., ancient *vs.* later). The road into yesterday's simplicity extends for a great distance, and later thinkers such as Rousseau would go back even farther to the noble savage. Today's mystics speak of previous lives detectable through hypnosis while others indulge in primal screams of birth. In all cases the past comes to redeem the present from some series of developments judged unfortunate and subject to elimination. The same blade that slashes tradition to the age of the apostles might cut more deeply to the time of Sinai, to Eden or before.

The problem posed by Christian-Hebraica was that the scalpel used had a Jewish blade. And lest one think it preposterous that fifteen hundred years of Christian tradition might fall prey to the lure of Hebraica, let us recall that Servetus rejected Christian tradition but accepted the validity of a three-thousand-year-old Jewish tradition. Surely Reuchlin's insistence that Cabbalah originated in Eden pushed this date farther into the past. Moreover, radicals dismissed the Trinity on the basis of Jewish thought, and orthodox thinkers clarified the Lord's Supper through examinations of Jewish table blessings. To cap it all, a score and more of talented Christian scholars translated and interpreted not only the OT but the NT according to Jewish theories and grammars. And once brought into the fold of usable Christian concept, it was not always easy to distinguish between acceptable and unacceptable Hebraica. Much as the Spanish had difficulty in determining true Christian from recent convert and had to depend upon the incredible argument of blood lines to determine old from new Christian, Protestant scripturalists had difficulty disputing the use of Jewish sources. One might claim that Jews knew no Hebrew, as Luther, Melanchthon, and Forster asserted; but that was absurd and perhaps unconvincing. One could damn both Jews and Christian-Hebraists as the devil's offspring, but such epithets were already abused, having been leveled at Huss and by everyone against everyone else thereafter. Moreover, Luther's enthusiasm of 1523 in which he justified much Jewish practice gave the lie to opposing charges written later.

In point of fact, the threat of Christian-Hebraica never materialized, for by midcentury almost all major Hebraists had died and the wars of religion forced men's minds elsewhere. As the magic of the Renaissance belief in the past slowly filtered out of the European intellectual bloodstream, it left not a judaized Christianity but an even greater crisis of faith than that witnessed during the Renaissance age of nostalgia. Descartes attempted to bolster Christian faith with the most obvious thing he could think of: himself. Spinoza faced the problems of rejecting the Christian culture around him and the Jewish culture of his birth. Perhaps he was too insecure to build an intellectual system predicated upon his own existence, but he utilized a foundation equally reasonable. If God existed, He was the world. Locke attempted to rid Christianity of miracles and other spiritual inconveniences and to predicate all wisdom upon sensory perception, and Bacon wrote of the need for "a total reconstruction of science, arts, and all human knowledge, raised upon proper foundations."

With the rise of such new thought and science based upon human experience and pragmatic demonstrations of proof, the ancients were finally laid to rest and the age of nostalgia came to an end. The classical studies were appreciated but no longer considered the source of truth and redemption of a fallen world. In time, anticipation of the future would replace the nostalgia for the past with new terms such as *progress, development*, and *enlightenment* expressing age-old hopes for something better than the present. Technology would become the new wonder-working word, and abstract mathematics would replace Cabbalistic numerology in providing a key to reality. Spheres and emanations lost their appeal but were replaced by theories of dialectical history and stages of development which also explained how the world got from there to here and from here to tomorrow, which in turn has become the repository of man's hopes previously entrusted to yesterday.

Christian-Hebraica was a road into yesterday in the same sense that dialectical materialism attempts to provide a pathway into the future or Freudian dream analysis attempts to provide a more telling understanding of the present. It would appear that each age finds its own solutions regarding the eclipse of the present for something more favorable and meaningful. Sometimes the rejection of the present takes on nostalgia for the past and sometimes it is the future that man longs for. The first half of the sixteenth century was a unique age, for never before had so many scholars looked to the past for redemption from the present. There must have been magic in this Renaissance search for the grail for now Jewish thought, while still anachronistic, was also the embodiment of a lost tradition; the rabbis were still blind but were also sources of scriptural insight; and rabbinic mysticism, still the perverted product of a God-rejected people, was also the intellectual awareness of an uncorrupted past.

Bibliography

Primary Sources

Agricola, Johannes. *Grüntlich anzergung was die theologen des chufürstenthums der Mark zur Brandenburgk von den christlichen Evangelischen lehre halten, lehren und bekunen.* Frankfort om Oder, 1552.

Aurogallus, Johannes. *Compendium Heb. et Chald. Grammatica.* Wittenberg, 1525.

Boschenstein, Johannes. *Elementale introductorium in hebreas literas . . .* Augsburg, 1514; Wittenberg, 1518.

Bucer, Martin. *Sacrorum Psalmorum Libri Quinque.* Basel, 1547.

––––––. *Von den Juden.* Strasbourg, 1539.

Calvin, Johannes. *Opera. (Corpus Reformatorum.)* Ed. Baum, Cunitz, Reuss. 59 vols. Braunschweig, 1863–1900.

Capito, Wolfgang. *In Habakuk Prophetam . . . enerrationes.* Strasbourg, 1526.

Charles V. *Privilegiorum Universorum Teutoniae nationis Hebraeorum Confirmatio. Jahrbuch der Gesellschaft für Geschichte der Juden in der Cecheslovakischen Republic.* Ed. A. Engel. Spire, 1544.

––––––. *Essential Erasmus.* Trans. J. P. Dolan. New York, 1964.

Erasmus. *Opus Epistolarum Des. Erasmi Roterdami . . .* Ed. P. S. Allen. Oxford, 1907–1947.

Fagius, Paul. *Precationes Hebraicae quibus in Solemnioribus Festis Iudaei . . .* Isny, 1542.

––––––. *Exegesis sive expositiones Dictionum Hebraicarum literalis et simplex in quatuor capita Geneseos pro studiosis linguae Hebraicae.* Isny, 1542.

––––––. *Liber Fidei.* Isny, 1542.

––––––. *Sententiae morales Ben Syrae, Vetustissimi authoris Hebraei.* Isny, 1542.

––––––. *Sententiae Vere Elegentes Piae . . .* Isny, 1541.

––––––. *Tobias Hebraice . . .* Isny, 1542.

Ficker, J., and Winchelmann, O. *Handschriften proben des sechzehnten Jahrhunderts . . .* Strasbourg, 1905.

Flacius, Matthias (Illyricus). *Clavis Scripturae.* Basel, 1567, 1580–81.

Forster, Johannes, *Dictionarium Hebraicum Novum, non ex Rabbinorum Commentis nec ex Nostratum Doctorum Stulta Imitatione Descriptum, sed ex ipsis Thesauris Sacrorum Bibliorum et eorundem accurata locorum Collatione Depromptum, cum Phrasibus Scripturae veteris et Novi Testamenti Diligenter Annotatis.* Basel, 1557.

Genevan Company of Pastors. *Registres de la Compagnie des Pasteurs de Geneve au temps de Calvin.* Ed. Robert M. Kingdon, Jean-Francois Bergier. Geneva, 1962.

Hunnius, Aegidus. *Calvinus judizans.* Wittembergae, 1593.

Hutton, Ulrich von. *Operum Supplementum.* Ed. E. Bocking. Leipzig, 1864, 1869.

Isaac, Johannes. *Contra Confussimum D. Joh. Fursteri Lexicon.* Cologne, 1558.

Josel of Rosheim. "Journal de Joselmann," ed. J. Kracauer. *Revue des Etudes Juives,* vol. 16 (1882), no. 22.

Kidde, B. J., ed. *Documents Illustrative of the Continental Reformation.* Oxford, 1911.

──────. *The Commentary of Rabbi David Kimchi on the Book of Psalms.* Ed. A. W. Greenup. London, 1918.

Kimchi, David. *The Longer Commentary of Rabbi David Kimchi on the First Book of Psalms.* Ed. R. G. Finch. New York, 1919.

──────. *Mikraot g'dolot.* (Bomberg's Rabbinic Bible.) Venice, 1517– .

Lefèvre d'Etaples. *Quincuplex Psalterium.* Paris, 1509.

Luther, Martin. *D. Martin Luthers Werke.* Kritische Gesamtausgabe. Weimar, 1883– .

──────. *Luther Works.* Gen. Ed. H. Lehman. Philadelphia, 1955.

──────. *Samtliche Werke.* Ed. Irmischer. Erlangen, 1830– .

──────. *Tischreden.* Ed. E. Kroker. Leipzig, 1903.

Melanchthon, Philip. *Corpus Reformatorum.* Vols. 1–28. *Opera Omnia.* Ed. C. G. Bretschneider et al. Halle and Brunswick, 1834– .

Mirandola, Pico della. *Opera Omnia.* Basel, 1572.

Münster, Sebastian. *Grammatica Hebraica Absolutissima.* Basel, 1525.

──────. *Havikuach: Christiani Hominis cum Judeo partinaciter prodigiosis suis opinionibus . . .* Basel, 1539.

──────. *Mashiach: Messias Christianorum et Iudaeorum . . .* Basel, 1539.

──────. *The Messiahs of the Christians and the Jews.* Trans. Paul Isaiah. London, 1655.

──────. *Mikdash YHVH: Hebraica Biblia.* Basel, 1534, 1546.

———. *Opus Grammaticum* . . . Basel, 1547.

———. *Torat ha-Mashiach*: *Evangelum Secundum Mattaeum in Lingua Hebraica cum versione Latina atque succincta annatationibus Sebastiani Münsteri.* Basel, 1537.

Oecolampadius, Johannes. *In Iesaiam Prophetam Hypomnematon.* Basel, 1525.

Pellican, Conrad. *Das Chronikon des Konrad Pellican.* Ed. Bernhard Riggenbach. Basel, 1872.

———. *Commentaria Bibliorum.* 7 vols. Zurich, 1532– .

Philip of Hesse. *Briefwechsel Landsgraf Phillipp's des Grossmüthingen von Hesse mit Bucer.* Ed. M. Lenz. Leipzig, 1880.

Reuchlin, Johannes. *De Verbo Mirifico.* Basel, 1494.

———. *De Arte Cabbalistica.* Basel, 1517.

———. *Briefwechsel.* Ed. L. Geiger Tübingen, 1875.

Servetus, Michael. *De Trinitatis Erroribus libri septem.* Hagenau, 1531.

———. *Biblia Sacra ex Santis Pagnini tralatione* . . . Lyon, 1542.

———. *De Restitutio Christianismi.* Vienne, 1553.

Talmud. Trans. and ed. I. Epstein. London, 1948– .

Tremelius, Immanuel. *Sefer Chinuch B'Chirei Yah.* London, 1554.

Troki, Isaac. *Hizzuk Emunah.* Ed. D. Deutsch. Breslau, 1873.

Welzig, W. *Erasmus' Werke.* Darmstadt, 1967.

Zwingli, Hulderich. *Selected Works of Hulderich Zwingli.* Ed. S. M. Jackson. Philadelphia, 1901.

Secondary Sources

Alcalá, Angel. *El Systema de Servet.* Madrid, 1978.

Amram, D. W. *The Makers of Hebrew Books in Italy.* Philadelphia, 1909.

Armstrong, E. *Robert Estienne, Royal Printer.* Cambridge, 1954.

Bacher, William. *Die Hebräischen Sprachwissenschaft vom 10 bis zur 16 Jahrhunderts.* Trier, 1892.

———. "Elija Lévitas Wisserchaftliche Leistungen." *Zeitschrift der Deutschen Morganländischen Gesellschaft,* 43:206–76.

Baer, Y. *A History of the Jews in Christian Spain.* 2 vols. Philadelphia, 1961.

Bainton, R. H. *The Hunted Heretic: The Life and Death of Michael Servetus, 1511–1553.* Boston, 1953.

Baker, J., and Nicholson, E. W. *The Commentary of Rabbi David Kimchi on Psalms CXX-CL.* Cambridge, 1973.

Baron, Hans. *The Crisis of the Early Italian Renaissance.* Princeton, 1966.

Baron, S. W. *A Social and Religious History of the Jews.* 16 vols. New York, 1969.

———. "John Calvin and the Jews" and "The Council of Trent and Rabbinic Literature." *Ancient and Medieval Jewish History.* New Brunswick, New Jersey, 1972.

Bauch, G. "Die Einführung des Hebraischen in Wittenberg," *Monatschrift der Gesellschaft für Wissenschaft des Judentums.* Vol. 48. Breslau, 1904.

Bayle, P. *Dictionnaire historique et critique.* 4th ed. Leiden, 1730.

Bebb, P. N. "Jewish Policy in Sixteenth Century Nürnberg." *Occasional Papers of the American Society for Reformation Research,* 1 (1977): 125–36.

Ben-Sasson, H. H. "The Reformation in Contemporary Jewish Eyes," *Proceedings of the Israel Academy of Sciences and Humanities.* Vol. 4. Jerusalem, 1971.

———. "Jewish-Christian Disputation in the Setting of Humanism and Reformation in the German Empire." *Harvard Theological Revue,* vol. 59, (1966), no. 4.

Benz, E. *Die Christliche Kabbala: Ein Stiefkind der Theologie.* Zurich, 1958.

Benzing, J. *Bibliographie der Schriften Johannes Reuchlin.* Wien, 1955.

Bettan, J. "The Sermons of Isaac Arama." *Hebrew Union College Annual,* vol. 12–13 (1937–38).

Blau, J. L. *The Christian Interpretation of the Cabala in the Renaissance.* New York, 1944.

———. "The Diffusion of the Christian Interpretation of the Cabala in English Literature." *Revue of Religion,* vol. 6.

Block, J. *Venetian Printers of Hebrew Books.* New York, 1932.

Blumenkranz, B. *Les Auteurs chrétiens latins du Moyen Ages sur les juifs et le judaisme.* Paris, 1963.

———. *Juifs et chrétiens dans le monde occidental.* Paris, 1960.

Bornkamm, H. *Luther and the Old Testament.* Philadelphia, 1969.

Bouwsma, W. J. *Concordia Mundi: The Career and Thought of Guillaume Postel.* Cambridge, Massachusetts, 1957.

———. "Postel and the Significance of Renaissance Cabalism." *Journal of the History of Ideas,* vol. 15 (1954).

Brod, Max. *Johann Reuchlin: Sein Leben und sein Kampf.* Stuttgart, 1965.

Brown, H. F. *The Venetian Printing Press.* New York and London, 1891.

Brückner, Alex. *Roznowiercy polscy.* Warsaw, 1905.

Burmeister, K. H. *Sebastian Münster: Versuch eines biographischen Gesamtbildes.* Basel and Stuttgart, 1963.

———. *Eine Bibliographie mit 22 Abbildungen.* Weisbaden, 1964.

Caplan, H. "The Four Senses of Scriptural Interpretation and the Medieval Theory of Preaching." *Speculum,* vol. 4 (1929).

Cassirer, E. "Giovanni Pico della Mirandola." *Journal of the History of Ideas,* vol. 3 (1942).

Centi, T. M. "L'attività letteraria di Santi Pagnini 1470–1536 nel campo delle scienza bibliche." *Archivum Fratrum Praedicatorum,* vol. 15 (1945).

Christ, Karl. *Die Bibliothek Reuchlins in Pforzheim.* Leipzig, 1924.

Churgin, P. *The Targum Jonathan to the Prophets.* New Haven, 1907.

Copenhaver, B. P. *Symphorien Champier and the Reception of the Occultist Tradition in Renaissance France.* Hague, 1978.

———. "Lefèvre D'Etaples, Symphorien Champier, and the Secret Names of God." *Journal of the Warburg and Courtauld Institutes,* 40 (1977): 189–211.

Daitches, D. *The King James Version of the English Bible.* Chicago, 1941.

Delapuelle, L. "Le séjour a Paris d'Agostino Guistiniani 1518–1522." *Revue du Seizième Siècle,* vol. 12 (1925).

De Lubac, Henri. *Exegese Médiévale: Les Quatre Sens de l'Ecriture.* 4 Vols. Paris, 1959– .

Dersauer, A. L. von, ed. *Gutachen über Jüdische Schriften.* Stuttgart, 1965.

Diehn, O. *Bibliographie zur Geschichte des Kirchenkampfes 1933–1945.* Göttingen, 1958.

Eells, Hastings. *Martin Bucer.* New Haven, 1931.

———. "Bucer's Plan for the Jews." *Church History,* vol. 6 (1937).

Falb, A. *Luther und die Juden.* Munich, 1921.

Feilchenfeld, L. *Rabbi Josel von Rosheim.* Strasbourg, 1898.

Ficher, Joh. *Die Anfänge der Akademischen Studien in Strassburg.* Strasbourg, 1912.

Finkelstien, L. *The Commentary of David Kimchi on Isaiah.* New York, 1926.

Fita, F. "Los Judaizantes españoles . . ." *Boletin de la Real Academia de la Historia,* Madrid, 33:330 f.

Fraenkel, P. *Testimonia Patrum: The Function of the Patristic Argument in the Theology of Philip Melanchthon.* Geneva, 1961.

Friedman, J. *Michael Servetus: A Case Study in Total Heresy.* Geneva, 1978.

———. "Luther, Forster, and the Curious Nature of Wittenberg Hebraica." *Bibliothèque D'Humanisme et Renaissance*, 42(1980):611–19.

———. "Michael Servetus: The Case for a Jewish Christianity." *Sixteenth Century Journal*, vol. 4 (April 1973).

———. "Michael Servetus: Exegete of Divine History." *Church History*, 43 (December 1974):460–69.

———. "The Reformation and Jewish Anti-Christian Polemics." *Bibliothèque D'Humanisme et Renaissance*, 41 (1979):85–97.

———. "Sebastian Münster, The Jewish Mission, and Protestant Anti-Semitism." *Archive für Reformationsgeschichte*, vol. 70 (1979).

———. "Servetus and the Psalms." Historia de l' *exégèse au XVIe siècle*. Ed. O. Fatio. Geneva, 1978.

———. "Sixteenth-Century Christian-Hebraica: Scripture and the Renaissance Myth of the Past." *Sixteenth Century Journal*, 11 (1980):67–85.

———. "Sixteenth-Century European Jewry: Theologies of Crisis in Crisis." *Social Groups and Religious Ideas in the Sxteenth Century*. Ed. M. Chrisman, O. Grundler. Kalamazoo, Michigan, 1978.

Fürst, Julius. *Bibliotheca Judaica*. 2 vols. Leipzig, 1849.

Galliner, H. "Agathius Guidacerius: An Early Hebrew Grammarian in Rome and Paris." *Historia Judaica*, 2 (October 1940):85–101.

Garin, E. *Giovanni Pico della Mirandola: Vita e Dottrina*. Florence, 1937.

Geiger, L. *Das Studium der Hebräische Sprache in Deutschland vom Ende des 15 bis zur mitte des 16 Jahrhunderts*. Breslau, 1870.

———. *Johannes Reuchlin: Sein leben und Seine Werke*. Leipzig, 1871.

Ginsberg, C. D *Jacob ben Chayim's Introduction to the Rabbinic Bible*. London, 1865.

———. *The Masoreth Ha-Masoreth of Elias Levita*. London, 1865.

Glaser, A. *Geschichte der Juden in Strasbourg*. 1894.

Gordis, R. *The Biblical Text in the Making: A Study of the Ketib-Qere*. Philadelphia, 1937.

Graetz, H. *Geschichte der Juden*. 4th ed. Leipzig, 1909.

———. *A History of the Jews*. 11 vols. Philadelphia, 1894.

Greenslade, S. L., ed. *The Cambridge History of the Bible. The West from the Reformation to the Present Day*. Cambridge, 1963.

Gurewicz, "The Medieval Jewish Exegetes of the Old Testament." *Australian Biblical Revue*, vol. 1 (1951).

Gundesheimer, W. L. "Erasmus, Humanism, and the Christian Cabbalah." *Journal of the Warburg and Courtauld Institutes*, 20:vi.

Hailperin, H. *Rashi and the Christian Scholars*. Pittsburgh, 1963.

————. "The Hebrew Heritage of Medieval Biblical Scholarship." *Historia Judaica*, vol. 5 (1943).

————. "Jewish Influence on Christian Biblical Scholars in the Middle Ages." *Historia Judaica*, vol. 4 (1942).

Hantsch, V. *Sebastian Münster: Leben, Werk, Wissenschaftliche Beduntung*. Leipzig, 1898.

Heckthorn, C. W. *The Printers of Basel in the XV and XVI Centuries*. London, 1897.

Hirsch, S. A. "Johannes Reuchlin: The Father of the Study of Hebrew Among Christians." *A Book of Essays*. London, 1905.

Hirschfeld, H. *Literary History of Hebrew Grammarians and Lexicographers*. Oxford, 1926.

Hobbs, R. G. "Martin Bucer on Psalm 22: A Study in the Application of Rabbinic Exegesis by a Christian Hebraist." In *Historie de l'exégèse au XVIe siècle*, Ed. O. Fatio. Geneva, 1978.

————. "An Introduction to the Psalms Commentary of Martin Bucer." Unpublished doctoral dissertation, University of Strasbourg, 1971.

Holmio, A. K. *The Lutheran Reformation and the Jews: The Birth of the Protestant Jewish Missions*. Hancock, Michigan, 1949.

Jannach, W. *Deutsche Kirchendocumente*. Zurich, 1946.

Kibre, P. *The Library of Pico della Mirandola*. New York, 1936.

Kisch, G. "The Jew in Medieval Law." In *Essays on Anti-Semitism*, ed. K. S. Pinson. New York, 1946.

————. *Erasmus' Stellung zu Juden und Judentum*. Tübingen, 1969.

————. *The Jews of Medieval Germany*. Chicago, 1949.

————. "Medieval Italian Juris Prudence and the Jews." *Historia Judaica*, vol. 6 (1944).

————. *Zasius und Reuchlin*. Constance, 1961.

Kittelson, J. *Wolfgang Capito: From Humanist to Reformer*. Leiden, 1975.

Kluge, O. "Die Hebräische Sprachwissenschaft . . ." *Zeitschrift für die Geschichte der Juden in Deutschland*, vol. 3 (1931) and vol. 4 (1932).

Koehler, W. *Hessische Kirchenverfassung im Zeitalter der Reformation*. Geissen, 1894.

Kot, S. *Polski stownik biograficzny* Krakow, 1938.

————. "Szymon Budny: Der grösste Häretiker Litauens in 16 Jahrhundert." *Studien zur Alteren-Geschichte Osteuropas*, 1 (Graz, 1956): 63–118.

Kraeling, E. G. *The Old Testament Since the Reformation*. London, 1955.

Krebs, M., ed. *Johannes Reuchlin, 1455–1522*. Pforzheim, 1955.

Kukenhein, L. *Contributions à l'Histoire de la grammaire . . . Hebraique*. Leiden, 1951.

Landsteiner, K. "Jacobus Palaeologus." In *XXIII Jahres Bericht über das K. K. Josefstadter . . .* Wien, 1873.

Lea, H. C. *A History of the Inquisition in Spain*. 4 Vols. New York, 1906–07.

Lewin, R. *Luthers Stellung zu den Juden*. Berlin, 1911.

Levi, J. *Elia Levita und seine Leistungen als Grammatiker*. Breslau, 1888.

Lilly, W. S. *Renaissance Types*. London, 1901.

Lipsius, R. A. *Die Apokryphen Apostelgeschichten und Apostellegenden*. Braunschweig, 1883.

Littel, F. H. *The Origins of Protestant Sectarianism*. New York, 1962. (This volume was previously published in 1952 and 1956 under the title *The Anabaptist View of the Church*.)

Longhurst, J. E. *Luther's Ghost in Spain*. Lawrence, Kansas, 1969.

Lowinger, S. D. "Selections from the Magen-Abraham of Abraham Farissol." (In Hebrew.) *Hazofe le-Hochmat Yisrael*. Budapest, 1928.

————. "Réchèrches sur l'oevre Apologistique d'Abraham Farissol." *Revue des Etudes Juives*, vol. 105 (1939).

Manzoni, C. *Umanesimo ed Eresia: M. Servet*. Naples, 1974.

Manzoni, G. *Annali Tipografici dei Soncino*. Bologna, 1883–86.

Marks, Alex. "Notes on the Use of Hebrew Type in Non-Hebrew Books." *Studies in Jewish History and Booklore*. New York, 1944.

Massetani, G. *La filosofia Cabbalistica di Giovanni Pico della Mirandola*. Empoli, 1897.

Maurer, W. "Reuchlin und das Judentum." *Theologische Literaturzeitung*, 77:533–44.

May, H. S. *The Tragedy of Erasmus*. St. Charles, Missouri, 1975.

Meier, K. "Zur Interpretation von Luthers Judenschriften." In *Festschrift für Franz Lau*, ed. James Atkinson et al. Gottingen, 1967.

Meinvielle, J. *De la Cábala al progresismo*. Salta, Argentina, 1970.

Moellering, R. "Miscellanea: Luther's Attitudes Toward the Jews." *Concordia Theological Monthly*, 19 (December 1948):920–34; 20 (January 1949):45–59; 20 (March 1949):194–215, 579.

Moerikofer, J. C. *Ulrich Zwingli*. Leipzig, 1867–68.

Muller, J. *Martin Bucers Hermeneutik*. Gütersloch, 1965.

Nauert, C. G. *Agrippa and the Crisis of Renaissance Thought*. Urbana, Illinois, 1965.

————. "The Clash of Humanists and Scholastics: An Approach to Pre-reformation Controversies." *Sixteenth Century Journal*. vol. 4 (April 1973).

Nestle, E. *Nigri, Bohm und Pellican*. Tübingen, 1893.

Neuman, A. A. *The Jews in Spain*. 2 vols. 1941. Reprint New York, 1969.

Newman, L. I. *Jewish Influence on Christian Reform Movements*. New York, 1925, 1966.

Niemoller, *Kampf und zeugnis der Bekennenden Kirche*. Bielefeld, 1948.

————. *Die Evangelische Kirche in Dritten Reich*. Bielefeld, 1956.

Norden, G. van. *Kirche in den Krise*. Düsseldorf, 1963.

Oberman, H. O. *Forerunners of the Reformation*. New York, Chicago, San Francisco, 1966.

Ortiz, A. D. *Los Judeoconversos en Espagna y America*. Madrid, 1971.

Overfield, J. H. "A New Look at the Reuchlin Affair." In *Studies in Medieval and Renaissance History*, Ed. H. L. Adelson. Vol. 8. Lincoln, Nebraska, 1971.

Ozment, S. *The Age of Reform, 1250–1550*. New Haven, 1980.

Parks, James. *The Conflict of the Church and Synagogue*. New York, 1934.

————. *The Jew in the Medieval Community*. New York, 1938.

Peritz, M. *Ein hebräischer Brief El. Levitas und Sebastian Münster*. Breslau, 1894.

Perles, J. *Beitrage zur Geschichte der Hebräischen und Aramäischen Studien*. Munich, 1884.

Pirnat, A. "Joacobus Palaeologus." *Studja nad Arianizmem pod redakcja Ludwika Chmaj*. Warsaw, 1959.

Poliakov, Leon. *The History of Anti-Semitism from the Time of Christ to the Court Jews*. Trans. R. Howard. New York, 1974.

Preisendanz, Karl. "Die Bibliothek Johannes Reuchlins." In *Johannes Reuchlin 1455–1522*, ed. M. Krebs. Pforzheim, 1955.

Preus, J. *From Shadow to Promise: Old Testament Interpretation from Augustine to the Young Luther*. Cambridge, Massachusetts, 1969.

Pulvermacher, D. *Sebastian Münster als Grammatiker*. Berlin, 1892.

Raeder, Sg. *Das Hebräische bei Luther*. Tübingen, 1961.

Rashdall, H. *The Universities of Europe in the Middle Ages*. 2 vols. Oxford, 1895.

Raubenheimer, R. *Paul Fagius aus Rheinzabern*. Grunstadt, 1957.

Rosenthal, E. I. J. "Sebastian Münster's Knowledge and use of Jewish Exegesis." In *Essays Presented to J. H. Hartz*, ed. I. Epstein et al. London, 1945.

Rosenthal, Frank. "The Rise of Christian-Hebraism in the 16th-Century." *Historia Judaica*, 7 (April 1945): 167–91.

———. "Christian Hebraists of Latin Europe." Unpublished doctoral dissertation, University of Pittsburgh, 1945.

Rosenthal, J. M. "Marcin Czechowic and Jacob of Belzyce: Arian-Jewish Encounters in 16th-Century Poland." *Proceedings of the American Academy of Jewish Research*, vol. 34. New York, 1966.

Roth, Cecil. *The Spanish Inquisition*. London, 1937.

———. *A History of the Jews in Venice*. New York, 1930.

———. *A History of the Marranos*. 4th ed. New York, 1974.

Roussel, Br. "Martin Bucer, exégète." *Strasbourg au coeur religieux du XVIe Siècle*. Strasbourg, 1971.

———. "Martin Bucer: Lecteur de l'Epître aux Romains." Unpublished doctoral dissertation, University of Strasbourg, 1971.

Rowan, S. W. "Ulrich Zasius and the Baptism of Jewish Children." *Sixteenth Century Journal*. Vol. 4 (October 1975).

Ruderman, D. "The Polemic of Abraham of Farissol with Christianity in its Historical Context." Unpublished doctoral dissertation, Hebrew Union College-Jewish Institute of Religion, New York, 1971.

Rupp, G. *Martin Luther and the Jews*. London, 1972.

Rupprich, H. "Johannes Reuchlin und seine Bedeutung im Europäischen Humanismus." In *Johannes Reuchlin 1455–1522*, ed. M. Krebs. Pforzheim, 1955.

Sacchi, F. *I Tipografi Ebrei di Soncino*. Cremona, 1877.

Scholem, G. "Zur Geschichte der Anfänge der christlichen Kabbala." *Essays Presented to Leo Baeck*. London, 1954.

———. *Major Trends in Jewish Mysticism*. New York and Jerusalem, 1954.

Schmidt, H. *Luther und das Buch der Psalmen*. Tübingen, 1933.

Schnerdemann, Gg. *Die Controverse des Lud. Cappelus mit den Buxdorfen über das alter hebräischen Punctation*. Leipzig, 1879.

Schnurer, Ch. F. *Biogr. und Literar. Nachrichten von den Hebräische Literatur in Tübingen*. Ulm, 1792.

Schwarz, W. *Principles and Problems of Biblical Translation*. Cambridge, England, 1955.

Sciroff, A. A. *Les Controverses des Statuts de "purité de sang" en Espagne du XVe au XVIIe siècles*. Paris, 1960.

Screech, M. A. *Ecstasy and the Praise of Folly*. Duckworth, 1980.

Secret, Fr. *Le Zôhar chez les Kabbalistes chrétiens de la Renaissance.* Paris, 1958.

―――. *Les Kabbalistes chrétiens de la Renaissance.* Paris, 1964.

―――. "Notes sur les hébräisants chrétiens." *Revue des Etudes Juives*, vol. 124.

Shulvass, M. A. *The Jews in the World of the Renaissance.* (Hebrew version published New York, 1955.) Trans. E. I. Kose. Leiden, 1973.

Siirala, A. A. "Luther and the Jews." *Lutheran World*, vol. 11 (July 1964).

Silberstein, E. *Conrad Pellican.* Berlin, 1900.

Silver, A. H. *A History of Messianic Speculation in Israel.* New York, 1927; Boston, 1959.

Singerman, R. *The Jews in Spain and Portugal: A Bibliography.* New York and London, 1975.

Smalley, B. *The Study of the Bible in the Middle Ages.* Oxford, 1941.

Smart, J. D. *The Interpretation of Scripture.* Philadelphia, 1961.

Soave, M. *Dei Soncino Celebre Tipografi Italiani nel secoli XV, XVI.* Venice, 1878.

Spicq, C. *Esquisse d'une histoire de l'exégèse latine au moyen age.* Paris, 1944.

Spinka, M. *John Hus at the Council of Constance.* New York and London, 1969.

Spitz, L. *The Religious Renaissance of the German Humanists.* Cambridge, Massachusetts, 1963.

Steinschneider, M. *Christliche Hebraisten.* Frankfort, 1901.

Stern, S. *Josel of Rosheim.* (German edition, Stuttgart, 1959.) Trans. G. Hirschler. Philadelphia, 1965.

Stobbe, O. *Die Juden in Deutschland Während des Mittelalters.* Braunschweig, 1866.

Stow, K. R. *Catholic Thought and Papal Jewry Policy, 1555–1593.* New York, 1977.

―――. "Conversion, Christian-Hebraica, and Hebrew Prayer in the 16th-Century." *Hebrew Union College Annual*, vol. 47 (1976).

Strack, H. L., and Billerbeck, P. *Kommentar zum Neuen Testament aus Talmud und Midrash.* Munich, 1922.

Strasser, O. "Un chrétien humaniste; Wolfgang Capito." *Revue d'Histoire et de Philosophie Religieuses*, vol. 20 (1940).

Sucher, C. B. *Luthers Stellung zu den Juden.* Munich, 1977.

Talmadge, F. *David Kimchi.* Cambridge, Massachusetts, 1976.

————. "David Kimchi as Polemicist." *Hebrew Union College Annual,* vol. 38 (1967).

————. "David Kimchi and the Rationalist Tradition." *Hebrew Union College Annual,* vol. 34 (1964).

Thorndike, L. *A History of Magic and Experimental Science.* Vol. 4. New York, 1934.

Trachtenberg, J. *The Devil and the Jews.* Philadelphia, 1943.

Trinkaus, Ch. E. *In Our Image and Likeness.* 2 vols. London, 1970.

Vekené, Emile van der. *Bibliographie der Inquisition: Ein Versuch.* Hildesheim, 1963.

Walde, H. *Das Studium der Hebräische Sprache in Deutschland am Ausgang des Mittelalters.* Münster i.w. 1916.

Walker, D. P. *The Ancient Theology.* Ithaca, New York, 1972.

————. *Spiritual and Demonic Magic from Ficino to Campanella.* London, 1958.

Weil, G. *Élie Levita: Humaniste et Massorete.* Leiden, 1963.

————. "Une Leçon de l'humaniste Elias Levita a' son élève Sébastian Münster." *Revue d'Alsace,* vol. 95 (1956).

Wilbur, E. M. *A History of Unitarianism.* Boston, 1949.

Willenski, B. Heller, *Rabbi Yizhac Arama u-Mishnato.* Jerusalem, 1957.

Williams, G. *The Radical Reformation.* Philadelphia, 1963.

————. "The Two Social Strands in Italian Anabaptism, ca. 1526–1565." In *The Social History of the Reformation,* ed. L. P. Buck, J. W. Zophy. Columbus, 1972.

Wirszubski, C. *Three Chapters in the History of the Christian-Cabbala.* (In Hebrew) Jerusalem, 1975.

Wolf, J. Chr. *Bibliotheca Hebraea.* 4 vols. Hamburg, 1715.

Yates, Fr. A. *Giordano Bruno and the Hermetic Tradition.* Chicago and London, 1964.

Zika, Ch. "Reuchlin's De Verbo Mirifico and the Magic Debate of the late Fifteenth Century." *Journal of the Warburg and Courtauld Institutes,* 39 (1976):104–38.

Zipfel, F. *Kirchenkampf in Deutschland, 1933–1945.* Berlin, 1965.

Zürcher, Ch. *Konrad Pellicans Wirken in Zürich.* Zürich, 1975.

Index